EXCHANGE RATE
SYSTEMS AND
POLICIES IN ASIA

EXCHANGE RATE SYSTEMS AND POLICIES IN ASIA

Editor

Paul S L Yip

Nanyang Technological University, Singapore

World Scientific

NEW JERSEY · LONDON · SINGAPORE · BEIJING · SHANGHAI · HONG KONG · TAIPEI · CHENNAI

Published by

World Scientific Publishing Co. Pte. Ltd.

5 Toh Tuck Link, Singapore 596224

USA office: 27 Warren Street, Suite 401-402, Hackensack, NJ 07601

UK office: 57 Shelton Street, Covent Garden, London WC2H 9HE

British Library Cataloguing-in-Publication Data
A catalogue record for this book is available from the British Library.

ISBN-13 978-981-283-450-8
ISBN-10 981-283-450-8

Typeset by Stallion Press
Email: enquiries@stallionpress.com

Printed in Singapore.

CONTENTS

Introduction: Important Lessons from Some Major Exchange Rate and
Monetary Experiences in Asia
Paul S. L. Yip   vii

The International Monetary Fund and Exchange Rate Crisis Management
Chong-Yah Lim   1

The Case for an Intermediate Exchange Rate Regime
John Williamson   11

Japan's Deflationary Hangover: Wage Stagnation and the Syndrome of the
Ever-Weaker Yen
Ronald McKinnon   25

Managing Flexibility: Japanese Exchange Rate Policy, 1971–2007
Shinji Takagi   51

China's Exchange Rate System Reform
Paul S. L. Yip   79

The Fog Encircling the Renminbi Debate
Yin-Wong Cheung, Menzie D. Chinn and Eiji Fujii   119

Insulation of India from the East Asian Crisis: An Analysis
Pami Dua and Arunima Sinha   135

Singapore's Exchange Rate Policy: Some Implementation Issues
Hwee-Kwan Chow   161

INTRODUCTION: IMPORTANT LESSONS FROM SOME MAJOR EXCHANGE RATE AND MONETARY EXPERIENCES IN ASIA

PAUL S. L. YIP

Division of Economics, School of Humanities and Social Sciences
Nanyang Technological University, Nanyang Avenue, Singapore 639798
aslyip@ntu.edu.sg

1. Introduction

This book volume, reprinted from the *Singapore Economic Review* (Vol. 52, No. 3), consists of eight insightful policy papers on the exchange rate systems and policies in Asia. As this volume is targeted at policymakers as well as academia and professionals in economics and finance, this Introduction links and elaborates the most important discussions in these papers on an issue-by-issue basis. This non-traditional format will enable me to highlight the important lessons from some major exchange rate and monetary experiences in Asia in a consistent and organic way. In addition, the Introduction links and elaborates only those discussions that the editor strongly agrees with. Thus, policymakers can be confident with the conclusions, which include some relatively revolutionary hypotheses drawn from the discussions. It is hoped that this volume will serve as a very useful handbook that policymakers can easily refer to whenever they encounter the major economic issues discussed here. This is particularly the case for other developing economies who are adopting a fixed exchange rate system, making the choice between capital control and capital account liberalization, seeking ways to reduce huge non-performing bank loans, or at the early stage of a rampant asset inflation era.

Before elaborating on the major lessons, let us first have a very brief overview of the eight papers collected in this volume. The first paper is on the International Monetary Fund and exchange rate crisis management, by Chong-Yah Lim. After giving a brief discussion of the economic performance of the old ASEAN 6 (i.e., Brunei, Indonesia, Malaysia, Philippines, Singapore and Thailand), the new ASEAN 4 (i.e., Cambodia, Laos, Myanmar and Vietnam) and China during and after the Asian financial crisis in 1997, Lim challenges the "Washington Consensus" which includes no capital control under any circumstances. It also highlights the enormous risk of having capital account liberalization before domestic economic liberalization.

Next is John Williamson's paper on the choice of exchange rate systems. After a concise and pertinent review on the advantages and disadvantages of fixed, floating, adjustable and

BBC (i.e., basket, band and crawl) regimes, Williamson challenges the Bipolarity Thesis (i.e., regimes other than firmly-fixed and freely-floating rates are infeasible) and highlights that an intermediate exchange rate regime such as a reference rate system could be a better choice.

The third and fourth papers are by Ronald McKinnon and Shinji Takagi, respectively, who have provided very detailed and insightful discussions on the exchange rate policies in Japan since the breakdown of the Bretton Woods System in 1971. In particular, McKinnon has made extremely insightful and interesting discussions on how: (i) the Japanese economy is currently caught by the perceived risk of yen appreciation; and (ii) the Bank of Japan is forced to stop the appreciation whenever there is a run for yen. As failure to contain future runs could imply disastrous global financial instability, I urge readers to have a very careful look at the paper with deep following-up thoughts on the consequences and solutions of the problem (see also the discussion in Section 4). Takagi's paper also suggests that: (i) Japan's exchange rate system is not as purely floating as many economists have been assuming; and (ii) Japan's experiences of using foreign exchange market intervention, change in capital control regulations, and other measures in influencing the exchange value of yen could be useful for other developing economies in the future.

The fifth paper, by Paul S. L. Yip, and the sixth paper, by Yin-Wong Cheung, Menzie D. Chinn and Eiji Fujii, are very up-to-date papers on China's exchange rate system, monetary policies and macroeconomic conditions. Yip notes that China's transitional exchange rate system reform in 2005 and banking reform in 2005–2006 were relatively successful, but the real risk of China and her reform are the stock market bubble, the rampant property inflation and rising CPI inflation since 2006–2007. If China fails to stop the asset bubble from expanding further, then a bursting of the bubble will be just a matter of time. In the worst scenario, this could result in political and social instability in China as well as serious economic disruptions or recessions in the regional, and perhaps the global, economies. In their policy paper in this volume and their econometric paper in the *Journal of International Money and Finance*, Cheung *et al.* highlight that empirical evidence for the US's claim of renminbi undervaluation is in fact very weak (i.e., statistically insignificant) with extremely imprecise estimates. Although this does not mean that there is no undervaluation, the paper emphasizes that renminbi appreciation in and of itself is unlikely to alter the basic problem of a massive US trade deficit. That problem is first and foremost a "made-in-America" issue, driven by collapsed household and public sector savings, and US's heavy dependence upon imported oil. It would also be an enormous mistake to think that a stronger renminbi is a panacea for what ails the US.

The seventh paper, by Pami Dua and Arunima Sinha, provides a detailed review of India's experience since her economic crisis in 1990–1991, the reforms made after the 1990–1991 crisis, and India's relative insulation from the Asian financial crisis in 1997–1998. Given the huge population and the rising importance of India, the paper also enables economists and policymakers in East Asia to have a relatively good understanding of an economy that could be extremely important to them in the future.

Finally, Hwee-Kwan Chow discusses some implementation issues on the exchange rate system and policies in Singapore. It should be noted that discussion on Singapore's exchange rate system is no less important than those of the three large Asian economies (i.e., Japan, China and India). The successful system in Singapore suggests that it could be a role model for other economies. In fact, as reported by Yip's paper in this volume, many of the useful settings and system designs were, and are going to be, adopted by China with appropriate modifications. If China is able to control her asset bubble and make no major mistake in her exchange rate system reform, there is a good chance that the useful settings and experience in Singapore will be adopted by many other developing economies (with appropriate modifications) in the future.

2. Lessons on the Choice of Exchange Rate Systems

Let us start with the lessons that can be drawn on the choice of exchange rate systems, which is in fact the first and most important international monetary decision of any economy. As we will see, the discussion is particularly important for those economies adopting a fixed exchange rate system, and those economies considering the costs and benefits of various exchange rate regimes.

2.1. *The risks and costs of a fixed exchange rate system*

In the second paper of this volume, Williamson provides a concise and updated review of the costs and benefits of a fixed exchange rate system. The paper first notes that the often-cited gain of lower transaction costs of a fixed exchange rate system may be true within a monetary area, but less true for a currency board and other fixed exchange rate system. Even for the former, the gain is likely to be rather small (i.e., it could not be a strong case for a fixed exchange rate system, especially if there are other major costs with a fixed exchange rate system). It also provides the following challenge on another often-cited argument for a fixed rate system: the provision of a nominal anchor of a fixed exchange rate involves an implicit and unrealistic assumption of zero-degree homogeneity among the economies in the fixed rate system. Williamson also highlights that there are many examples of countries that have disruptive adjustments of their real exchange rate in a manner contradictory to the nominal anchor argument: one might, for example, cite the East Asian countries in 1997 and India in 1991–1992 (see Dua and Sinha, the seventh paper of this volume).

On the other hand, the costs of a fixed exchange rate system are that it will deprive the economy of (i) a potent expenditure-switching instrument (i.e., using exchange rate changes to switch demand between domestic and foreign outputs); and (ii) an independent monetary policy (i.e., to finetune domestic aggregate demand) if there is free mobility of capital. Besides, under a fixed exchange rate system, the restoration of full employment output will rely on the adjustment of prices and wages. However, it is well-known that prices and wages are highly sluggish in the downward direction (see Yip and Wang, 2001, 2002 for the empirical evidence on Singapore and Hong Kong). As a result, any shock causing a reduction in internal or external demand, or an overvaluation of domestic currency could imply huge economic adjustment costs in terms of low output and high unemployment for a prolonged period. One very good example is detailed in Yip (2005a, 2002): after detailed theoretical and empirical discussions, the book and paper conclude that the fixed exchange rate in Hong Kong's currency board system and the greater flexibility of exchange rate in Singapore were the main reasons for a less severe recession in Singapore during the 1997 Asian crisis and post-crisis period, although Singapore's economic, financial and trading relationships with the crisis-hit economies were much greater than that of Hong Kong.

After highlighting the likelihood (and high cost) of an eventual abrupt adjustment in real exchange rate under a fixed rate system, Williamson lists a set of conditions for a policy of fixing exchange rate to make sense. From the list, one can easily recognize that many economies adopting a fixed exchange rate system do not satisfy these conditions. In particular, Williamson regards Hong Kong's peg with the US dollar as anomalous as her economic relationship with China and other East Asian economies are much greater than that with the US (i.e., violation of the zero-degree homogeneity assumption).

2.2. *Major misalignments could also happen in a floating regime*

Williamson notes that major exchange rate misalignments could also happen in a floating regime. The currently well-known undervaluation of the yen is one example (see the discussion in Section 4 and McKinnon's paper), and the overvaluation of the US dollar at the end of the dollar bubble in 1981–1984 is another example. Furthermore, Yip notes that the phenomena of herding behavior and exchange rate overshooting could result in big cycles and high volatility of exchange rate under a floating regime. In fact, we have seen, on and off, quite a number of big and long cycles of major floating currencies such as the US dollar, euro, yen and sterling over the last few decades. Thus, policymakers should bear in mind that exchange rate experiences and theoretical developments since the 1970s suggest that flexible exchange rate is not as perfect as that presumed by proponents of the regime in the late 1960s (e.g., Johnson, 1969; Friedman, 1969).

2.3. *The real choice of exchange rate system for most economies*

In view of the relatively small benefits as well as the huge economic adjustment costs and vulnerability to speculative attacks under the fixed exchange rate system, Williamson believes that the real choice for most countries lies between freely floating rates and some kind of intermediate regime such as floating rates with a reference rate system, managed floating or BBC regime. Yip also notes that the phenomena of herding behavior and exchange rate overshooting could result in undesirable outcomes in China if she adopts a floating regime in the 2000s. Instead, he recommends more detailed studies of the interesting and desirable features in: (i) the monitoring band system in Singapore;[1] and (ii) a floating regime with occasional major interventions. Chow also reports that the exchange rate system in Singapore has enabled her to cope with the Asian financial crisis, even though her neighbors were seriously hurt by the crisis.

---

[1] Note that Yip also warns that a mere adoption of Singapore's system without appropriate adaptations could be disastrous. Thus, appropriate modifications of the monitoring system to suit the major economic characteristics of the adopting economy are important to the success of reform.

Despite reservations on the feasibility of the reference rate system in Williamson's current paper, the editor agrees with him that it is possible to design an intermediate regime in a form that avoids the hard bands that provoke crises, e.g., BBC regimes without hard edges to the bands. One promising and proven to be successful example is the monitoring band system that was first proposed by Williamson (2000), further refined and improved by Yip (2003, 2005a), and actually implemented in Singapore. Policymakers are highly recommended to have a careful reading of the articles and book for more details, including its advantages in: (a) maintaining credibility and yet allowing for sufficient exchange rate flexibility with respect to normal internal or external shocks as well as extremely adverse shocks such as the Asian financial crisis in 1997; (b) discouraging herding behavior and hence, big cycles in the exchange rate; and (c) allowing continuous adjustment of exchange rate to avoid accumulation of exchange rate misalignments that could provoke crises. Finally, the editor believes it is better to avoid grouping various types of non-polar regimes (i.e., neither fixed rate nor free floating regimes) into a big group of intermediate regimes. As highlighted by Yip in this volume, a viable exchange rate system involves right and mutually consistent decisions in all the relevant dimensions or characteristics of the systems (e.g., degree of flexibility, width of band, soft or hard bands, etc.) as well as other characteristics of the adopting economy. In particular, inconsistent decisions on the different dimensions could result in a complete failure. Thus, grouping the multidimensional exchange rate systems into a simple intermediate regime could be misleading and dangerous.

3. Capital Control and Speculative Attacks

Lim's paper in this volume notes that China and the new ASEAN 4 were not much affected by the Asian financial crisis, mainly because there was capital control in these economies. Meanwhile, with a reasonably high degree of capital mobility and inherent weakness in the economic system, Indonesia, Thailand, Philippines and Malaysia suffered a lot from the speculative attacks in 1997–1998. On the other hand, after the adoption of capital control in August 1998, Malaysia was no longer subject to speculative attacks and was able to recover from the recession without resorting to the IMF loans. Lim also notes that Japan, South Korea and Taiwan all had important capital control at their early stage of (rapid) economic growth. Thus, at the early stage of economic growth, when speculative attacks on their currencies can be frequent and disastrous, capital control can help insulate the developing economies from speculative attacks and hence contribute to exchange rate stability. While admitting that capital control is never the most desirable option or target to pursue, Lim also highlights that capital account liberalization could and should usher in the liberalization of the domestic economy, particularly the strengthening of the financial infrastructure and the liberalization of both foreign and domestic trade. [Postscript: With excessive capital inflows and monetary growth, rampant asset inflation and then high CPI inflation for years, there was eventually an outbreak of crisis in Vietnam in June 2008. The Editor is of the view that there are important lessons to be learned from (a) the causes and experiences of Vietnam's crisis; and (b) the differences and similarities between China's and Vietnam's latest experiences. He also believes that the effectiveness of capital control in Vietnam will be the key on whether the country can go through the crisis with less unbearable economic and political damages.]

Lim's view is in fact shared by many prominent economists, including McKinnon who has in the past expressed a similar view. In the detailed discussion of China's exchange rate system reform in this volume, Yip also uses the doctrine of Impossible Trinity to highlight China's needs to maintain a sufficient degree of capital control in the medium future (i.e., at least in the next 8–10 years) so that she can control her money supply (to finetune the aggregate demand) and monitor the appreciation rate of renminbi (to avoid coordination failure in the economic system as well as unnecessary disruptions to exports, output and employment). Drawing from the experience of crisis-hit Asian economies in 1997, he also notes that a list of prerequisites should be satisfied before China can consider complete liberalization of her capital account. For example, China should maintain a sufficient degree of capital control at least until (i) the problem of non-performing bank loans and extensive moral hazard activities are cleared, and (ii) the real exchange rate has gradually adjusted to levels reasonably close to its equilibrium level. That is, removing capital control should be the last step of the reform.

For Japan in the 1970s to mid-1980s, Takagi also notes the contribution of changes in capital control regulations in smoothing the abrupt changes in the value of the yen. Dua and Sinha also report that, unlike the crisis-hit economies who adopted complete or a significant degree of capital control before 1997, India's capital account reforms with reasonable degree of capital control after the 1991–1992 crisis have contributed to her relative insulation from the Asian financial crisis in 1997.

Thus, a few conclusions can be drawn from the discussion on capital control. For small developed city-economies such as Hong Kong and Singapore whose benefit of becoming an international financial center is relatively large, it is advisable to have free capital mobility which is a prerequisite of an international financial center. Similarly, for developed economies whose financial system is reasonably sound (i.e., no significant inherent weakness) and real exchange rate is not significantly misaligned, the contributions of free capital mobility (i.e., more efficient allocation of capital) will be greater than that of capital control. However, for large and medium (developing) economies whose financial system and exchange rate level are vulnerable to speculative attacks, one has to be extremely careful in liberalizing her capital account. In fact, as noted by McKinnon and Takagi, with a significantly misaligned dollar value and rapidly growing international capital mobility by 1971, even the US was unable to stand against speculative attacks on the dollar.

4. Undervaluation of Yen: A Threat to Global Financial Stability?

Let us now come to McKinnon's discussion on the current undervaluation of the yen and the low interest rate in Japan, which is related to the very hot topic of "yen carry trade"[2] and could be a potential cause of global financial turmoil in the future.

---

[2]An example of yen carry trade noted by McKinnon is as follows: a speculator, who need not be a Japanese national, borrows short in Tokyo in yen at less than 1% in order to invest long-term in 10-year Australian government bonds bearing 6.27%.

4.1. *Currency mismatch, low interest rate, carry trade and run of yen*

Both Williamson and McKinnon in this volume indicate that the current yen is substantially undervalued, reflecting that this could be a common view among policymakers and economics academia in the US. Williamson believes the undervaluation of yen could be as much as 30%; McKinnon's comparison of real wages in Japan, Europe and the US also suggests that the real undervaluation of yen is substantial. McKinnon goes further in explaining how Japan is trapped by the undervalued yen and the currency mismatch between the huge US dollar claims and yen liabilities of Japanese mainline financial institutions such as insurance companies and banks:

> "... Although Japan is the world's largest creditor country, it does not lend much in yen because of the currency asymmetry associated with the dollar standard. Instead, the country's large current account (saving) surpluses are partially financed by outward foreign direct investment, but mainly by building up foreign currency claims (mainly dollars) on foreigners (Table 2). This leads to a currency mismatch within Japan's economy.
>
> In the private sector in particular, financial institutions such as insurance companies or banks acquire higher-yield dollar assets even though their liabilities are mainly in yen — as are their annuity obligations to policyholders or to depositors. Although these financial institutions have come to depend on the higher yield on dollar over yen assets, they fear any fluctuation in the yen/dollar exchange rate that would change the yen value of their dollar assets relative their yen liabilities. Even a random upward blip (appreciation) in the yen could wipe out their net worth. So they will hold dollar assets only if they are given a substantial risk premium for doing so."

> "... Because of the currency mismatch, this negative risk premium will be higher (more negative) the greater the fluctuations in the yen/dollar rate and the larger are Japan's private holdings of dollar assets. Figure 13 shows that, in the absence of secular appreciation of the yen since 1995, the yen/dollar rate has still fluctuated very substantially.
>
> Japan's current account (saving) surpluses only became significant in the early 1980s. But more than 20 years later, the cumulative total of liquid dollar claims held by the economy is now much greater relative to GNP than it was back in the 1980s — and it is continually growing (Table 2)..."

Thus, Japanese banks, insurance companies, trust funds and even some individuals are willing to hold the existing huge amount of US dollar assets only if they are given a substantial risk premium (i.e., substantial differential between the US and Japanese interest rates). However, with a close to zero interest rate and hence a limit in the risk premium, the system becomes vulnerable to any news that could trigger an expectation of yen appreciation or run for yen, and the Bank of Japan (BoJ) is forced to intervene in the foreign exchange market to stop the yen from appreciating:

> "… once there is a run, during which the BoJ buys dollar assets from the private sector on a large scale, Japanese insurance companies, banks and so forth, eventually become happy holding their remaining smaller stocks of dollar assets if and when they finally decide that the BoJ can hang on without letting the yen appreciate (further). After a run, these institutions may even be willing to rebuild their depleted stocks of higher-yield dollar assets for many months or years — thus providing finance for the ongoing current account surplus without the BoJ's intervening at all."

McKinnon also notes that: (i) the above mechanism also applies to yen carry trade; (ii) the size of the currency mismatched assets held by mainline Japanese financial institutions is much greater than that of carry trade; and (iii) carry traders have raised the exchange rate risk, and hence the required risk premium, of mainline Japanese financial institutions, which could in turn increase the likelihood and frequency of run for yen:

> "… the carry trade does contribute to the potential volatility of the yen/dollar exchange rate. With any hint of, or rumor that, the yen might appreciate, carry-trade speculators with their short-term yen liabilities may well react first. They rush to cover their short positions in yen by not renewing loans or simply buying offsetting yen assets. This quickly adds to the upward pressure on the yen so as to trigger a run that induces mainline financial institutions to start selling off their dollar assets as well, which the BoJ buys as per the positive spikes of official reserve accumulation in Figure 15. By making the yen/dollar rate more volatile, carry traders heighten the exchange risk to mainline financial institutions. Thus, indirectly, do carry-trade speculators widen the interest differential between dollar and yen assets necessary to maintain (an uneasy) portfolio equilibrium where mainline Japanese financial firms hold some of both."

4.2. *Japan is caught*

According to McKinnon, because of the worry of an abrupt appreciation of the yen,

(a) Japanese exporters were extremely cautious in revising wages up with productivity growth (i.e., with wage increment based on the current (undervalued) yen, a sudden reversal of the yen can easily change their business from profit-making to loss-making). As a result, Japanese wage increments have lagged behind those in Europe and the US, which has in turn increased the real undervaluation of the yen. The sluggish wage has also dampened Japan's private consumption and hence recovery from the lost decade, even though Japanese exports have achieved moderate growth in recent years.[3]

---

[3]Note that this is likely to be an argument for a delay in wage increment instead of a permanent stagnation of wages. With greater and greater relative real wage gap between Japan and the industrialized economies of the US and Europe, relative real wage in Japan will sooner or later be revised up, albeit with a delay.

(b) Japanese lending and deposit rates were low, with the deposit rate being close to the floor of zero.[4] This in turn implies a low lending-deposit interest margin which has contributed to the slow clearing of non-performing bank loans caused by the bursting of the asset bubble. With banks' lending ability still constrained by the non-performing loans, it is hard for Japan to emerge from the lost decade in a more promising pace.[5]

4.3. *A potential threat to global financial stability?*

So far is what has been discussed in McKinnon. What I would like to go further from here on is the following question: if a run for yen is big enough, is it possible that the BoJ might eventually choose not to intervene? What would happen in such a case? To answer these questions, first note that the BoJ foreign exchange market intervention (to stop the yen from appreciating) involves purchases of the US dollar and sales of yen, and the BoJ has the right to print as much yen as it likes. Thus, if it ever wishes to, the BoJ can deal with any size of run for yen. Nevertheless, it is still possible that the BoJ may no longer wish to stop the yen from appreciating when the cost of intervention (say, in terms of excessive money supply and inflationary pressure) is higher than the cost of not intervening. To see this, let us first discuss the mechanisms during the normal period and run for yen period with the help of Tables 1(a) and 1(b).

Table 1(a). Normal Period

Activities and Counteracting Force	Effect on the Foreign Exchange Market	
Japanese FIs and yen carry traders use their yen borrowings to acquire US dollar claims	demand US dollar	supply yen
Japan's current account surplus	supply US dollar	demand yen

Table 1(b). Run for Yen Period

Activities and Counteracting Force	Effect on the Foreign Exchange Market	
Japanese FIs and yen carry traders run for yen to unwind their currency mismatch exposures	supply US dollar	demand yen
BoJ's FOREX market intervention	demand US dollar	supply yen

---

[4]As explained in McKinnon, the risk premium on US dollar claims and internationally determined US interest rate would imply low interest rates in Japan. In addition, the sluggish economy has also resulted in a low lending rate in Japan.

[5]Note, unlike the case of wage increment, this argument could be permanent (i.e., with the required risk premium, Japanese interest rate could stay low forever). In addition, Japan could stay in a vicious cycle of low aggregate demand and weak bank lending activities.

During the normal period, most of the effect of Japan's substantial current account surplus will be offset by Japanese mainline financial institutions' (FIs) and yen carry traders' borrowing and investment activities (i.e., use their yen borrowings to acquire US dollar, or other foreign currency, claims). Thus, during the normal period, the BoJ was able to control Japan's money supply with only a small open market operation.

During the run for yen period, the BoJ will supply huge amounts of yen (and demand US dollar) in the foreign exchange market to meet the Japanese financial institutions' and yen carry traders' demand for yen. If the BoJ's intervention manages to, as it has been able to, clam the market so that the run is only temporary and Japanese financial institutions and yen carry traders are thereafter happy to hold the US dollar claims, then things will very soon return to normal. In the whole process, only a small portion of the US dollars was unwound for a short period, with which the Japanese economy and the global financial market have no problem to absorb. However, suppose there is a change in market fundamentals that eventually convince the Japanese bank and non-bank sectors to unwind their dollar claims on a more long-term basis, the BoJ intervention will imply a huge supply of yen and hence a multiple creation of Japan's domestic money supply for a prolonged period. Unless the Japanese government is able and willing to sterilize this with sufficient issuance of government bond, this will be extremely inflationary.[6] According to McKinnon, Japan's cumulative total of banks' and non-banks' net liquid dollar claims has already reached a huge sum. I am not sure whether this would exceed the Japanese government's capacity or willing limit of sterilization. If yes, then the implied inflationary pressure would eventually force the BoJ to give up the foreign exchange market intervention. By then, the substantially undervalued yen will start to shoot up, which would induce more inflows, and run, for yen. Obviously, the BoJ will try to smooth the yen appreciation even if it has decided to give up the intervention eventually, but the shock to the global financial and property market associated with the currency-match unwinding and the induced speculative inflows for yen could be sufficient to cause a crisis and hence, a global recession. The shock and disturbance to the Japanese and global economies arising from these relatively fast major realignments of the yen's exchange value against other currencies will also be huge.

How likely is this horrible scenario? My tentative view is: not that easy, but not impossible. Given the potential damage of not intervening amid a run for yen, it is obvious that the BoJ will intervene and the Japanese government will sterilize the implied money creation whenever possible. So, the key here is the relative size of the potential run (i.e., sum of Japanese private sectors' net dollar claims, yen carry traders' borrowings and speculative inflows) and Japanese government's willing limit of sterilization. However, even if the former is still within the limit of the latter, continued undervaluation of yen and continued accumulation of liquid dollar claims by the Japanese private sector could one day reverse the situation. Another question is what "market fundamentals" can convince Japan's private sector to unwind its liquid dollar claims on a more long-term basis and in a large enough

---

[6]Because of the floor of zero interest rate, Japan's interest rate may not be able to fall further to discourage the inflows.

scale. Will a recovery of the Japanese economy, which could cause a stock market boom or strong recovery of property price, be able to do so? Will the growing risk of a plunge in global financial asset price, which would induce the unwinding (and hence increase the likelihood and depth of the crisis), be able to do so? As it is too ambitious an aim for this Introduction to provide an answer to the whole issue, I will leave these very important questions for further rigorous study by national or international policy research institutes or academia.

Another related issue, and perhaps a solution of the above problem, is on the latest developments. With the recent substantial depreciation of the US dollar, the undervaluation of Japan's nominal effective exchange rate (NEER) could have been reduced. However, this would also mean an emergence or deepening of Europe's NEER overvaluation. That is, Europe and other floating currencies are not just losing their relative price competitiveness relative to the US, but are also losing their competitiveness relative to Japan, whose currency is more or less following the fall of the US dollar. Worse still, with the sustained years of sluggish wage in Japan and the relatively high wage growth in Europe highlighted by McKinnon, Europe's NEER could have been substantially overvalued. If so, after further rallies of the euro, will there be substantial depreciation of the euro in the longer future? That is, we might be seeing big cycles in major currencies such as the euro, sterling, Australian dollar and so on. This comes back to our Section 2's reminder against the presumed perfection of the floating exchange rate regime. [Note, with the depreciation of the US dollar in the first stage and the depreciation of other floating currencies in the second stage,[7] perhaps the above problem of yen undervaluation will be cleared. Of course, we have to hope that this happens before an uncontrollable run for yen.] [Postscript: Since the publication of this article in the *Singapore Economic Review* in December 2007, there were further depreciations of the US dollar *vis-à-vis* the euro and a temporary run for yen in February–April 2008 due to the sub-prime crisis in the US. However, from May 2008 onwards, changes in the expected market fundamentals (i.e., the market expected no further cut in interest rate and anticipated that the forthcoming election would mean the end of the weak-dollar Bush regime) had resulted in a rebound of the US dollar, and suggested that the US dollar might have already gone through its local trough and there could be major correction of the euro from the current unsustainably high level in the longer future. If so, it is possible that the world could clear the yen undervaluation and avoid the above run-for-yen crisis with a major correction of the US dollar at the first stage (already happened), and then another major correction of the euro and other floating currencies in the second stage (could happen in the longer future). For example, despite temporary runs for yen, the yen–US dollar rate on 16 June 2008 was 108.08, not much different from the 108.94 on 16 June 2005. On the other hand, the US dollar had depreciated by more than 20% against the euro during the same period (i.e., from 1.2115 to 1.5459). Of course, even if we could avoid the run-for-yen crisis in this way, there would still be big exchange cycles in the US dollar and the euro along the whole process. These would in turn have substantial impacts on the outputs of the related economies.]

---

[7]Note that both the US dollar and the euro will probably overdepreciate in the first and second stage. That is, there is likely to be overshooting and cycles of exchange rates in the whole adjustment process.

Which economy can better deal with the potentially big cycle of exchange rate discussed above? I believe the answer is Singapore, which would usually maintain her NEER appreciation target unless there are changes in real factors or inflation. By targeting the Singapore dollar against a basket of currencies, the fluctuations of the Singapore dollar will be much smaller than that of the euro: when the euro rises (falls) against the US dollar, the Singapore dollar will rise (fall) against the US dollar by a smaller amount and fall (rise) moderately against the euro. That is, despite large nominal swings in individual floating currencies, Singapore can avoid changes in her competitiveness through an appropriate choice in her NEER target. For example, in the absence of changes in real factor and foreign-domestic inflation differential, maintaining a fixed trade-weighted NEER would mean no change is her relative price competitiveness during the whole exchange rate cycle. That is also why I have kept recommending the Chinese government to start convincing and send strong signals to the market that she is constantly "observing" the exchange value of her currency against a basket of currencies instead of against the US dollar. That is, given the various types of imperfections in China's financial system, China should leave the difficult job of dealing with the cycles in the US dollar (euro) to Europe (the US), but she would do her duty by following the nominal swings in a smaller scale through a relative stable NEER which would be adjusted with changes in real factors or relative inflation. Such a shift of focus to the NEER from the rate against the US dollar will also mitigate the US pressure for further renminbi appreciation.

5. Remarks: Other Major Lessons

Finally, I would like to list a few other important lessons as follows. Interested readers could refer to the related articles for more details.

5.1. *Control of asset inflation*

Yip notes that one underlying reason for the Asian financial crisis in 1997 was the prolonged and rampant asset inflation era before 1997. It also highlights that the major risk to the Chinese economy and her exchange rate system reform is in fact the stock market bubble and rampant property inflation formed in recent years. To keep asset inflation under control,

(a) it is always better to curb any potential rampant asset inflation (or asset bubble) during the early stages; and
(b) if an expectation of rampant asset inflation has been formed, much greater curbing measures are needed before the asset inflation can be properly controlled.

Policymakers should also be careful about rebounds in asset price from a trough. If the rebound has resulted in an established upward inertia and an expectation of further rises in the asset price, it could cause changes in economic behaviors, a few macroeconomic vicious cycles and herding behaviors, which will fuel the rise in asset price and bring the asset market into an automatic path towards the bubble. Past experiences in the US and Hong Kong as well as the recent experience in China suggest that such likelihood is much greater than most people believe. Finally, experiences in the East Asian economies before 1997 and China since 2006 suggest that the asset inflation will sooner or later spillover to the CPI inflation. It is sad that a substantial number of insufficiently or improperly trained economists in China has caused delay in the curbing of China's CPI inflation through their ignorant comments and recommendations.

5.2. *Exit strategy from a fixed exchange rate system*

In Section 2, we explained that a fixed exchange rate system is probably not the best choice for most economies. Nevertheless, an exit from a fixed rate system could involve a huge exit cost, especially if the currency is substantially undervalued or overvalued. Thus, careful exit strategy is necessary to bring the exit costs to an affordable level. In the fifth paper of this volume, we see how China has used a gradual appreciation with narrow band (i.e., an upward-sloping variant of a fixed exchange rate system) to get out from the horizontal fixed rate system *vis-à-vis* the US dollar, before proceeding to the next stage of reform. Yip (2005b) has also provided a discussion on the exit costs of, and exit strategy from, the currency board system in Hong Kong.

5.3. *China's experience of banking reform*

In Yip's paper in this volume, we see that the non-performing loan ratio in China's banking industry was at a vulnerably high level before the banking reform in 2005–2006. However, after the injections by the Chinese government, then by the new foreign strategic partners, and then by the new shareholders through IPOs, the capital adequacy ratio in the Chinese banking industry has increased to a much more healthy level. Despite the Chinese banks' high non-performing loan ratio at the early stage, foreign strategic partners are interested in investing because they regard the injection as a fee paid to buy the "right" of doing, or participating in, banking business in the fast-growing Chinese economy. With the participation of the foreign strategic partners, there is a better likelihood of proper internal control in the future. This, together with the expected profit from the IPO allotments, has induced a lot of individual and institutional investors to inject funds into the Chinese banks through IPO subscriptions. Hence, China's experience in banking reform has provided a theoretically viable strategy for improving banks' capital adequacy ratio in other developing economies. Nevertheless, as noted by Yip, China still has to prove that the foreign strategic partners will be able to establish proper internal control and business-oriented lending mentality within the Chinese banks. Here, the role of foreign strategic partners is important as the size of their interests in the Chinese bank is much higher than the monitoring cost. On the other hand, shareholders' interests are so diffused such that the size of their interests is small relative to the monitoring cost. That is, one cannot rely on the shareholders to monitor the banks' behavior towards the desired direction.

5.4. *US bashing could be misleading*

McKinnon is very much against the US bashing for yen appreciation, and believes the yen appreciation has caused the syndrome of the ever-higher yen:

> "The expectation of an ever-higher yen led first to reduced nominal interest rates on yen assets, and contributed to the great bubbles in Japanese stock and land prices in the late 1980s. When the bubbles burst in 1990–1991, the deflationary pressure was reinforced by the further sharp appreciation of the already overvalued yen through to April 1995. The combination of an overvalued yen and the aftermath of the collapsed asset bubbles forced Japan's economy into a deflationary slump from which it has yet to fully recover."

He also recommends China to resist pressure for renminbi appreciation. Cheung *et al.* also note that the mere act of quickly revaluing renminbi — or of moving to a relatively free float — might in itself change the equilibrium exchange rate if it triggers corporate defaults or causes changes in the balance sheets of unhedged firms. The end of capital controls, either by fiat or by slow erosion, might also alter the equilibrium exchange rate. They believe that the US trade deficit is first and foremost a "made-in-America" problem, and it would be an enormous mistake to think that a stronger renminbi is a panacea for what ails the US. Other economists in the US also express concern that a rapidly appreciating renminbi would harm the US (say, in terms of consumer loss and inflation).

In the fifth paper of this volume, we can also see that China did not follow Japan's mistake by accepting secular appreciation. In fact, in my other recommendations to the Chinese government, I have indicated that if China bows to the US pressure for sharp appreciation, it will cause a lot of problems (e.g., enormous capital inflows though the illegal channels and abuse of legal channels, which will fuel the appreciation and/or cause rampant asset inflation through the greater money supply; the sharp appreciation will also cause a surge in China's unemployment rate to a socially painful level). By then, the Chinese leaders will be blamed by the Chinese people, and the US would have no incentive to correct the mistake. On the other hand, if China resists the US pressure, Chinese people will stand on the side of their leaders even if there is a trade sanction. As the US will also suffer from the trade sanction, there are incentives for the US to correct the mistake in the future. In a subsequent policy comment, I have also used the standard game theory result to highlight that the US threat of trade sanction is in fact a non-credible threat for a large economy such as China (i.e., it is not to the advantage of the US to honor the threat). By now, it is clear that China will not bow to the US pressure for sharp appreciation and capital account liberalization, although she does not mind making other non-detrimental concessions such as purchasing more US planes for the expansion of her airline fleets.

5.5. *Variable wage component*

Finally, Yip notes that the adoption of Singapore's variable wage component in the wage system will enable the adopting economy to cut the wage when deemed necessary. In view of the empirical evidence of substantial wage and price sluggishness, this will increase the flexibility of wages in the adopting economy. For example, in case of an overvaluation of domestic currency and an externally triggered recession such as that in Singapore in 1985–1986, the adopting economy can facilitate the recovery by cutting the variable wage component. In case of speculative attacks such as those in the Asian economies in 1997, a cut in the variable wage component will change the equilibrium exchange rate and help to fend off speculative attacks: a cut in wage amid a moderate depreciation will cause a rebound in exchange rate and hurt the speculators; in fact, speculators will have less tendency to attack the currency if they know the adopting economy can announce a nation-wide cut in wage when deemed necessary.

References

Friedman, M (1969). Round table on exchange rate policy. *American Economic Review*, 59(2), 364–366.

Johnson, HG (1969). The case for flexible exchange rates. *Federal Reserve Bank of St. Louis Review*, 51(6), 12–24.

Williamson, J (2000). Crawling bands or monitoring bands: How to manage exchange rates in a world of capital mobility. In *International Economics and International Economic Policy: A Reader*, P King (ed.). McGraw-Hill.

Yip, PSL (2002). A note on Singapore's exchange rate policy: Empirical foundations, past performance and outlook. *Singapore Economic Review*, 47(1), 173–182.

— (2003). A restatement of Singapore's monetary and exchange rate policies. *Singapore Economic Review*, 48(2), 201–212.

— (2005a). *The Exchange Rate Systems in Hong Kong and Singapore: Currency Board vs Monitoring Band*. Singapore: Prentice Hall.

— (2005b). On the maintenance costs and exit costs of the peg in Hong Kong. *Review of Pacific Basin Financial Markets and Policies*, 8(3), 377–403.

Yip, PSL and RF Wang (2001). On the neutrality of exchange rate policy in Singapore. *ASEAN Economic Bulletin*, 18(2), 251–262.

— (2002). Is price in Hong Kong that flexible? Evidence from the export sector. *Asian Economic Journal*, 16(2), 193–208.

THE INTERNATIONAL MONETARY FUND AND EXCHANGE RATE CRISIS MANAGEMENT*

CHONG-YAH LIM

Albert Winsemius Chair Professor of Economics
Director, Economic Growth Centre (EGC)
School of Humanities and Social Sciences (HSS)
Nanyang Technological University (NTU)
S3-01B-38, Nanyang Avenue, Singapore 639798
acylim@ntu.edu.sg

The article analyzes the limits of the IMF as a global multilateral economic agency to handle serious balance of payments disequilibria. Capital control and growth rates in developing Asia and the twin deficit problem of the United States are also discussed. It also assesses the probability of the reemergence of an exchange rate crisis in Southeast Asia and the wisdom of having an Asian IMF.

> "Lenin was right. There is no subtler, no surer means of overturning the existing basis of society than to debauch the currency."
>
> — John Maynard Keynes
> *The Economic Consequences of Peace*

Keywords: Exchange rate crisis; capital control; growth rates in China and ASEAN; East Asian financial crisis; US twin deficits; IMF; AMF.

1. Post-Crisis Per Capita Income

A not well-known fact is that *all* the six economies in Southeast Asia adversely affected by the 1997/1998 financial crisis have not, until today (November 2005), some eight years later, recovered from the pre-crisis per capita income level in US dollar terms (see Table 1). Thailand's per capita income in 1996 was US$3,084. After the impressive post-crisis recovery eight years later in 2004, it decreased by 18.3% to US$2,519. Indonesia's per capita income declined by 10.4%. In other words, the damage the exchange rate crisis did to the Southeast Asian economies is serious enough that utmost attempts must be made to prevent its recurrence. However, should there be another massive speculative attack on the exchange rate, and should external help be required, where could these countries turn to?

---

*This article is based on a Special Lecture presented at The Launch of Philip Kotler Center for ASEAN Marketing Forum on "Ten Countries, One Market", at the ASEAN Hall, The ASEAN Secretariat, Jakarta, on 24 November 2005.

Table 1. Per Capita Income of Crisis ASEAN
Countries, 1996 and 2004 (US$)

Countries	1996	2004	% Change
Brunei	17, 361	14, 454	−16.7
Indonesia	1, 141	1, 022	−10.4
Malaysia	4, 827	4, 731	−2.0
Philippines	1, 186	1, 059	−10.7
Singapore	25, 681	25, 002	−2.6
Thailand	3, 084	2, 519	−18.3

Source: United Nations (http://unstats.un.org).

It is also a not well-known fact that the exchange-rate-based crisis hit *only* the old ASEAN 6 — namely Thailand, Malaysia, Singapore, Indonesia, the Philippines and Brunei — but not the new ASEAN 4, namely, Myanmar, Laos, Cambodia and Vietnam. What is the explanation? The answer is that the new four all had exchange and capital control before the crisis struck. Today, in November 2005, some eight years later, contrary to some expectations, all four of them have, by way of contrast, much higher levels of per capita income in US dollar terms than before the crisis. Vietnam, for example, had in 2004 a per capita income that was 66% higher than the pre-crisis level, and Laos, 56% higher (see Table 2).

2. China and Capital Control

China had (and still has) exchange and capital control before, during and after the 1997 crisis. The economy continued to gallop, in real terms, at around 9% to 10% per annum, despite the existence of capital control. Or, is it because of the existence of capital control? If capital control shielded China from the Asian exchange and financial crisis of 1997/1998, the capital control mechanism must have contributed importantly to the continuation of the phenomenal income growth in China. Put differently, capital control certainly did not disenable China from attaining phenomenal real GDP growth rates from the time China went through the economic reforms of the opening-up process in 1979. IMF (International Monetary Fund) statistics show that China's per capita income in 1996, before the crisis, was US$667, and

Table 2. Increase in Per Capita Income of
Non-Crisis ASEAN Countries, 1996 and
2004 (US$)

Countries	% Increase
Cambodia	+9.0
Laos	+56.3
Myanmar	+17.7
Vietnam	+66.0

Source: United Nations (http://unstats.un.org).

this increased steadily to US$1,269 by 2004. Throughout this metamorphosis, including the Asian financial crisis years, China had capital control.

It is also often claimed that capital control would inhibit the inflow of foreign direct investment (FDI). China, as is well-known, attracted very much more foreign investments than all the six non-capital control Southeast Asian economies combined. Indeed, the massive inflow of FDI for the 1990s and thereafter came to as high as 3.9% of China's GDP (see Figure 1). This massive FDI inflow must have significantly contributed to China's most spectacular GDP advance, the phenomenal increase in external trade, and the impressive accumulation of foreign exchange reserves. Throughout the period of phenomenal capital inflow, China had capital control. There was no FDI in China before the 1979 "opening-up" period.

3. East Asia and Capital Control

The other East Asian economies that showed phenomenal economic advance at an earlier period, namely Japan, South Korea and Taiwan, all had important capital control and for a long period at that. Of course, capital control *per se* was, and never is, the magic wand for economic and social development. Nor is it *per se* the most desirable option or target to pursue. It was just a means to an end. At the early stage of economic growth, when speculative attacks on their currencies can be frequent and disastrous, capital control could contribute to the stability of the exchange rate. It could also allow for orderly exchange rate adjustments and the orderly shifting of gears. Hopefully, this phase could and should usher in the liberalization of the domestic economy, particularly the strengthening of the financial infrastructure and the liberalization of trade, both foreign and domestic trade. The

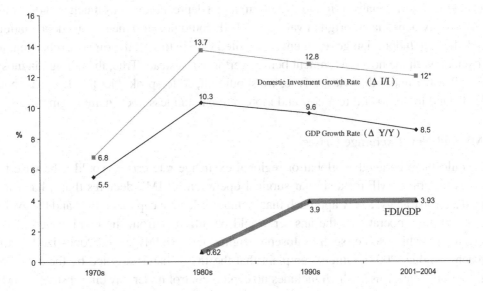

Figure 1. China: Relationship between Growth and Investment
Source: Lim (2005).

sequence should *not* be the opposite: exchange rate liberalization before domestic economic liberalization.

When IMF was invited by the Thai and Indonesian governments to help them halt their exchange rates from further precipitous fall in 1997, IMF unfortunately did not succeed. With hindsight, IMF was doomed to failure. Their exchange rates continued the precipitous slides (see Table 3, particularly column 7). Two main reasons why IMF did not succeed will be discussed here: one reason was doctrinaire, and the other, wrong timing or doing the right things at the wrong time. Ideologically, IMF was and still is anathema to any form of capital control, including any restriction on very short-term speculative capital movements, including by hedge funds. IMF has, therefore, in our view, deprived itself of a very useful and powerful instrument of exchange stabilization and orderly exchange adjustment. It is analogous to saying that IMF does not believe in the use of anesthesia, when modern surgery requires it. As is well-known, at the time of the crisis, Malaysia rightly broke rank. Much against the strong advice of IMF and others, Malaysia introduced selective capital control (Lim, 2004). As shown in Table 3, Malaysia succeeded in stopping the serious foreign exchange hemorrhage. Thailand lost so much foreign exchange reserves that the amount far exceeded the IMF loan she later received as a rescue operation (Lim, 2004).

In addition, when Thailand and Indonesia were faced with a serious crisis of confidence in the baht and the rupiah, the IMF advised the Thai and Indonesian governments to close down 56 finance companies in Thailand and 16 commercial banks in Indonesia (Djiwandono, 2005). These were done in the midst of the crisis of confidence in the financial system in these countries. As expected, there were runs on the banks in both countries. The already badly eroded confidence in the baht and the rupiah were further badly eroded. As Table 3 shows, at the beginning of the crisis, the exchange rate for the baht was US$1 = 25.8 bahts. By January 1998, it fell to US$1 = 53.8 bahts, a loss of 52% in value. In Indonesia, it began with US$1 to 2,450 rupiahs. It fell to 14,900 rupiah; a depreciation of as much as 84% of the already greatly depreciated original value. The IMF could not stop the serious depreciation. Indeed, the then Indonesian government had invited IMF in to save the rupiah exchange rate, and it ended with the host government being overthrown instead. True, the telling diagnosis is now all water under the bridge. True, we should all, so to speak, "let the dead past bury its dead", and look forward to a new and more rational and less doctrinaire beginning.

4. IMF and New Exchange Crises

But, should there be another global or regional exchange rate crisis, would it be wise for countries to turn to IMF for a similar surgical operation? If IMF declares that it has since adopted a new strategy, a new approach that includes selective capital control and the avoidance of untimely operations, the answer would be different from the continuance of the same remedy, which some, such as Joseph Stiglitz, have rightly called "one-size-fits-all" approach (Stiglitz, 2002). Others complain that the IMF's hands are tied by the so-called "Washington Consensus", which includes no capital control under any circumstances. IMF loan is conditional on the liberalization and further liberalization of the exchange rate. But the Washington Consensus also advocates the liberalization of the domestic economy and

Table 3. IMF and Depreciation of Exchange Rate (Per US$)

(1) Some Crisis Currencies	(2) Rates Before Crisis (June 1997)	(3) Rate at Time of IMF Intervention	(4) Lowest Rate	(5) Lowest Month	(6) First Depreciation [(2) − (3)/(3)]× 100%	(7) Depreciation Since IMF Intervention [(3) − (4)/(4)]× 100%	(8) Total Depreciation [(2) − (4)/(4)]× 100%
Indonesian Rupiah	2,450	3,648 (Nov 97)	14,900	Jun 98	−33%	−76%	−84%
Thai Baht	25.78	32.48 (Aug 97)	53.82	Jan 98	−21%	−40%	−52%
Korean Won	890.5	1,484.1 (Dec 97)	1,707	Jan 98	−40%	−13%	−48%
Malaysian Ringgit	2.57		3.8 (ringgit peg)	Sep 98 (start of capital control)		0% (after capital control)	−42% (before capital control)

Source: CEIC database.

Note: Malaysia did not adopt an IMF-supported program, unlike Indonesia, Thailand and South Korea.

the strengthening of the domestic financial infrastructure, which in our view, should come first before the crisis: otherwise, according to the S-Curve sequential theory (Lim, 2004), it would amount to putting the cart before the horse.

If the domestic value of a currency is not placed under a *laissez faire* footing, why should the external value be thus placed? It is good food for thought for the currency regulators, particularly IMF, especially in relation to serious short-term speculative capital movements. Money, including the exchange rate, is a means of exchange. If the internal value of money is subject to regulation in its supply by the central bank, why not the external value?

5. Future Exchange Crises

Is there a danger of a global exchange rate crisis, say, within the next five years, engulfing the Southeast Asian economies as well? There is some real danger, and this danger has not faded away with the persistent twin deficits in the USA.

One danger, hanging like the sword of Domiciles, is the selling away of a substantial US dollar stockpile from their huge accumulated US dollar reserves by important creditor nations like China, Japan and South Korea. This action may result, or is likely to result, in the serious depreciation of the US dollar generating adverse contagion effect all round, including all of Southeast Asia. The sizeable selling of US dollar reserves need not necessarily mean the swapping of US dollars for other currencies like the Euro dollar or the Japanese yen. They can be exchanged into other stockpiles of imports of irreplaceable assets like gold and fossil oil.

Another danger lies in the persistent and significant rise in the price of fossil oil, seriously aggravating further the balance of payments position of the USA. An important and persistent rise in fossil oil price will increase this danger, as never before in US post-war history has the US been so dependent on oil imports than she is today. Oil is an important common input in all modern production processes, and could easily trigger a cost-push and demand-pull circular cumulative inflationary process. The symptom is the frequent increases in interest rate to cut inflationary pressures or, exchange rate depreciation, or both.

The important increase in oil price can arise from many causes that result in the sudden and persistent or long-term curtailment of world supply. However, in the last few years, in response to persistent high fossil oil prices, the search for alternative energy sources has resulted in the discovery of replaceable bio-diesel fuels such as from the perennial oil palms. Besides, important new sources of fossil oil and gas outside the Middle East such as in Northeast China and Sichuan province are likely to moderate too great a jump in current fossil oil prices.

Thus far, the US has been able to maintain a fairly strong and stable US dollar, despite serious balance of payment disequilibrium on current account. Three factors are involved here. One, the use of interest rate differentials to stamp out the outflow of US dollars. Two, the very important, substantial autonomous long-term capital inflow (FDI) into the USA. Debates on the US dollar often miss this very important point. Three, the willingness and ability of balance of payments surplus and high savings nations such as China and Japan to lend to the US to finance its twin deficits, thus strengthening the external value of the US dollar.

Let us now pause for a minute to recall that in August 1971, the US was forced to abandon the international gold exchange standard. No longer could the US dollar be changed at a fixed rate of US$35 to one fine ounce of gold. A serious global exchange rate crisis thus erupted. The gold price is now US$672.64 to the same one fine ounce of gold. The world then moved to today's floating exchange system, with varying degrees of floating. What was once condemned as "dirty float" by the IMF has become acceptable "managed float". In short, most unfortunately, the US dollar today is not immune from originating and generating a global financial crisis, as it had come to pass in August 1971.

Oil price in 1971 was US$1.90 per barrel. Today, it is about US$65 per barrel. In 1973 and 1974, when oil price went up to US$2.80 and US$10.40 per barrel respectively, serious global inflation followed. If oil price today were to escalate from US$65 per barrel, to, say, US$120 per barrel within the next few years, for sure, serious global inflation or global stagflation would follow. Then, in the early 1970s, US was self-sufficient in oil. Today, US imports 25% of its domestic oil demand. An oil crisis, with further adverse impact on US balance of payments deficit, can thus easily turn to a US dollar crisis, with a serious downslide in the US dollar. If countries cannot pay for the high oil import price, an exchange crisis can also develop. (The Indonesian experience in August 2005 confirms this possibility, nay, probability.) Then, when a global or regional crisis breaks, where do the crisis countries turn to for help? The IMF, as in 1997/1998?

One most frequently discussed US balance of payments problem is her serious trade deficit with China (the PRC). The solution often advocated by the US, and supported by the IMF, is the deliberate appreciation of the Chinese yuan. But the facts are that the US has trade deficit problems, in varying degrees of seriousness, with nearly all, if not all, its major trading partners (see Table 4). In fact, as Table 4 shows, the US's trade deficit in 2006 with the European Union and Mexico and Canada ($253 billion) even exceeded that of China ($232 billion). Thus, a more flexible exchange rate policy of China is no guarantee

Table 4. United States' Merchandise Trade
Deficits, 2005 and 2006 (US$ bn)

Country/Region	Balance on Visible Trade	
	2005	2006
China	−218	−232
Japan	−87	−87
East Asian countries*	−58	−50
Middle East	−34	−31
European Union	−131	−116
North America (Canada, Mexico)	−81	−137
Africa	−52	−62
Deficit with the world	−782	−818

*East Asian countries here refer to Hong Kong, Malaysia, Korea, Singapore, Taiwan and Thailand.
Source: US Census Bureau.

that the overall trade deficit of the US will disappear, from serious overall disequilibrium to equilibrium or surpluses. Is the gradual orderly depreciation of the US dollar the solution for the USA and for the whole world? Can this orderly gradual depreciation be brought about, if other important trading partners also depreciate *pari passu*, as would automatically be the case, if their currencies are rigidly pegged to the US dollar, as in the case of China before 1979?

6. Asian IMF Proposal

Under the circumstances, will an Asian IMF (AMF) be helpful? During the 1997/1998 Asian exchange rate crisis, Japan, then with by far the largest foreign exchange reserves in Asia and in the world, proposed the setting up of an AMF. The proposal received hardly any support from the USA or from Asia. A regional IMF using the same tools for stabilization and following the same policy options as the IMF obviously could not be of benefit to member countries in Asia or the world. The AMF, when constituted, must stick to the original Keynesian objective of the IMF, with the mission for an orderly exchange rate adjustment arising from fundamental disequilibrium in the balance of payments. This means the AMF must not be a regional replica of the present IMF, together with its blemishes and self-imposed handicaps. But if the global IMF adopts a new policy of strategic pragmatism, the case against an AMF should, in my view, be considerably weakened. But an Asian IMF too could hardly be expected to solve the serious US balance of payments problem without the orderly depreciation of the US dollar.

7. Another Southeast Asian Crisis

However, as it is, if for any reason the US dollar, which is the world's pivotal currency, strengthens significantly or weakens significantly, it does not follow in the present circumstances that Southeast Asian countries would *pari passu* come under serious exchange rate pressure. As Figure 2 shows, one, unlike in 1997/1998 when many of the Southeast Asian countries had had serious long-term balance of payments disequilibria, they all have had impressive yearly balance of payments surpluses after the catastrophic collapse of their exchange rates. Two, contrary to the pessimistic forecast of natural rubber price by the World Bank (World Bank website), rubber price has steadily increased from US$0.58 per kilo in 2001 to US$1.50 per kilo in 2004 and US$1.66 per kilo in 2005 (see Table 5). With a spectacular increase in rubber price, and given that Thailand, Indonesia, Malaysia and Vietnam are the largest producers and exporters of natural rubber in the world, a rubber export boom in Southeast Asia is not off the cards. The inflated export earnings would be a direct or indirect boon to many Southeast Asian economies, though not to the extent of the Korean War boom in the early 1950s.

However, also of immense importance is the spectacular increase in palm oil prices (see Table 5). Southeast Asia, particularly Indonesia and Malaysia, produces nearly all the palm oil supply in the world. As a large part of this supply is expected to take the form of replaceable bio-diesel fuels from palm oil, the factor would further boost up the commodity

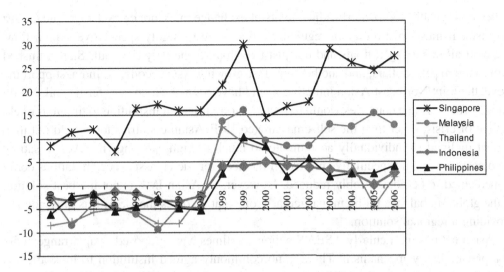

Figure 2. Current Account Balance as a Percentage of GDP, 1990–2006

Source: Lim (2001, p. 313).

Note: 2000–2006 data extracted from ADB, *Asian Development Outlook 2005, 2007*.

Table 5. Natural Rubber and Palm Oil Prices
(US$)

Year	Natural Rubber	Palm Oil
2001	$0.58/kg	$286 mt
2003	$1.08/kg	$443 mt
2004	$1.50/kg	$471 mt
2005	$1.66/kg	$422 mt
2006	$2.31/kg	$478 mt
2007 (April)	$2.48/kg	$708 mt

Source: International Rubber Study Group (IRSG);
United Nations Conference on Trade and Development (UNCTAD); World Bank.

export boom of Southeast Asia, reducing further the fear of a foreign exchange disaster of the sort experienced in 1997/1998.

Nonetheless, the conclusion is that should any of the Southeast Asian countries be faced with an exchange rate crisis, the wisdom to turn to IMF for help is still in serious doubt. If IMF adopts a more flexible policy in handling crisis management, that doubt might disappear. If an AMF is formed, it must abandon the two basic pillars of the Washington Consensus strategy and policy, adopting instead a New IMF Consensus based on strategic pragmatism. With so many Asian nations now flushed with so much foreign exchange reserves, perhaps the time is ripe for Japan, China and South Korea to take the lead to form a new Asian Monetary Fund as a precautionary and preemptive move. The new regional institution must be based on strategic pragmatism, on orderly adjustments of exchange rates, not on exchange rate *laissez faire*-ism. It must have room for regulation on short-term highly speculative capital flow. It should allow managed floats and not just free float. If the very rich Gulf States, flushed with so much petrodollars, and another very fast-growing Asian economy, India, support the move, the joint Northeast Asian initiative would have been sown on very fertile soil, not on slippery rocks. Asian countries would have another multilateral institution to turn to for help in time of crisis, other than the self-emasculated IMF. Asian countries too would not then be that inclined to individually accumulate so much foreign exchange reserves to satisfy the precautionary and speculative motives if the need for such massive accumulations could be perceived to be considerably reduced. However, an Asian IMF is not the best solution to the global imbalance problem, particularly one that involves the USA. It is only good in providing a regional solution.

Asian nations, particularly ASEAN nations, at times have proposed swap arrangements as a precautionary mechanism. There is no commonly agreed institution to look after its implementation. Prior to the 1997/1998 Asian financial crisis, ASEAN too had initiated an exchange swap arrangement. It turned out to be toothless when the crisis emerged. That Asian nations have continued each to stockpile huge foreign exchange reserves is indicative of their trust in their own individual responsibility and individual solution to any possible exchange storm, rather than to regional or global arrangements such as the IMF.

Acknowledgments

The views expressed herein are the author's personal views. He would like to thank Ms Sarah Chan, his Research Associate, for the preparation of this paper.

References

Djiwandono, S (2005). *Bank Indonesia and the Crisis: An Insider's View*. Singapore: ISEAS Publications.
Lim, CY (2001). *Southeast Asia: The Long Road Ahead*. Singapore: World Scientific.
Lim, CY (2004). The Asian financial crisis. In *Southeast Asia: The Long Road Ahead*, 2nd Ed. Singapore: World Scientific.
Lim, CY (2005). Economic theory and the East Asian region. *Singapore Economic Review*, 50, 495–512.
Stiglitz, J (2002). *Globalization and Its Discontents*. New York: WW Norton & Company, Inc.

THE CASE FOR AN INTERMEDIATE EXCHANGE RATE REGIME*

JOHN WILLIAMSON

Senior Fellow, Peterson Institute
1750 Massachusetts Ave, NW
Washington DC 20036, USA
jwilliamson@petersoninstitute.org
JWilliamson@iie.com

The argument that any exchange rate regimes other than firmly fixed and freely floating rates were infeasible — the so-called bipolarity thesis — acquired great popularity in the wake of the Asian crisis of a decade ago, but it has almost vanished today. One reason is surely the unkind empirical evidence, which shows that intermediate regimes — measured as those where both reserve and exchange rate changes lie in an intermediate range — are not in fact tending to disappear (Levy Yeyati and Sturzenegger, 2002). Another reason is the recognition that exchange rate policy should have other objectives besides avoiding crises, and that in the world we live in today it is reasonable to give these other objectives a significant priority. And perhaps a third factor is growing recognition that it is possible to design or operate intermediate regimes in ways that avoid exposing them to the dangers that were focused on by the disciples of bipolarity.

This article starts by distinguishing the options that countries face in choosing an exchange rate regime. It examines the advantages and disadvantages of each of them, finally suggesting that for most countries the real choice lies between freely floating rates, floating rates disciplined by a reference rate system, and an ill-defined managed floating with the management undefined. Three issues may influence the choice between those alternatives: transparency; perceived consistency with that pillar of current macroeconomic thinking, inflation targeting; and the theory of what determines exchange rates. In the latter context, it is argued that the current conventional wisdom of the economics profession is wrong, and that a more convincing diagnosis of the process of exchange rate determination lends support to the proposal for a reference rate system.

Keywords: Exchange rates; fixed versus floating; intermediate regime; IMF; behavioral finance.

1. A Taxonomy of the Options

There are many ways of classifying the set of exchange rate arrangements from which countries must choose. For example, it is possible to classify them according to their combinations of exchange rate volatility and reserve volatility, as Levy Yeyati and Sturzenegger (2002) do. For some purposes this is a useful procedure, but it does not focus directly on the set of rules that a country must adopt, as a more traditional taxonomy does. Adopting that approach, one

---

*An article commissioned for publication in the *Singapore Economic Review*. Copyright Peterson Institute: All rights reserved.

might get a taxonomy similar to that presented below:

- Fixed rates (really fixed: dollarization or currency board)
- Floating, either free or managed, by:

  ○ Seat of the pants intervention (e.g., "countering disorderly markets")
  ○ Intervention to counter the trend of the market
  ○ Intervention to push the rate toward equilibrium (the Reference Rate Proposal)

- Adjustable peg (Bretton Woods' "stable but adjustable")
- Intermediate = BBC (basket, band and crawl).

"Fixed rates" mean what they say. They are rates that are intended to stay fixed for all time, not until the next crisis. Dollarization (i.e., the use of a foreign currency as money) surely guarantees that the rate will remain fixed, as, according to their advocates, do currency boards. Until the Argentine crisis we all bought that line, and afterwards the advocates of currency boards were quick to point out that the Argentine arrangements differed in significant respects from an orthodox currency board. But the Argentine crisis made one realize that a currency board holds reserves only equal to M0 but has to guarantee the convertibility of a multiple of that amount (M3), at pain of creating a crisis. There is no reason in principle why this should always be possible without provoking a crisis, and the fact of national sovereignty means that there can be no assurance that the government will not respond to the crisis by changing the exchange rate.

The term "floating" encompasses two very different regimes. One is that discussed in economic textbooks, in which the authorities treat the exchange rate with benign neglect (or at least with neglect). Purists sometimes worry about whether such a thing as a freely floating exchange rate is possible, since the dates at which the government's own transactions are put through the market are bound to have an impact on exchange rates. The non-purists among us dismiss this worry as *de minimis*. Of vastly greater importance is the distinction between a market-determined floating rate and a system in which the government has such a major influence in determining the exchange rate as to justify calling it "managed" floating. These two systems will be analyzed separately in what follows, although the difference is not always readily apparent from public pronouncements and hence, these two systems are often classified together in statistical presentations.

The third regime listed is the "adjustable peg". This is the most descriptive name for the system officially described by the oxymoron "stable but adjustable exchange rates" that was the basis of the Bretton Woods system.

Last is what Dornbusch and Park (1999) termed the "BBC Regime". In this context, BBC stands for basket, band and crawl. The band, and its center, is defined in terms of a *basket* of currencies so as to keep the effective exchange rate reasonably constant in the face of changes in the exchange rates between the major currencies. The authorities give scope for the market exchange rate to respond to market forces within a *band*, but they place limitations on that flexibility by undertaking to intervene to prevent the rate going outside the (wide) band. They further undertake to make changes in the band, and its center, gradually in relatively small steps (i.e., by *crawling*) rather than in the sudden discrete jumps characteristic of the adjustable peg.

2. Fixed Rates

An obvious advantage of fixed exchange rates is that transactions costs within the monetary area will be lower. This will be much less true if there remains a separate currency with a currency board as opposed to using a foreign currency, and even where there is a single currency the experience of the euro area indicates that the benefits can be slow in materializing, but the benefits are relatively certain. (In all probability they are also rather small, though we do not have a good estimate of their size.)

Economists (e.g., Frankel, 1999) customarily cite the provision of a nominal anchor as the other great benefit of a fixed exchange rate. They rely on the postulate of zero-degree homogeneity to argue that if one locks in the foreign price level by a fixed exchange rate, then this will guarantee that the domestic price level approaches a determinate equilibrium level. I do not give much shrift to this argument. We have many examples of countries that have achieved major adjustments of their real exchange rates in a manner contradictory to the theory: one might, for example, cite the East Asian countries in 1997. More persuasively still, Brazil hung on to an overvalued exchange rate until early 1999 because of a fear that devaluation would reignite its multi-decade hyperinflation that had been ended by the Plano Real in 1994. When the devaluation finally came, the inflationary acceleration was no more than a blip. What matters to stabilizing inflation is a domestic policy that is prepared to stop inflation — which is why inflation targeting has been such a success.

Most economists also recognize two important costs to giving up the exchange rate as a policy instrument by fixing the exchange rate. One is that this deprives a country of its most potent expenditure-switching instrument, implying that — especially if there is a real danger of exchange rate misalignment against the anchor currency — adjustment becomes a whole lot more costly. The other is the impossibility of pursuing an independent monetary policy.[1] This is, however, a good deal less unambiguous a gain than has traditionally been portrayed. One wonders whether we would have been such enthusiastic supporters of every ex-colony acquiring its own independent central bank and running its own monetary policy if we had understood in 1960 how many of them were going to abuse the power of the printing press. Fortunately, this is now history and most countries have learnt from bitter experience that fast inflation is not a clever policy, which implies that nowadays the conventional wisdom is probably an acceptable formulation.

---

[1]This cost is frequently cited by the IMF as the reason for wanting China to revise its exchange rate policy. Unfortunately, this would require China to allow its exchange rate to become market-determined, which is a pipe-dream in the short run. A faster rate of appreciation, which is the realistic objective, might well increase the incentive to move into yuan and therefore *increase* the needed level of Chinese intervention, despite which it would gradually contribute to resolving the global payments imbalances.

Based on the foregoing considerations, my list of conditions for a policy of fixing the exchange rate to make sense is as follows:

(1) The country and its prospective partner(s) satisfy the conditions for an optimum currency area.
(2) Its trade is focused principally on its prospective currency partner(s). (This is the ground on which I regard Hong Kong's choice as anomalous; the policy of pegging to the currency of a minor trading partner is the source of the severe macroeconomic pressures to which Hong Kong is notoriously subject.)
(3) Its inflation target is consistent with that in its prospective partner(s).
(4) It is prepared to adopt an institutional arrangement that will guarantee continued credibility of the fixed-rate commitment. (In practice, this is likely to imply a currency board.)

3. Freely Floating Rates

The advantages of a policy of free floating of the exchange rate are the obverse of the costs of a decision to fix the exchange rate. In the first place, this implies that adjustment will be less costly, because the exchange rate can change in order to promote adjustment. Second, it means that macroeconomic policy can function without an artificial external constraint being imposed by the need to satisfy an exchange rate objective. (Of course, it is still true that there will be an external constraint, because countries cannot finance deficits larger than those for which the rest of the world is prepared to advance finance.) Note also that it is not true, if it ever was, that floating countries need suffer the absence of a nominal anchor: they can adopt a policy of inflation targeting.

The disadvantage of a policy of free floating is, however, shared with the policy of fixing the exchange rate. This is shown very clearly in East Asia today, where the two large currencies, the Chinese renminbi and the Japanese yen, have diametrically opposed exchange rate policies (one being essentially fixed and the other floating with no intervention), but are both undervalued by upwards of 30% against the US dollar. So misalignment is as much a problem with a floating exchange rate as with a fixed exchange rate. In my view this is of major importance, because the evidence is now accumulating that a big misalignment is bad for growth. The evidence that this is true in developed countries is mixed, but it seems to be unambiguously true of emerging markets and developing countries (Razin and Collins, 1999; Prasad, Rajan and Subramanian, 2006; Aguirre and Calderón, 2006). These are, of course, the countries where growth really matters. Note that although overvaluation is the most damaging type of misalignment, large undervaluations are also empirically bad for growth — which is not theoretically surprising, given that an undervaluation siphons off real resources into reserve accumulation that could be invested in growth under alternative policies.

4. The Adjustable Peg

If one wishes to avoid misalignments, then it is necessary to adopt an exchange rate regime that gives priority to the objective of avoiding them. This was a hope of the adjustable peg regime adopted at Bretton Woods: that it would allow the conveniences of fixed exchange rates in normal times, while allowing the possibility of using the exchange rate as an adjustment instrument when a large misalignment had emerged. Had the world remained permanently with the capital immobility that was a fact of life at the time of Bretton Woods, maybe this regime would have worked. But of course it did not. Capital mobility gradually revived. Already by the 1960s, it was apparent that exchange rates among the industrial countries needed to be consistent with the new reality of capital mobility. The hope of the Committee of Twenty (1972–1974) that it could design a revised international monetary system on "stable but adjustable exchange rates" by encouraging prompt exchange rate changes when these were needed was naïve: a resolve to change exchange rates promptly would have been met by the market by prompter speculative flows. It was necessary instead to go to an alternative exchange rate regime.

5. The BBC Regime

Some of us argued in the late 1960s that the answer was to make parity changes through a series of small steps, via a crawling peg, rather than in the occasional large steps that characterized the adjustable peg. That way the market could be well aware that an exchange rate change was impending, but still not be motivated to indulge in large destabilizing capital flows between currencies, so long as differential interest rates offset the expected exchange rate change. If a currency was expected to depreciate at 3% per year, then the interest rate would need to be 3% higher to neutralize the incentive the expected depreciation would otherwise provide to shift funds out.

Before long, the question arose as to how large were the "small steps" that were acceptable. The answer was provided by Johnson (1970), who showed that as long as the old and new bands overlapped, then the market could not be confident of making a profit by correctly speculating on an impending change. Thus emerged a realization that the two forms of limited flexibility that had been discussed in the 1960s, the crawling peg and the wide band, were interdependent. So, in due course, the two ideas were merged in proposals for limited flexibility under the heading of "target zones" or "crawling bands". It was argued that the band needed to be wide for four reasons:

(1) Because estimates of equilibrium exchange rates were imprecise. There was no point in wasting financial resources and the authorities' credibility in defending a disequilibrium exchange rate, as might happen with a narrow band.
(2) Because a wide band is necessary to allow scope for anti-cyclical variations in monetary policy. For example, even if the public anticipated everything correctly, a band of ±10% would allow the authorities to hold the short-term interest rate 5% above that in the rest of the world for two years. The exchange rate would initially appreciate to the strong edge of the band, and then the expected depreciation would offset the higher interest rate and leave the incentive to arbitrage unchanged.
(3) A wide band is needed to allow exchange rate changes to be made without provoking disequilibrating capital flows, as already explained.

(4) The last reason for wanting a wide band was to allow strong but temporary capital movements to have a part of their counter in exchange rate movements, rather than compelling all of them to be financed by reserve changes.

The last element of the BBC regime (which happens to be the first term in its title) arose from the literature on the optimal behavior of developing countries in a world of floating exchange rates among the main industrial countries. This suggested that a country with diversified trade would do better to peg to a basket of currencies that kept its effective exchange rate roughly constant than to follow the traditional practice of pegging to a single other currency. This would tend to stabilize its inflation rate and employment levels against the shocks that would otherwise be created by the exchange rate of the currency to which it pegged changing against the exchange rates of its other trading partners. The classic example of the importance of this factor was provided by several East Asian currencies in 1997, when their dollar pegs resulted in their effective exchange rates appreciating in parallel to the dollar, thus helping provide the conditions in which the Asian crisis could emerge.

6. Managed Floating

The distinction between free and unmanaged floating was emphasized above, but up to now there has been no analysis of a system of managed floating. The problem is that there is no agreed view on *how* floating should be managed. At one extreme, a regime of managed floating may be one in which the government determines the exchange rate by administrative fiat: it simply gives no guarantee that the rate it decides tomorrow will bear any relation to the rate it decides today. That varies all the way to a system in which the market ordinarily determines the rate, but the government retains the right to intervene when it feels the outcome of market forces to be unsatisfactory. Often, intervention is described as aiming to counter disorderly markets or prevent unrealistic rates. Both these cases are examples of what I describe as "seat of the pants intervention": the government intervenes if it feels like it, but it gives no information to the market which might help in understanding when or under what circumstances to expect intervention or what objectives might be pursued. So long as the government refuses *ex ante* to explain what it means by such terms as disorderly markets or unrealistic rates, then it falls in my category of seat of the pants intervention.

There are two suggestions in the literature as to how one could define *ex ante* the type of intervention that would be acceptable. One (due to Wonnacott, 1958) is that intervention should always "lean against the wind", i.e., resist the recent trend of the exchange rate. The other (due to Ethier and Bloomfield, 1975) is that any intervention that may occur should always push the exchange rate toward its estimated equilibrium, i.e., resist misalignments. (Since that equilibrium is named as the reference rate, this proposal goes under the term "the reference rate proposal".) In neither case is it implied that there is a *duty* to intervene under certain conditions: the implied obligation is only on the direction of any intervention there may be. In both cases, it is defensible to describe this as a managed floating exchange rate: it is a rate that is determined as the outcome of an interaction between market forces and official management described with some transparency to the market. Governments have automatic permission to discipline the market, but only if the discipline they wish to administer goes in a socially-approved direction.

The main suggestion as to how one might introduce some international discipline into what I have described as seat of the pants intervention is due to my colleague Morris Goldstein (2004), who wishes to give some substance to the existing IMF Articles by defining exchange rate "manipulation" (which is proscribed but undefined) as substantial and prolonged intervention in the same direction. In itself, this definition would tend to prohibit the intervention that is most needed, as well as that which is most pernicious. For example, the yen is currently greatly undervalued by the market, and this situation has persisted for a long time. Ergo, Goldstein's rule taken by itself would prohibit intervention to strengthen the yen, which seems to me to be just as badly needed as a prohibition on intervention to keep the renminbi weak. However, the remainder of the IMF's Article IV, Section 1(iii) might be construed to limit manipulation to that which prevents adjustment or tends to beggar-thy-neighbor, since it obliges member countries to:

> "Avoid manipulating exchange rates or the international monetary system in order to prevent effective balance of payments adjustment or to gain an unfair competitive advantage over other members."

Wonnacott's (1958) proposed rule suffers from a similar problem. If the yen were to start to recover, it would allow intervention to slow the rate of appreciation. But when the yen is greatly undervalued, the objective should be to encourage appreciation, not to discourage it. The rule would only make sense in conjunction with something like a reference rate rule.

So long as one regards the real problem as one of misalignment, the only rational basis for authorizing intervention is whether or not the intervention would tend to reduce the misalignment. One is thus led to the reference rate rule. No one should imagine that this rule is some sort of panacea. Where capital mobility is high, the existence of the rule will not alter the fact that there is little scope for altering market outcomes. But it will be argued subsequently that it is a mistake to believe that there is no scope at all, and so long as there is any scope it is undesirable to allow governments unfettered ability to exert influence without any international disciplines. Exchange rates are inherently a subject involving more than one country, and in a multi-country world, the international interest is best taken into account by subjecting each country to a symmetrical set of rules.

7. The Bipolarity Thesis

In the wake of the Asian crisis, there arose a school of thought which claimed that the world was being driven to consider firmly fixed and freely floating exchange rates as the two only feasible systems (Eichengreen, 1999; Fischer, 2001). The thesis was that any intermediate regime would be overwhelmed by speculative pressures. It had long been accepted that this was true of the adjustable peg (a system that tended to be classified as an intermediate regime, despite the fact that the initial analyses of intermediate regimes arose as a reaction against the adjustable peg), but the same was claimed to be true of the BBC regime. And there was an element of truth in this contention. Indonesia had a well-functioning BBC regime which showed no sign of macroeconomic trouble in June 1997, despite which it found itself forced to abandon its BBC regime two months later as contagion from Thailand changed Indonesia's situation abruptly. Perhaps a BBC regime provided enough flexibility to avoid being overwhelmed by domestic shocks, but shocks that originated abroad were another matter.

The bipolarity thesis has since become much less appealing, for reasons additional to the empirical observation that intermediate regimes are not in fact tending to disappear. One is the realization (already mentioned) that currency boards do not guarantee that crises are not possible. A second is acceptance that there are other objectives to economic policy besides avoiding crises. Specifically, there is increasing concern that misalignments, and in particular overvaluation, may disrupt growth, particularly in emerging markets and developing countries (Razin and Collins, 1999; Prasad, Rajan and Subramanian, 2006; Aguirre and Calderón, 2006). Whether or not it should be, this is the dominant objective of economic policy. A third element is the increasing acceptance that it is possible to design intermediate regimes in a form that avoids the hard bands that provoke crises. For example, it is possible to conceive of the BBC regime without hard edges to the bands, or one may have a system of managed floating based upon reference rates. Either results in an intermediate regime without the vulnerability that arises from having a hard edge to the band.

8. Choices

Where does this leave policymakers? For some countries, primarily small ones or else those with neighbors prepared to share monetary sovereignty, the option of a fixed exchange rate may be attractive. For the remainder, free floating is one option, but some form of intermediate regime is another. If transparency as well as invulnerability to speculative pressures are regarded as essential, then the choice is essentially between a BBC regime with soft margins and a reference rate system. However, since a BBC regime with soft margins is more or less indistinguishable from a reference rate system, this is not in practice much of a choice. The more important issue may in fact be that of transparency. Academics tend to take it for granted that transparency is a virtue, and to dismiss any system that does not maximize the clarity of what is happening. Policymakers tend to be much more attracted by what they see as the virtues of non-transparency, which allows them to escape accountability when mistakes are made. Presumably, non-transparent policymakers can eventually win market trust (as one assumes those of Singapore have done), but the process can surely be hastened by adopting a set of rules that enable the market to check whether the policymakers are systematically doing as they claim. I am not aware of any evidence that presently bears on this issue.

In choosing between free floating and managed floating disciplined by a reference rate system, two issues have been held to be relevant. One is the issue of inflation targeting (see the report of de Rato's interview in the *Financial Times*, 28 January 2006). It is widely accepted that inflation targeting has proved an effective principle for conducting monetary policy. Many of us even regard it as the best way of interpreting the Keynesian concept of internal balance. Hence, if de Rato was right in arguing that there is an inconsistency between a reference rate rule and inflation targeting, this would be a serious issue. The argument is, however, ill-conceived. A reference rate rule merely specifies that if there is any intervention, then it has to be in a certain direction. It never compels a country to intervene, and hence it cannot influence the growth of the money supply in a direction that is counterproductive to that desired by the authorities. There cannot be an obligation imposed on a government that may conflict with an inflation-targeting objective.

The other issue is the legitimacy of the standard model of exchange rate determination. Some of the empirical implications of this standard model are (Williamson, 2007):

(1) That exchange rates respond systematically to changes in such fundamentals as money supplies, income levels, interest rates, expected inflation rates, terms of trade, and productivity, at least insofar as current events influence perceptions of permanent values.
(2) That in the absence of such "news", exchange rates will not change.
(3) Money is made by having a good notion of the implications of the fundamentals for exchange rates, and it will be lost by extrapolating past exchange rate changes, as chartist rules do.
(4) That there is no scope for "bubble-and-crash" dynamics.

All these implications run strongly counter to massive empirical evidence:

(1) The study of Meese and Rogoff (1983), which found that a random walk outperformed all the models of exchange rate determination at time horizons of up to a year. This is still the dominant conclusion of students in the field, although Gourinchas and Rey (2005) have argued that adding the exchange-rate induced change in wealth to the current account can permit a degree of short-run forecastability to the exchange rate.
(2) No one has suggested any "news" that might account for the great rollercoaster in the rate between the US dollar and the DM/euro over the decade 1993–2003.
(3) Chartist rules are widely and profitably used in the foreign exchange market.
(4) There frequently appear to have been instances of bubble-and-crash dynamics in the foreign exchange market (e.g., the surge in the dollar that peaked in early 2002, or the peak of the yen in 1995, or the dollar in 1985, or the pound sterling after Margaret Thatcher came to power).

It is difficult to avoid the conclusion that the standard model of exchange rate determination is an empirical failure. It is well-known, however, that models are not abandoned just because of empirical failures, but that they are replaced only by a better model. De Grauwe and Grimaldi (2006) argue that the standard model should be replaced by what they term a behavioral model. This has a similar structure to that first presented by Frankel and Froot (1986), although it is more firmly grounded in the now proliferating literature of behavioral finance. They postulate that the foreign exchange market is populated by agents who use either fundamentalist or chartist trading strategies, where the former involves forecasting the exchange rate will move part way back to the estimated equilibrium, while the latter extrapolates the recent change in the exchange rate. Any particular agent may adopt either strategy, but is "boundedly rational" in changing tactics to the other rule if it is proving more profitable over a recent period. They adopt a rule of thumb motivated by bounded rationality because the real world is too complex for them to imagine that they are able to command the perfect knowledge that would enable them to optimize rationally.

The model is too complex to permit an analytical solution, so the authors resort to simulations. On the basis of several thousand simulations, they conclude that:

(1) Exchange rate changes are disconnected from the fundamentals, although the level of the exchange rate is cointegrated with its fundamental value.
(2) Exchange rates may change in the absence of news.
(3) Chartist rules tend to be more profitable than fundamentalist ones, although a better strategy is to switch between one and the other.
(4) Exchange rate changes have fat tails.
(5) The exchange rate is sometimes, but unpredictably, disconnected from its fundamental value, and instead involved in bubble-and-crash dynamics.

In other words, the model appears to be consistent with the stylized facts about the operation of the foreign exchange market.

One very interesting feature of the De Grauwe–Grimaldi model is that intervention in the foreign exchange market can be an effective policy tool. It "works" through neither of the channels recognized by standard theory, namely the portfolio channel and the signaling (of future monetary policy) channel, but instead by increasing the profitability of the fundamentalist trading strategy, and thereby inducing a greater percentage of market operators to use that strategy and abandon chartism. This is important because it gives the authorities an instrument with which to pursue a BBC or reference rate rule. It remains true that the authorities cannot hope to pursue successfully any old exchange rate target they want. If they try to hold a disequilibrium exchange rate target, they will still be killed (as they should be). But if they confine themselves to the objective of limiting misalignments, they can hope to succeed. However, a given level of intervention will be less effective the greater the volume of funds that shifts in response to a given differential in expected rates of return (i.e., the greater the degree of capital mobility).

The IMF will have to be at the center of such a system. It would be responsible for developing and securing political agreement to the set of reference rates. One would expect it to use the CGER[2] group to develop a set of mutually consistent proposals, and then to lay these before the Executive Board for approval. No doubt many countries will be somewhat dissatisfied, but at least the obligations which go along with a reference rate are limited. No country will be required to intervene against its wishes; it will simply be required to refrain from intervening except when in a direction that will be implicitly determined as in the international interest. Since such intervention will be receiving international sanction, one would expect that "oral intervention" pointing that way would be somewhat more effective than unilateral pronouncements. And since most interventions that countries will anyway wish to make are likely to receive such international support, countries will have a strong

---

[2]The Consultative Group on Exchange Rates, an internal working group of IMF staff.

incentive to agree procedures that will ensure that agreement is ultimately reached. Of course, these will need to include the right of the Executive Board to refer back a proposed set of reference rates for revision if it is dissatisfied, and in principle this might happen more than once. But it would be necessary to agree a procedure which would ultimately give the Board the right to impose a set of reference rates on a recalcitrant minority. While one would hope that agreement on a set of reference rates would normally be based on consensus, it would be necessary to provide for the worst.

In assessing the likelihood of the IMF having difficulty reaching agreement on a set of reference rates, it would help if the IMF were to publish the figures for equilibrium exchange rates that it is already producing. It published a very helpful description of the techniques that it uses (IMF, 2006), which outlined the three methods that it applies. The first asks what exchange rates (real effective rates, obviously) would be needed in the medium-term to generate a set of current account targets that represent a conception of equilibrium capital flows. A second is essentially a variant on this, in which the current account targets would be at the levels needed to keep existing NIIP/GDP ratios constant. The third is quite distinct, and asks what exchange rates would produce the average outcome over a previous period, taking account of changes in variables that are known to affect equilibrium exchange rates like net foreign assets and trend productivity growth. It would be of much help to outsiders in assessing likely difficulties in agreeing on equilibrium exchange rates if the results of these exercises were published, so that we could see whether they in fact produce significantly different figures for most currencies. If not, and if such differences as exist are readily explicable (e.g., because during the period of observation one country was going ever deeper into international debt), it would strengthen confidence in the feasibility of producing figures that would command general assent.

9. Concluding Remarks

The option that has received relatively little discussion in this paper is the one that prevails at the moment and is likely, I fear, to prevail in the future. This is a regime in which many countries float, in the sense of not accepting any published limits on where their exchange rates may go, but intervene without any articulated principles governing their intervention. The reason that this regime has not been analyzed more systematically is that it is impossible to analyze something that is incapable of definition. Nevertheless, one may identify three reasons why this regime does not seem very desirable:

(1) It does not appear to be feasible to superimpose a system of international management without individual countries adopting a set of principles governing their economic policy. The most that anyone has suggested is to make effective — by defining — a proscription on exchange rate "manipulation", and even that would require an interpretation of balance of payments equilibrium (for otherwise there cannot be knowledge of whether intervention is such as to prevent adjustment).
(2) Individual economic agents have no basis other than inertia and their own private expectations on which to base their presumption of what will transpire in the future.

There would be advantage in a system that increased the assurance about the form of the future.

(3) It is not transparent, and this prevents public servants being held accountable as well as impeding the public learning that is the basis for an orderly and well-behaved foreign exchange market.

Most countries will not wish to embrace the constraints of a fixed-rate system in order to escape from the current *laissez faire*. Unless sufficient can be persuaded of the virtues of free floating, a well-defined system will be possible only on the basis of the sort of reference rate system that I have described above. The bipolarity thesis had things exactly backwards: the extremes remain unattractive to most countries, but it is entirely possible to conceive of an attractive and crisis-free middle ground.

Acknowledgments

The author is indebted to his colleague Edwin Truman for useful discussions, but absolves him for responsibility of the results.

References

Aguirre, A and C Calderón (2006). The effects of real exchange rate misalignments on economic growth. Mimeo.

De Grauwe, P and M Grimaldi (2006). *The Exchange Rate in a Behavioral Finance Framework*. Princeton: Princeton University Press.

Dornbusch, R and YC Park (1999). Flexibility or nominal anchors? In *Exchange Rate Policies in Emerging Asian Countries*, S Collignon, J Pisani-Ferry and YC Park (eds.). London and New York: Routledge.

Eichengreen, B (1999). *Toward a New International Financial Architecture*. Washington: Institute for International Economics.

Ethier, W and AI Bloomfield (1975). *Managing the Managed Float*, Princeton Essays in International Finance, No. 112. Princeton: International Finance Section.

Fischer, S (2001). Exchange rate regimes: Is the bipolar view correct? *Journal of Economic Perspectives*, 15(2), 3–24.

Frankel, J (1999). *No Single Currency Regime is Right for All Countries or at All Times*, Princeton Essays in International Finance, No. 215. Princeton: International Finance Section.

Frankel, JA and KA Froot (1986). Understanding the US dollar in the Eighties: The expectations of fundamentalists and chartists. *Economic Record*, 62, 24–38.

Goldstein, M (2004). Adjusting China's exchange rate policies. Paper presented to an IMF seminar on China's Foreign Exchange System, Dalian, May.

Gourinchas, P-O and H Rey (2005). International financial adjustment. Mimeo.

IMF (International Monetary Fund) (2006). *Methodology for CGER Exchange Rate Assessments*. Occasional Paper No. 209.

Johnson, H (1970). A technical note on the width of the band required to accommodate parity changes of particular size. In *Approaches to Greater Flexibility of Exchange Rates: The Burgenstock Papers*, CF Bergsten, GN Halm, F Machlup and RV Roosa (eds.). Princeton: Princeton University Press.

Levy Yeyati, E and F Sturzenegger (2002). On the endogeneity of exchange rate regimes. Business School Working Paper, Universidad Torcuata Di Tella.

Meese, R and K Rogoff (1983). Empirical exchange rate models of the 1970s: Do they fit out of sample? *Journal of International Economics*, 14, 3–24.

Prasad, ES, RG Rajan and A Subramanian (2006). Foreign capital and economic growth. Mimeo, IMF.

Razin, O and SM Collins (1999). Real exchange-rate misalignments and growth. In *The Economics of Globalization: Policy Perspectives from Public Economics*, A Razin and E Sadka (eds.). Cambridge: Cambridge University Press.

Williamson, J (2007). Exchange rate economics. Paper prepared for the Growth Commission sponsored by the World Bank.

Wonnacott, P (1958). Exchange stabilization in Canada, 1950–1954: A comment. *Canadian Journal of Economics and Political Science*, 24(2), 262–265.

JAPAN'S DEFLATIONARY HANGOVER: WAGE STAGNATION AND THE SYNDROME OF THE EVER-WEAKER YEN

RONALD MCKINNON

William Eberle D. Professor of Economics
Economics Department, Landau Economics Building
Stanford University, Stanford
California 94305-6072, USA
mckinnon@stanford.edu

Japan still suffers a deflationary hangover from the great episodic yen appreciations of the 1980s into the mid-1990s. Money wages are still declining, and short-term interest rates remain trapped near zero. After Japan's "lost decade" from 1992 to 2002, however, output has begun to grow modestly — but through export expansion and associated investment rather than domestic consumption. This export-led growth has been helped by a passive real depreciation of the yen: prices and wages in Europe and the United States have grown, and are growing, faster than in Japan. As the yen becomes weaker in real terms, American and European industrialists and politicians are again complaining that the yen is too weak (Japan bashing II?) — although the pressure on Japan to appreciate is not yet as great as it now is on China.

But Japan is trapped. If it does appreciate the yen, its fragile economy will be driven back into outright deflation. The only solution is to stabilize the nominal dollar value of the yen over the long-term, but this step will not necessarily be immediately effective in placating foreign mercantilists. Under foreign pressure to appreciate the renminbi, China, with its booming economy, is now in a similar position to Japan's of more than 20 years ago. Policymakers in China should resist pressure to go down the same deflationary road as Japan.

Keywords: Japan; exchange rate risk; deflation.

1. Introduction

In early February 2007, a phalanx of incoming Democratic committee chairmen — Levin, Rangel, Frank and Dingel — worrying particularly about a 32% increase in automobile imports from Japan from 2005 to 2006 and which continue to increase strongly in 2007, wrote a letter to US Treasury Secretary Paulson:

> "The weak yen reflects (Japanese) monetary and fiscal policies, including setting low interest rates and failing to stimulate consumer demand. We believe that the weak yen is a reflection of Japanese government policy. It reflects the Japanese government's massive intervention earlier in the decade, an intervention which still reverberates in the value of its currency."

On 30 March, the *Financial Times* reported: "A lobbyist for GM, Ford and Chrysler said the Treasury Secretary needed to be pushed into spearheading a coordinated international effort that would lead to Japan selling down its excess reserves to stimulate a stronger yen".

On 16 July, *The Japan Times* reported that The Bank for International Settlements has issued a warning against the current trend of yen undervaluation. Its Annual Report states, "There is clearly something anomalous in the ongoing decline in the external rate of the yen".

In Europe, the financial press has also been full of quotes from politicians complaining about the yen being unduly weak against the euro and pound sterling, making Japanese exports too competitive. In its 10 February 2007 issue, *The Economist* pontificated: "A country with one of the world's largest current-account surpluses and low inflation (but no longer deflation) should have a much stronger currency. Japan's economy is no longer flat on its back. Last year it grew by an estimated 2.3% and is forecast to maintain a similar pace this year. As a result Japan does not need such low interest rates or a super-cheap currency anymore. Indeed, Japan's abnormally low interest rates (the short-term interbank rate is just one quarter of one percent) could be viewed as a form of intervention to hold down the yen" (p. 77).

The Economist produced a graph showing a sharp fall in the real trade-weighted yen of more than 30% over the last eight years. (The euro and pound have appreciated even more against the yen in real terms.) *The Economist* also showed that, by February 2007, the "real" yen had depreciated just below where it was in 1970 — just before the Nixon shock of August 1971 drove the dollar down against all the major currencies.

Without contradicting any of these statistics, I will show that the Japanese have been rather hapless victims of international monetary events. Foreign exchange risk (fear of yen appreciation) has kept Japanese interest rates mired close to zero for more than a decade, and still prevents the Bank of Japan from properly stimulating domestic consumption demand. Even though output resumed growing modestly from 2003 to 2007 after the preceding "lost decade", wages continue to stagnate. The recovery remains so fragile that the Japanese government is divided and uncertain on the question of raising interest rates and strengthening the yen. In this paper, the historical roots of Japan's continuing macroeconomic fragility, resulting in today's syndrome of the ever-weaker yen, are examined.

2. The Historical Origins of Japan's Deflationary Trap

Should the Bank of Japan, and the Japanese government more generally, now be faulted for striving for a deliberately undervalued (beggar-thy-neighbor) currency? Are they cheating in the international money game? Essentially no to both questions. The Japanese authorities are trapped into allowing an ever-weaker yen to continue.

The roots of today's trap go back to the 1970s. Worried about Japan's increasing mercantile competitiveness and rising trade surpluses, the United States pressured Japan — by numerous threats of trade sanctions arising out of industry-specific disputes — to keep appreciating the yen. The yen rose from 360 to the dollar in August 1971 (at the end of the Bretton Woods period of fixed exchange rates) to touch 80 in April 1995, before Treasury Secretary Robert Rubin announced a new "strong dollar" policy and ended overt Japan bashing to appreciate the yen. The Bank of Japan and the US Federal Reserve intervened several times

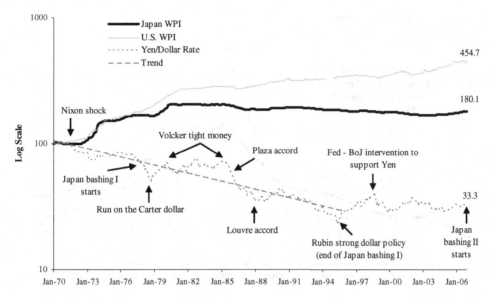

Figure 1. Wholesale Price Indexes for Japan and the US versus the Yen/Dollar Rate from 1970 to 2006 (1970 = 100)
Source: *IFS*.

in the summer of 1995 to put a ceiling on further appreciations of the yen. Rubin's new policy was, in the main, successful. In the late 1990s, the yen retreated from its extraordinary 1995 high, and has averaged about 118 to 120 yen per dollar over the past eight years — albeit with the fairly wide fluctuations shown in Figure 1.

However, the deflationary damage, including heightened fear of foreign exchange fluctuations, had been done. In 1997, McKinnon and Ohno in *Dollar and Yen: Resolving Economic Conflict between the United States and Japan* described what they called "the syndrome of the ever-higher yen", which arose arising from recurrent mercantile (protectionist) pressure from the United States to get the yen up (Chapter 1). Yen appreciation began forcing down the yen prices of tradable goods in the mid-1980s. The expectation of an ever-higher yen led first to reduced nominal interest rates on yen assets, and contributed to the great bubbles in Japanese stock and land prices in the late 1980s (Chapter 5). When the bubbles burst in 1990–1991, the deflationary pressure was reinforced by the further sharp appreciation of the already overvalued yen through to April 1995. The combination of an overvalued yen and the aftermath of collapsed asset bubbles forced Japan's economy into a deflationary slump from which it has yet to fully recover.

Japan's surprisingly long deflationary hangover can be better understood by looking at relative wholesale (tradable goods) prices in Japan and the United States arising out of yen appreciation (Figure 1). By the mid-1970s, inflation in Japan's WPI fell below the high inflation rate in the US, but was still positive. However, when the American price level stabilized in the mid-1980s, Japan's WPI inflation turned sharply negative from the massive appreciation of the yen over 1985–1987 — coming out of the 1985 Plaza Hotel Accord to depreciate the dollar. Subsequently, Japan's WPI drifted down more slowly until

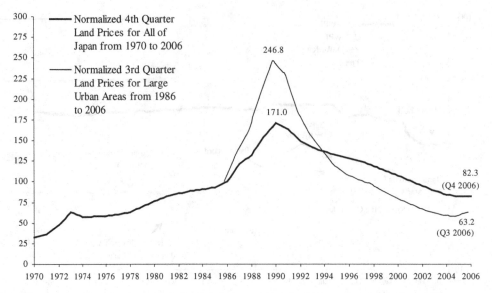

Figure 2. Index of Land Prices for All of Japan versus Large Urban Areas (1986 = 100)
Source: Bank of Japan.

the international price of oil increased after 2002. But Japan's WPI inflation remained (and remains) far below that in the US.

Another measure of Japan's deflationary hangover is how long land prices continue(d) to fall after the property bubble burst in 1991. Figure 2 shows the sharp rise in Japanese land prices from 1986 to 1990 when they more than doubled, and then fell by two-thirds — albeit more gradually — from 1990–1991 through 2005. Although urban land prices turned up slightly in 2006, land prices continue to fall elsewhere. Unsurprisingly, residential construction remained virtually dormant over this deflationary period.

3. Wage Growth and the Exchange Rate

What does the historical record tell us about the link among alternative exchange rate arrangements and growth in nominal wages? From 1950 to 1971, Japan provided a useful case study of wage behavior in a very high-growth economy with its exchange rate securely fixed at 360 yen per dollar — the dominant international money.

First, keeping the fixed rate anchored Japan's price level for tradable goods as Japanese wholesale prices rose at about the same speed as those in the US — only 1% per year (Table 1). Because the bulk of world trade was (is) invoiced in dollars, fixing the exchange rate to the dollar was (is) a stronger anchor for the price level than the size of Japan's bilateral trade with the United States would suggest.

Second, Japanese money wages in manufacturing grew substantially faster — about 10% per year in Japan versus only 4.5% in the US. From the 1950s into the 1970s, Japan's catch-up phase, productivity growth in manufacturing was much higher than in the US. But international competitiveness was roughly balanced by Japan's much higher wage growth when the

Table 1. Japan and the United States, 1950–1971, with the Yen Fixed at 360 per Dollar (Average Annual Percent Changes)

Wholesale Prices		Money Wages (Mfg)		Consumer Prices		Industrial Production	
US	Japan	US	Japan	US	Japan	US	Japan
1.63	0.60[a]	4.52	10.00	2.53	5.01	4.40	14.56

Real GDP		Nominal GDP		Narrow Money		Labor Productivity	
US	Japan	US	Japan	US	Japan	US	Japan
3.84	9.45[a]	6.79	14.52[a]	3.94	10.10[b]	2.55	8.92[c]

[a] 1952–1971.
[b] 1953–1971.
[c] 1951–1971.
Source: *IFS, Japan Economic Yearbook, Economic Survey of Japan, OECD Economic Surveys,* and Bureau of Labor Statistics.

yen–dollar exchange rate was fixed. In China from 1994–2005 when the renminbi–dollar exchange rate was fixed, the same phenomenon was observed: the much higher productivity growth in Chinese manufacturing was matched by much higher growth in money wages relative to those of the United States (McKinnon and Schnabl, 2006). Thus, a rough balance in international competitiveness was preserved.

Why, in a rapidly growing open economy, should wage growth better match productivity growth when the nominal exchange rate is fixed? From the old Scandinavian model of wage determination in high export-growth-led economies (Lindbeck, 1979), the tradables sector — with its much higher growth in productivity than in non-tradables — naturally becomes the leading sector in wage setting. Employers in export activities bid vigorously for skilled and unskilled workers, subject to remaining internationally competitive at the fixed exchange rate. Thus, workers in export-oriented manufacturing receive the main fruits from the high productivity growth there. But then, from "labor solidarity" (as the Scandinavian model would have it), these high wage settlements spread into the rest of the economy, largely non-tradable services where productivity growth was much lower.

In Japan, the price of services rose relative to goods prices over 1950–1971: Japan's CPI, which includes services as well as goods, increased more than 4 percentage points faster per year than its wholesale price index (which contains only goods), and faster than the US CPI (Table 1). However, under the fixed yen/dollar exchange rate leading to rapid wage increases, Japan's international competitiveness in its high-growth tradables sector remained balanced with the United States — as reflected in the similar rates of price inflation in tradable goods measured by their respective WPIs.

In this bygone high-growth era, finding a purely domestic monetary anchor for Japan's price level would have been difficult. As in China today, restrictions on domestic interest rates and capital controls proliferated, and growth in the money supply was high and unpredictable

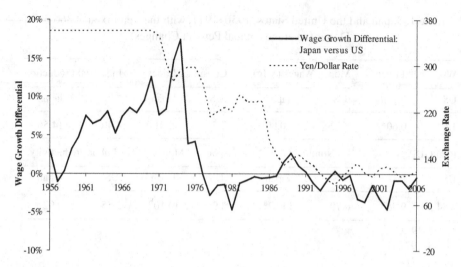

Figure 3. The Yen/Dollar Exchange Rate and Differential Manufacturing Wage Growth between Japan and the US, 1956–2006
Source: *IFS*, OECD.

as Japanese households rebuilt their financial assets after World War II. Thus, having the Bank of Japan simply key on the dollar exchange rate conveniently anchored Japan's tradable goods price level while promoting high growth in money wages. By the end of the 1960s, however, American monetary policy became too inflationary for the dollar to provide a stable anchor, and the Bretton Woods system of fixed exchange rates collapsed.

How did the switch to a "floating" but ever-appreciating yen affect relative wage growth in the two countries? After 1971, episodic Japan bashing led to ongoing yen appreciation as reflected in the dashed line in Figure 3. The expectation of an ever-higher yen (from recurrent US pressure) eventually undermined the system of relative wage adjustment. As employers began to anticipate further yen appreciation, growth in Japanese wages slowed — albeit with a lag. Before 1975, money wage growth in Japan remained much higher than in the United States; but then in 1975–1976, Japan's money wage growth slowed sharply — the bold line in Figure 3. Since then, wage growth in Japan has been even *lower* than that in the United States. While imposing general deflationary pressure on the Japanese economy, *the erratically appreciating yen undermined the natural process of adjustment in relative wages for balancing international competitiveness.*

In addition, the slump in Japanese absorption reduced imports, which offset the slower growth in exports from the higher yen. Thus, Japan's large trade surplus, measured as a share of its own GDP, did not decline (McKinnon, 2007; Qiao, 2007). Although this earlier episode of Japan bashing to push the yen up failed in its principal objective of reducing Japan's trade surplus, it did cause severe deflationary disorder within Japan's macroeconomy that continues to the present day.

But why should wage stagnation continue 12 years after Secretary Rubin announced his strong dollar policy and the end of American arm-twisting to get the yen up? The answer is twofold. First is the stagnation in Japanese GDP growth from 1992 to 2002 — its "lost decade" — with only weak growth subsequently. Second, because of a currency mismatch within Japan's financial system (to be explained below), the threat of sudden upward ratchets in the dollar value of the yen is still very much alive — and heightened by the return of US and European Japan bashing in 2007. Employers could face bankruptcy if they granted a generous wage settlement and the yen then shot upward. Thus, risk-averse Japanese employers remain unduly timid in granting higher wage settlements — leading to the phenomenon of an ever-weaker yen, i.e., real exchange depreciation.

4. Parsing the Yen's Real Depreciation

Changes in real exchange rate depend both on relative rates of price inflation and changes in the nominal exchange rate. Consider first the underlying rates of price inflation. Figure 4 plots the paths of the consumer price indexes (CPIs) for Japan, the Euro Zone and the United States, from 1 January 1999 — when the euro officially came into existence — to the last quarter of 2006. Over this eight-year period, inflation was 22.8% in the United States, 18.5% in the Euro Zone, and −2.3% in Japan.

Figure 5 then plots the nominal (undeflated) exchange rates for the yen/dollar, the euro/dollar, and the yen/euro. Despite a few ups and downs, the nominal yen/dollar rate was little changed: the dollar had appreciated just 4.7% against the yen from January 1999 through January 2007. By adding the CPI inflation differential to the change in the nominal exchange rate, 29.8% approximates the real appreciation of the dollar against the yen. More precisely, if we double deflate the nominal yen/dollar rate by the Japanese and US CPIs, Figure 6 shows the actual real appreciation of the dollar against the yen to be 28.7%. Either

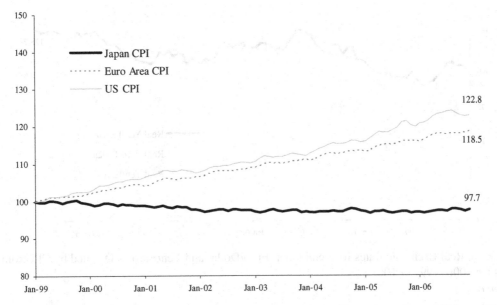

Figure 4. Consumer Price Indexes for Japan, the US and the Euro Area from 1999 to 2006 (1999 = 100)
Source: IFS.

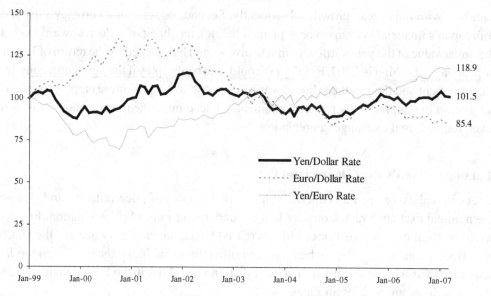

Figure 5. Nominal Yen/Dollar, Euro/Dollar and Yen/Euro Exchange Rates from January 1999 to March 2007 (1999 = 100)
Source: IFS, The Economist.
Note: Actual market rates as of 31 March 2007: Yen/Dollar: 117.93; Euro/Dollar: 0.750; Yen/Euro: 157.23.

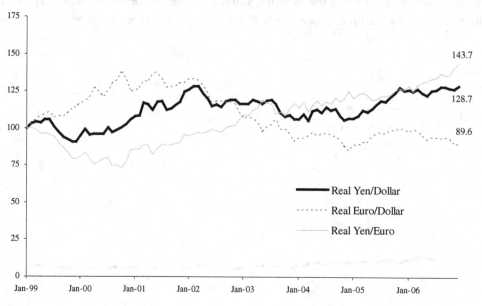

Figure 6. Real Exchange Rates for Yen/Dollar, Euro/Dollar and Yen/Euro as Deflated by CPI from 1999 to 2006 (1999 = 100)
Source: IFS.

way, the real appreciation of the dollar came mainly from the 25.1% inflation differential, i.e., the higher inflation in the US, and not from the dollar's modest nominal appreciation against the yen.

The story of the yen/euro rate is somewhat different. From January 1999 to the last quarter of 2006, the euro appreciated 19.2% against the yen in nominal terms (as shown in Figure 5). If the CPI inflation 20.8% differential between Japan and the Euro Zone (Figure 1) is added to this nominal euro appreciation, the approximate real appreciation of the euro against the yen is close to 40%. When the real exchange rate is calculated more precisely by double-deflating the nominal exchange rate by the CPIs in Japan's and the Euro Zone, Figure 6 shows the euro's real appreciation against the yen to be 43.7%. Thus, the euro's more visible nominal appreciation was almost as important as the inflation differential in explaining the euro's large real appreciation against the yen, which now so irritates European mercantile interests and their governments.

Changes in the euro/dollar exchange rate have been less dramatic. From January 1999 to January 2007, the euro also appreciated against the dollar by 12.1% in nominal terms (Figure 5), and by 10.4% in real terms (Figure 6).This real appreciation of the euro against the dollar was slightly muted because CPI inflation in Europe was moderately lower than in the United States (Figure 4). Although some Europeans — notably the makers of Airbus aircraft — are worried about the relatively small decline in the dollar, most see Japan with its weak yen to be the greater mercantile threat to European heavy and high-tech industries.

Unit labor costs. To check on these calculations of "real" exchange rates deflated with broadly based CPIs, consider the OECD's estimated unit labor costs more narrowly in manufacturing — the only sector for which comparable quarterly data are available across all three areas. Unit labor costs are wage costs in local currencies less productivity growth per unit of output.

Figure 7 compares the course of manufacturing wages in Japan, the Euro Area and the United States from the first quarter of 1999 through the fourth quarter of 2006. American nominal wages in manufacturing rose by 24%, European by 27.8% and Japanese by only 7.9%. Figure 8 then shows that Japanese unit labor costs fell by 24.2%, whereas those in the Euro Area fell by just 3% and those in the US by 5.9%. (Although this general fall of unit labor costs in manufacturing is striking, it need not hold in other sectors within our three economies.) Thus, manufacturing unit labor costs in the Euro Area rose relative to those in Japan by 21.3 percentage points. But on top of this, the euro appreciated in nominal terms against the yen by 19.2% (Figure 5). To be more precise, double-deflating the nominal yen/euro exchange rate with manufacturing unit labor costs, Figure 9 shows *the "real" appreciation of the euro against the yen to be a remarkable 55% from early 1999 through the fourth quarter of 2006.*

Can this increase in Japan's international competitiveness be explained by its superior productivity growth? Somewhat surprisingly, from first quarter 1999 to fourth quarter 2006, manufacturing productivity growth rates across all three areas were similar. Changes in labor productivity can be backed out of the OECD data on wages (Figure 7) and unit labor costs (Figure 8) to show that growth in labor productivity was 32.1% in Japan, 29.9% in the US

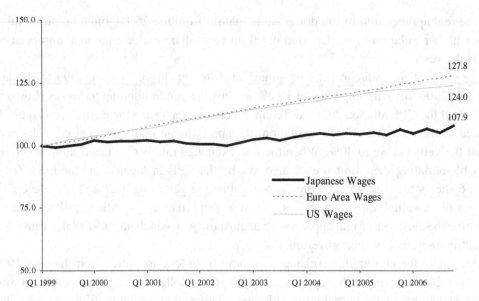

Figure 7. Japan, Euro Area and US Manufacturing Wages from Q1 1999 to Q4 2006 (1999 = 100)
Source: OECD.

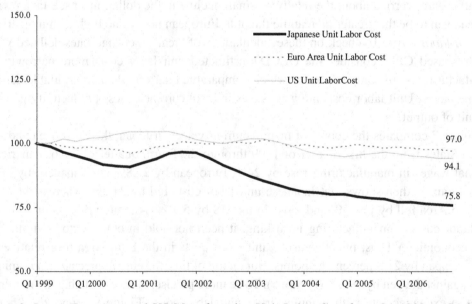

Figure 8. Japan, Euro Area and US Manufacturing Unit Labor Cost from Q1 1999 to Q4 2006 (1999 = 100)
Source: OECD, European Central Bank.

and 30.8% in the Euro Area. Although the Euro Zone's slightly lower productivity growth (1.3 percentage points in manufacturing) contributed to its loss of competitiveness relative to Japan, this effect was dwarfed by the euro's nominal appreciation of 19.2% against the yen, and by European wage growth being 19.9 percentage points higher than Japan's.

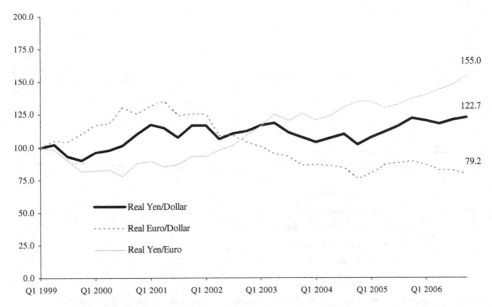

Figure 9. Yen/Dollar, Euro/Dollar and Yen/Euro Real Exchange Rates as Deflated by Relative Manufacturing Unit Labor Costs, Q1 1999 to Q4 2006 (1999 — 100)
Source: *IFS*, OECD, European Central Bank.

Based on unit labor costs, the dollar's real appreciation against the yen was "only" 22.7% (Figure 9), but still very substantial. However, most of the loss in US competitiveness relative to Japan's came from the faster growth in US wages, or, to put it differently, wage stagnation in Japan. From 1999 through the fourth quarter of 2006, American wages grew by 16.1 percentage points above their Japanese counterparts in manufacturing when US productivity growth was only 1.2 percentage points less.

To erase any doubt about the persistent deflationary pressure on prices and wages in Japan, Figure 4 shows a 2.3% fall in Japan's CPI from 1999 to fourth quarter 2006. Beyond just manufacturing, Figure 10 provides comparable wages across the whole of the private sectors of Japan, the United States, France and Germany. (No such general series was available for the Euro Area as a whole.) Japanese nominal wages actually *fell* by 3.4%, while those in the US rose by 27.8%, by 33.4% in France and by only 16.5% in Germany. And wage deflation in Japan continues. *The Economist Intelligence Unit* (June 2007, p. 27) reports that in April 2007, monthly cash wages per worker in Japan actually fell 1.4% compared with a year earlier. Wage deflation in Japan continues to be unique relative to the other large industrial countries.

Does this persistent wage stagnation simply reflect Japan's low or non-existent GDP growth during its lost decade after the stock and land bubbles burst in 1990–1991? Perhaps not. Remarkably, from 2003 through 2006, when Japan's real output and GDP growth finally began to grow a modest 2% per year (Figure 11 shows nominal GDP growth), Japanese money wages still fell in private industry generally. Because Japan's unit labor costs continue to fall

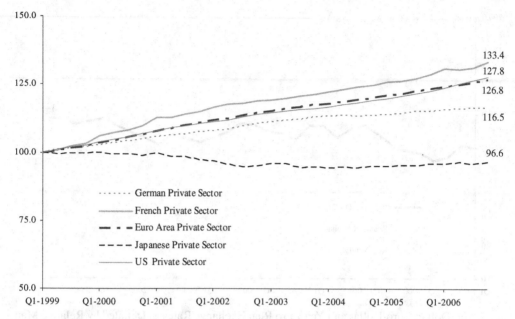

Figure 10. Private Sector Wages for Germany, France, the Euro Area, Japan and the US from Q1 1999 to Q4 2006 (1999 = 100)
Source: OECD.

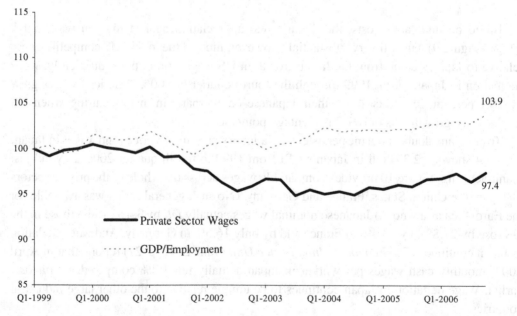

Figure 11. Japan: Private Sector Wages versus GDP Divided by Civilian Employment, from 1999 to 2006 (1999 = 100)
Source: OECD, Cabinet Office (Government of Japan).

from wage stagnation, Japanese exports became even more competitive in world markets — thus triggering the return to Japan bashing in 2007.

5. Intra-European Differences in Wage and Productivity Growth: An Aside

The euro's real appreciation against the yen (and even against the dollar) affects some countries within the Euro Area much more than others. Before the advent of the euro in January 1999, all the potential member countries had to show substantial convergence in their CPI inflation rates (which they did) and keep their nominal exchange rates stable for a year or more before entry. After the change to a common currency, wage costs and productivity within the Euro Area — and more generally in the European Union — were expected to gradually converge. For a fringe of the least developed, low per capita income, smaller countries — led by Ireland and some in Eastern Europe — rapid growth in their catch-up phases has led to some convergence.

Surprisingly, however, measures of competitiveness among some of the more mature industrial countries in the Euro Zone have *diverged*. Based on unit labor costs in manufacturing, Figure 12 compares the evolution of unit labor costs from 1999 through 2006 for Germany, Italy and France to the United States and Japan. Within the euro group, unit labor costs ranged from a rise of 20.8% in Italy to a fall of 13.5% in Germany. France was about the Euro Zone average: its manufacturing unit labor costs fell about 4%. The experiences of Greece, Portugal and Spain's are closer to Italy's, whereas Austria's is similar although not quite as good as Germany's (De Grauwe, 2006). Germany, with its large current account

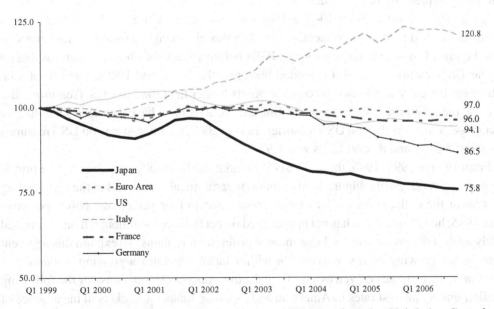

Figure 12. Italy, France, Germany, Euro Area, Japan and US Manufacturing Unit Labor Costs from Q1 1999 to Q4 2006 (1999 = 100)
Source: OECD, European Central Bank.

surplus, is much better in retaining its international competitiveness in the face of an appreciating euro.

Unsurprisingly, German politicians have been relatively silent about the problems of a strong euro (weak yen), whereas their Italian and French counterparts have openly criticized the European Central Bank for letting the euro get too strong because European interest rates are too high, and the Bank of Japan for letting the yen get too weak because Japanese interest rates are too low. Just what was the origin of "unduly low" interest rates in Japan, and why have they persisted for so long?

6. Interest Rates and Japan's Currency Mismatch

Like wage setting in labor markets, interest rates in financial markets are also forward-looking and sensitive to currency risk — perhaps more immediately so. When future changes in exchange rates are well-signaled from some easily identifiable source, such as continual foreign mercantile pressure, interest rates begin to adjust.

After the yen first appreciated, about 17% from the "Nixon Shock" of 1971, most analysts felt that this was a one-time devaluation of the dollar against the currencies of all the major industrial countries. However, by the late 1970s, the United States began to single out Japan, its foremost mercantile competitor, for applying overt political pressure to appreciate the yen. In 1977, in the midst of trade disputes and the threat of US trade sanctions on imports from Japan, US Secretary of the Treasury Michael Blumenthal stated that the yen should be appreciated. This contributed to a run on the "Carter dollar" in 1978 with a sharp yen appreciation. At this point, the financial markets began to behave as if the yen would continually appreciate into the indefinite future.

Long-term interest rates on 10-year Japanese government bonds (JGBs), which are not directly controlled by the government, best reflect this big change in exchange rate expectations. Figure 13 shows the interest rate on JGBs before 1978 to be about the same as that on 10-year US Treasuries — and if extended back into the 1950s and 1960s, interest rates on JGBs were typically one to two percentage points higher than those on US Treasuries. But by 1978, the relationship turned around. Since then, JGB rates have averaged three to four percentage points *less* than on US Treasuries. In July 2007, the interest rate on US Treasuries was about 5.04%, and that on JGBs was 1.97%.

From 1978 to 1995–1996, this interest differential can be readily explained by the principle of *open-interest parity*. Figure 13 also shows logarithmically the trend of the appreciating yen against the dollar from 1971 to 1995, about three to four percentage points per year. Since 1995, however, the yen has not appreciated on net balance — although it has fluctuated widely against the dollar. But the large interest differential remains. To explain this apparent anomaly, the growing *currency mismatch* within Japan generates a growing *negative risk premium* in interest rates on yen assets. To make this concept clearer, consider the following equation linking interest rates in American and Japanese financial markets in the absence of capital controls:

$$i = i^* + E(e) + \varphi, \tag{1}$$

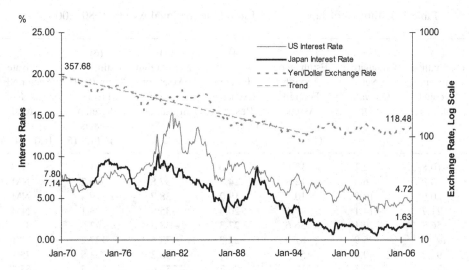

Figure 13. The Yen/Dollar Exchange Rate and Long-Term Interest Rates (10-Year Bonds) in the United States and Japan (January 1970 to February 2007)
Source: IFS.

where i is the interest rate on yen bonds, and i^* that on dollar bonds at the same term to maturity. The interest differential, $i - i^*$, between yen and dollar bonds is partitioned into two components: $E(\hat{e})$ is the expected change in the yen/dollar rate (negative if appreciation is expected), and φ is the risk premium (negative in the Japanese case). Because both these components are negative, $i < i^*$.

In the Japan bashing period before April 1995, one could reasonably expect that the yen would continue to appreciate so that the $E(\hat{e})$ term was dominant. Similarly, today's China bashing to appreciate the renminbi is forcing down nominal interest rates on renminbi assets within China (McKinnon, 2007). Because entrenched expectations often change with a lag, after 1995 the expectation of a secular appreciation of the yen may have decayed only gradually so that $E(\hat{e})$ remained important while slowly losing its dominance.

However, for the interest rate differential to remain so large today, one must appeal to the value of the negative risk premium φ. Although Japan is the world's largest creditor country, it does not lend much in yen because of the currency asymmetry associated with the dollar standard. Instead, the country's large current account (saving) surpluses are partially financed by outward foreign direct investment, but mainly by building up foreign currency claims (mainly dollars) on foreigners (Table 2). This leads to a currency mismatch within Japan's economy.

In the private sector in particular, financial institutions such as insurance companies or banks acquire higher-yield dollar assets even though their liabilities are mainly in yen — as are their annuity obligations to policyholders or to depositors. Although these financial institutions have come to depend on the higher yield on dollar over yen assets, they fear any fluctuation in the yen/dollar exchange rate that would change the yen value of their dollar assets relative their yen liabilities. Even a random upward blip (appreciation) in the

Table 2. Estimates of Japanese Net Liquid International Assets, 1980–2006

	(1) Cumulative Current Account Surplus	(2) Cumulative Net Outward FDI	(3) Estimate of Liquid Foreign Assets (1) + (2)	(4) Official Foreign Exchange Reserves	(5) Net Foreign Assets of Banking Institutions	(6) Estimate of Non-Bank Private Foreign Assets (3)−(4)−(5)	(7) Private Sector NFA as % of Total [(3)−(4)]/(3)
1980	−10.8	−2.1	−12.9	21.6	−39.1	4.7	NM
1981	−6.0	−6.8	−12.8	24.7	−37.8	0.2	NM
1982	0.9	−10.9	−10.1	19.2	−38.7	9.4	NM
1983	21.7	−14.1	7.6	20.4	−35.9	23.1	NM
1984	56.7	−20.1	36.6	22.3	−48.3	62.6	39%
1985	107.8	−25.9	81.9	22.3	−77.6	137.2	73%
1986	193.7	−40.4	153.3	37.7	−148.2	263.8	75%
1987	278.0	−59.5	218.5	75.7	−256.6	399.5	65%
1988	357.3	−95.5	261.8	90.5	−265.3	436.6	65%
1989	420.5	−142.6	277.9	78.0	−241.8	441.8	72%
1990	464.6	−191.3	273.3	69.5	−283.9	487.7	75%
1991	532.8	−221.6	311.2	61.8	−175.4	424.8	80%
1992	645.3	−236.2	409.1	61.9	−88.4	435.6	85%
1993	777.0	−249.9	527.1	88.7	223.9	214.4	83%
1994	907.2	−267.1	640.1	115.1	273.8	251.2	82%
1995	1018.3	−289.6	728.7	172.4	335.2	221.0	76%
1996	1084.1	−312.8	771.3	207.3	210.7	353.2	73%
1997	1180.9	−335.7	845.2	207.9	280.7	356.6	75%
1998	1299.6	−357.0	942.6	203.2	249.9	489.5	78%
1999	1414.2	−367.0	1047.2	277.7	227.1	542.4	73%
2000	1533.9	−390.3	1143.6	347.2	205.5	590.9	70%
2001	1621.7	−422.6	1199.0	387.7	187.1	624.3	68%
2002	1734.1	−445.6	1288.6	451.5	196.1	641.0	65%
2003	1870.3	−468.1	1402.2	652.8	199.5	550.0	53%
2004	2042.4	−491.3	1551.1	824.3	227.5	499.3	47%
2005	2208.2	−533.5	1674.7	828.8	348.2	497.7	51%
2006	2379.0	−591.7	1787.3	874.9	357.7	554.7	51%

Source: *International Financial Statistics*, Bank of Japan and *The Economist*. All values in billions of USD.
Memo: Official Foreign Exchange Reserves reported to be US$888.3 billion as of March 2007.

yen could wipe out their net worth. So they will hold dollar assets only if they are given a substantial risk premium for doing so.

Because American interest rates are mainly determined in world markets, portfolio equilibrium within Japan's economy requires that interest rates on yen assets be bid down [as in Equation (1)] by the amount of the negative risk premium to make Japanese investors at the margin willing to hold dollar assets. Because of the currency mismatch, this negative risk premium will be higher (more negative) the greater the fluctuations in the yen/dollar rate and the larger are Japan's private holdings of dollar assets. Figure 13 shows that, in the absence of secular appreciation of the yen since 1995, the yen/dollar rate has still fluctuated very substantially.

Japan's current account (saving) surpluses only became significant in the early 1980s. But more than 20 years later, the cumulative total of liquid dollar claims held by the economy is now much greater relative to GNP than it was back in the 1980s — and it is continually growing (Table 2). Private sector finance for acquiring counterpart dollar claims is always chancy because of ongoing high volatility in the yen/dollar exchange rate — the risk that offsets the higher yield on dollar assets relative to yen assets. For the private sector to keep acquiring dollar claims, the interest rate differential may have to increase — i.e., the risk premium becomes more negative so as to depress yields on yen assets [Equation (1)]. But what happens when Japanese short rates approach zero?

7. The Liquidity Trap and Portfolio Instability

Japanese banks, insurance companies, trust funds and even some individuals hold dollar assets over a wide spectrum maturities. But interest rate adjustment for currency risk is more difficult at the shorter end of the maturity structure than for the 10-year bonds shown in Figure 13. First, governments in industrial countries tend to target some short-term interbank rate — federal funds in the US, *gensaki* in Japan — as an instrument of monetary control, thus leaving it rigid for extended periods. Consequently, these rates cannot change to counteract short-term shifts in currency risk. Second, if the currency risk is sufficiently great, nominal interest rates on yen assets — particularly those at short-term — are eventually forced toward zero. Figure 14 shows the near-zero interest rate on short-term yen assets, the so-called liquidity trap, that has persisted since early 1995.

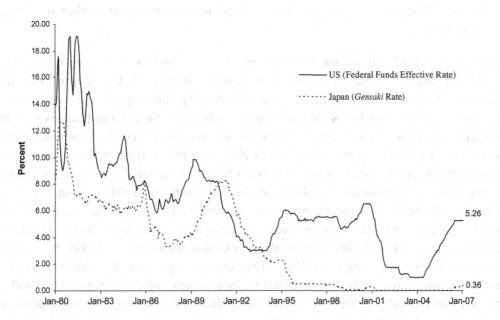

Figure 14. US Federal Funds and Japan *Gensaki* Rates (Overnight) from January 1970 to February 2007
Source: *IFS*, Federal Reserve.

The liquidity trap has major implications for economic policy:

(1) During Japan's lost decade and even today, the central bank has not been able to stimulate domestic demand by the traditional technique of lowering short-term interest rates when they are bounded from below by zero. Once deflation was set in motion by the greatly overvalued yen in the early 1990s, within the liquidity trap there was (is) nothing the central bank could do to stop it. Engineering a major devaluation of the yen against the dollar in nominal terms, if technically possible, was and is out of the question after the previous episodes of Japan bashing to get the yen up.

(2) Having short-term interest rates compressed toward zero greatly reduced(s) the profit margins, the spread between loan and deposit rates, of Japanese commercial banks. After the real estate and stock market bubbles burst in 1990–1991, numerous defaults on bank loans led to a rash of non-performing loans (NPLs) on bank balance sheets. No surprise there. What is surprising, however, is that the banks had not grown out of their NPL problem more than a decade later — even after several subsidized recapitalizations. Goyal and McKinnon (2003) attributed this anomaly to the artificially reduced bank profit margins arising out of the persistent liquidity trap.

(3) Once yen interest rates fall near zero, greater portfolio instability in the holding of dollar versus yen assets within Japan is generated. Because yen interest rates cannot be forced below zero, the condition for portfolio stability — Equation (1) — is violated at shorter terms to maturity, with echo effects at longer terms. With private Japanese financial institutions fearful of another big yen appreciation, episodic runs out of dollars into yen become more likely. And, to prevent the yen from appreciating sharply, the BoJ becomes the residual buyer of the surplus dollars — resulting in a substantial build-up of official exchange reserves.

Points (1) and (2) are obviously important for understanding Japan's past economic malaise and deflationary hangover into the present, but point (3) is less obvious. For any given interest rate on a dollar asset, in the low-interest liquidity trap the rate on the same-maturity yen asset cannot be forced low enough for Japanese financial institutions to hold the riskier dollar asset at the margin. But where the margin is depends on how large the existing stocks of dollar assets are in Japan's private sector. If, from the ongoing current account surplus, private holdings of dollar assets become large relative to the net worth of Japanese financial institutions, then the system becomes very vulnerable to a run.

On the other hand, once there is a run, during which the BoJ buys dollar assets from the private sector on a large scale, Japanese insurance companies, banks and so forth, eventually become happy holding their remaining smaller stocks of dollar assets if and when they finally decide that the BoJ can hang on without letting the yen appreciate (further). After a run, these institutions may even be willing to rebuild their depleted stocks of higher-yield dollar assets for many months or years — thus providing finance for the ongoing current account surplus without the BoJ's intervening at all.

Figure 15 captures the remarkably episodic nature of (internal) runs from dollars into yen since 1980 by simply plotting the monthly percentage changes in the BoJ's official foreign

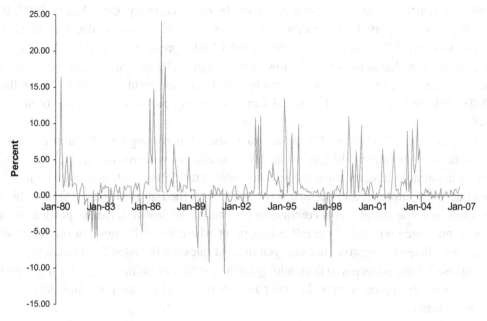

Figure 15. Monthly Percentage Changes in Japanese Official Foreign Exchange Reserves from January 1980 to February 2007
Source: IFS.

exchange reserves — which we know to be mainly dollars, although the authorities do not reveal the exact currency composition of the reserves. The episodes of concentrated upward spikes in official reserves clearly indicate the presence of runs — often followed by quiescent periods, sometimes with some reserve decumulation. However, a single satisfactory metric for measuring runs is not easy to find. Indeed, the absolute scale of the official intervention from late 2002 to early 2004 of $330 billion was much greater than previous interventions (Table 2). But it was not particularly large in monthly percentage terms, as reflected in the spike in reserves for 2003–2004 (Figure 15).

With Japanese short-term interest rates mired close to zero and without overt Japan bashing to appreciate the yen, the behavior of US interest rates becomes the biggest determinant of whether or not there will be a run. After the collapse of the high-tech bubble in 2001, US short-term interest rates came down very sharply, with the rate on federal funds touching the unprecedented low level of 1% in January 2004 (Figure 14). Because Japanese short-term interest rates were bounded from below by zero, the differential of American over Japanese rates narrowed sharply. Consequently, net dishoarding of dollar assets by Japan's private sector led to a sharp jump in official exchange reserves. From the end of 2002 through early 2004, official reserves almost doubled (Table 2). These episodic runs into official reserves, followed by quiescent periods, were also part of Japan's earlier experience (McKinnon, 2005, Chap. 3).

In their letter to Secretary Paulson in 2007, American lawmakers and Michigan automobile executives in particular were harking back to this three-year-old intervention episode as evidence that Japan has been unfairly manipulating its currency. On 9 March 2007, the Bloomberg Press reported, "Democrats say a book, *Global Financial Warriors* (January 2007) by former US Treasury Undersecretary John Taylor proves that the Bush Administration went along as Japan tried to hold down the foreign exchange value of the yen, hurting American manufactures. Taylor writes that he acquiesced as Japan sold yen to buy dollars in 2003–2004 to help the world's second largest economy pull out of a decade of anemic growth."

However, after March 2004, US interest rates started increasing back to "normal" levels so as to increase the interest differential at shorter maturities with yen assets. Japan's private financial institutions have returned to acquiring most of the dollar assets generated by Japan's current account surpluses and the BoJ has hardly intervened at all (Figure 15). But this is only a lull. Because dollar assets continue to accumulate in private Japanese portfolios, the currency mismatch will again cumulate to a point where the risk premium on yen assets cannot be sufficiently negative (because yen interest rates are bounded from below by zero) for Japanese private investors to keep adding to their stocks of dollar assets. Then any mere rumor of currency appreciation will prompt another run out of private portfolios into official exchange reserves.

8. The Yen Carry Trade

In the liquidity trap, Japan's ultra-low short-term interest rates lead to a phenomenon popularly referred to as the "yen carry trade". Defined narrowly, carry trade refers to transactions that combine term-structure risk with currency risk. Suppose a speculator, who need not be a Japanese national, borrows short in Tokyo in yen at less than 1% in order to invest long-term in 10-year Australian government bonds bearing 6.27%. That is hyper risk-taking beyond the ordinary course of business or household behavior. There is the risk that short-term rates will increase relative to long everywhere, or that long rates in Australia increase further so as to reduce the capital value of the bonds, and then there is the specific risk that the yen will appreciate against the Australian dollar. In this last case, our speculator could have trouble repaying or rolling over his short-term yen loan.

How much of Japan's large current account surplus today is intermediated by the yen carry trade so narrowly defined is anybody's guess. But I suspect that it is much less than that done through the more traditional forms of international financial intermediation associated with insurance companies and the like — and thus much less than what the financial press thinks.

However, the carry trade does contribute to the potential volatility of the yen/dollar exchange rate. With any hint of, or rumor that, the yen might appreciate, carry-trade speculators with their short-term yen liabilities may well react first. They rush to cover their short positions in yen by not renewing loans or simply buying offsetting yen assets. This quickly adds to the upward pressure on the yen so as to trigger a run that induces mainline financial institutions to start selling off their dollar assets as well, which the BoJ buys as per the positive spikes of official reserve accumulation in Figure 15. By making the yen/dollar rate more volatile, carry traders heighten the exchange risk to mainline financial institutions.

Thus, indirectly, do carry-trade speculators widen the interest differential between dollar and yen assets necessary to maintain (an uneasy) portfolio equilibrium where mainline Japanese financial firms hold some of both.

But our concern here with the mechanics of runs and negative risk premia in interest rates should not detract from how expensive foreign exchange instability has been for Japan's economy. The extraordinary appreciations of the yen through the mid-1990s threw the economy into a deflationary slump. The subsequent low interest rate liquidity trap prevented the Bank of Japan from reinflating the economy to escape from the slump. And, during Japan's lost decade from 1992 to 2002, massive fiscal deficits have also failed to stimulate private spending, whilst leaving the Ministry of Finance very leery of increasing today's huge public debt even further.

9. Fragile Export-Led Recovery: 2003–2007

Fortunately, since 2002, the world economy has been sufficiently buoyant to attract Japanese exports and stimulate investment in export-related activities. In 2003, Japan's economy began recovering: real GDP has been increasing about 2.3% per year. Table 3 shows GDP's various components from 2002 to 2006 in undeflated nominal terms — which, because of mild ongoing deflation, tends to understate real growth rates. Overall *nominal* GDP grew from 2002 to 2006 by just 3.33%.

Figure 16 summarizes the relative contributions to overall GDP growth over these four years as proportion of Japanese GDP in 2002. What is remarkable is the lack of growth in private consumption. Despite being a "normal" 57% of GDP, consumption was just 30% of the overall GDP growth from 2002 to 2006. Moreover, private residential investment was virtually stationary. In contrast, corporate investment (which is normally just 17% of GDP) contributed an astonishing 100% of the increment in Japan's overall GDP. To square the accounts, government spending was the big negative — falling 1.14 percentage points or

Table 3. Components of Annual Japanese GDP (2002–2006) (Not Deflated)

In Billions of Yen	2002	2003	2004	2005	2006
GDP (Expenditure Approach)	491, 312	490, 294	498, 328	501, 342	507, 653
Private Consumption	283, 254	281, 791	284, 428	286, 530	288, 096
Private Residential Investment	18, 031	17, 844	18, 367	18, 280	18, 815
Coporate Investment	64, 431	66, 747	71, 048	74, 718	80, 777
Government Expenditures	119, 184	115, 937	114, 859	114, 859	113, 616
Government Consumption	88, 306	88, 503	89, 468	90, 684	90, 920
Public Investment	30, 751	27, 310	25, 215	23, 918	22, 445
Net Exports	6, 412	7, 976	9, 626	6, 956	6, 349
Net Exports Ex Oil	10, 985	13, 304	15, 691	15, 779	17, 884
Gross Exports of Manufactured Goods	42, 894	44, 868	50, 123	52, 974	60, 262
Gross Imports of Basic Inputs	10, 696	12, 008	13, 750	18, 065	23, 390

Source: Cabinet Office, Government of Japan.

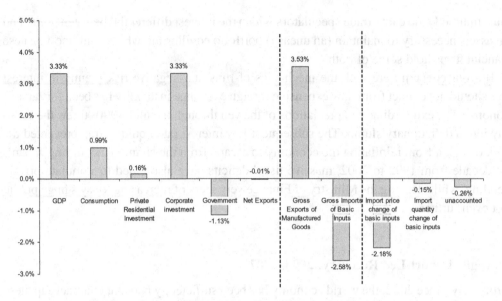

Figure 16. Change in Components of GDP from 2002 to 2006 as a Percentage of 2002 GDP
Source: Japanese Cabinet Office, Japanese Statistics Bureau and Japanese Ministry of Finance.
Note: Basic Inputs include raw materials and mineral fuels (which includes crude oil).

34% of the incremental growth in GDP. Table 3 shows that the bulk of this fall in government spending was in public sector investment.

Exports also made a substantial contribution to Japan's modest recovery. But the standard presentation of the GDP accounts (the bars to the left of the first vertical broken line in Figure 16) shows growth in Japan's *net* exports to be slightly *negative*. However, this masks the huge increase in *gross* exports from Japan after 2002 when the price of oil and related petroleum products began to increase substantially — and Japan is completely dependent on oil imports. Without any significant change in the quantity of oil imported, the yen cost of oil imports rose almost 150% through 2006 (Table 3). Thus, Japan had to export more in real terms just to pay for the more expensive oil.

But the problem is more general than just oil. The prices of many important basic inputs — iron ore, copper, various minor metals, agricultural raw materials as well as mineral fuels — sharply increased after 2002. Thus, without any increase in Japan's net trade surplus, manufactured exports had to expand dramatically — if only to offset the adverse change in Japan's terms of trade. Figure 16 and Table 3 show gross exports of manufactured goods expanding by even more than GDP from 2002 through 2006.

The large increases in Japan's domestic corporate investment can now be better understood. Although both consumption and public expenditures have languished since 2002, increased investment was induced by, and supported, expanding manufactured exports. Reinforcing this effect, the depreciation in Japan's *real* exchange rate against both the euro and the dollar, and against other Asian currencies with exchange rates more closely tied to the dollar, makes investment in Japan look relatively inexpensive (McKinnon, 2005, Chap. 2).

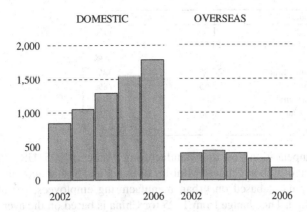

DOMESTIC   OVERSEAS

Figure 17. Domestic Factory Construction in Japan and New Overseas Operations Started by Japanese Companies
Source: Japanese Ministry of Economy, Trade and Industry.
Notes: This figure is reproduced from the *Wall Street Journal* article by Yuka Hayashi on 12 June 2007. According to the original notes, the year in overseas operations data covers from April of the previous calendar year to March of the year indicated.

In particular, Japanese multinational firms, which normally engage in outward foreign direct investment (FDI), may instead be investing more at home — mainly in export activities.

This result is neatly portrayed in Figure 17 taken from the *Wall Street Journal* article "Japan Inc. comes back home", by Yuka Hayashi (2007). Since 2002, it shows a virtual doubling of new factory construction within Japan, while factory construction in Japanese companies (and their affiliates) overseas has declined: "Japanese companies registered to build 1,782 factories in Japan last year, up from 844 four years ago, and the highest number in 14 years according to government figures. Meanwhile, they are building fewer plants abroad — 182 in the year ended March 31, down from 434 four years earlier, according to a government survey of 19,000 companies" (Hayashi, 2007, p. 14).

While it is all well and good to analyze the decline in the real exchange rate of the yen against the dollar and the euro as presented earlier in the paper, Hayashi's article also compared the changes in hourly nominal compensation costs for manufacturing workers from 1995 to 2005 across the broader spectrum of countries shown in Figure 18. Notably, "the average dollar denominated wage for a Japanese manufacturing worker was $21.76 in 2005, down 7.3% from a decade earlier according to the US Bureau of Labor Statistics. During the same period, the average wage in the US soared 38% to $23.65, while the German average climbed 9.6% to $33". Figure 18 also shows wages in other East Asian countries rising faster than in Japan. Korean wages rose a remarkable 86%, while a guesstimate for China is 211%. However, China's absolute wage level of $1.33 is still so low relative to Japan's that this high percentage increase is less meaningful.

The data on which Hayashi drew from the US Bureau of Labor Statistics provides another striking perspective on the relative stagnation of money wages in Japan, falling 7.3% from 1995 to 2005, compared to its neighbors (Figure 18). Figure 4 shows the official Japanese CPI fell about 2.3% over a comparable period — implying that Japanese real take-home

Country	Cost	Change from 1995	
China	1.33	211%	
South Korea	13.56	86%	
Mexico	2.63	55%	
United States	23.65	38%	
Hong Kong	5.65	18%	
Germany	33.00	10%	
Taiwan	6.38	7%	
Japan	21.76	−7%	

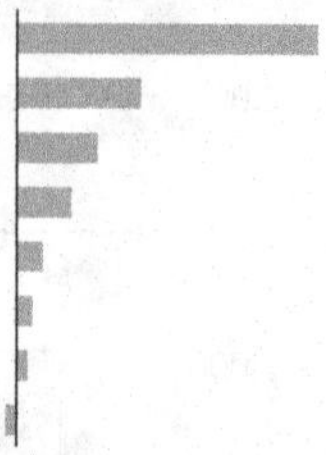

Figure 18. Hourly Compensation Cost for Manufacturing Workers, 2005 (US dollars)
Source: US Department of Labor, Chinese Ministry of Labor and Social Security, EIU.
Note: The cost for China is based on urban manufacturing employees, calculated by Lett and Banister's (2006) method. The change from 1995 for China is based on the average wage of urban manufacturing employees.

wages have been falling about 0.5% per year. But this weakness in Japanese wage setting, including the surprising quiescence of trade unions, could be partly a statistical illusion.

In a recent intriguing paper by Broda and Weinstein (2007), they show that Japan's official CPI could well be overestimating Japan's inflation, i.e., *underestimating* the rate of deflation, by 0.8% per year. Japan's statistical bureau still uses an old fashioned fixed-weight Laspeyres price index rather than the more modern cost-of-living index (COLI) used by the United States. The Japanese method fails to take substitution effects into account when relative prices in the consumer basket change, and does not sufficiently allow for improved product quality from technical progress.

In a complex statistical exercise, Broda and Weinstein recalculate Japan's CPI inflation rate using the American COLI methodology. Their result is shown in Figure 19. From 1998 to 2006, the COLI methodology shows Japan's CPI falling by 8%, whereas the official (Laspeyres) methodology shows a fall of just 3%. Referring back to Figure 18 showing the 7.3% fall in money wages, the COLI methodology is consistent with approximately stable real wages — whereas the official CPI shows them in decline. Real wage stability, rather than persistent decline, is easier to accept intuitively.

True enough. But the COLI methodology shows that Japan's deflationary hangover is worse than the official statistics show — and remains very puzzling indeed.

10. Stabilizing the Yen: A Concluding Note

Japan is many years away from working itself out of its deflationary trap without relying on "excessive" export expansion. But a necessary first step would be to reduce the foreign exchange risk that causes the low-interest-rate liquidity trap and undermines the ability of the BoJ to expand the domestic economy, and causes international financial intermediation to finance Japan's current account surpluses to be excessively volatile.

Counterintuitive as it may seem from today's low real valuation of the yen, stabilizing the nominal dollar value of the yen is the preferred strategy. If the yen is credibly fixed within a narrow band over the long run, Japanese nominal interest rates must rise to American levels as the negative risk premium vanishes and fear of future deflation erodes. The dollar exchange

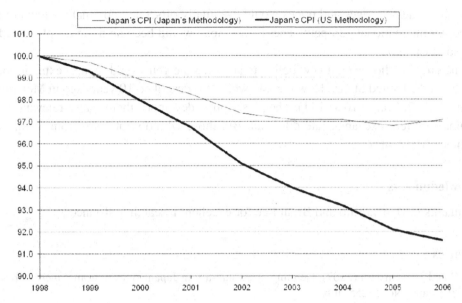

Figure 19. Japanese Prices Computed with US and Japanese CPI Methodologies (1998–2005)
Source: Broda and Weinstein (2007).

rate would again be the nominal anchor — as in the 1950s and 1960s. Moderately higher nominal interest rates need not have a deflationary impact if risks in capital and labor markets are reduced, and if fears of future deflation are eliminated. Once Japanese employers become more confident that the yen would not again ratchet upwards, they would feel freer to grant more generous wage settlements (McKinnon and Schnabl, 2006). Then private consumption could well increase more generally along with personal disposable income and residential construction.

Credibly fixing the yen dollar rate, with the BoJ allowing domestic nominal interest rates to rise, would spring the liquidity trap and restore some — albeit limited — power to the central bank. The yen carry trade would disappear and be replaced by a more normal international financial intermediation: private purchases of overseas financial assets by Japanese insurance companies, banks and pension funds would increase, while the government's role in acquiring foreign exchange reserves would diminish. With surplus saving even if somewhat lessened by greater private consumption, Japan would remain a large international creditor. But once foreigners know that the yen could not ratchet up, they would become more willing to borrow in yen, and would complain less once the BoJ stopped accumulating dollar reserves.

While technically feasible, a credible stabilization of the yen/dollar rate presents a major political problem. It conflicts with recent calls in both Europe and the United States to appreciate the yen — either directly by the BoJ selling dollars to buy yen in the foreign exchange markets, or indirectly by raising domestic interest rates to attract more foreign capital. But officially induced nominal yen appreciations with the fear of more to come would accentuate the deflationary pressure that Japan now faces. As in the 1980s and 1990s, declines in domestic wages and prices would eventually offset any nominal appreciation in its effect on international competitiveness, and Japan would become more deeply mired in its deflationary trap.

To be credible, however, a new policy to stabilize the yen would require explicit cooperation with the United States. How it could work was described 10 years ago in McKinnon and Ohno (1997, Chaps. 10 and 11). The prescription developed there is also relevant today for China's current exchange rate dilemma. But those who do not learn from history are condemned to repeat it.

Acknowledgments

Many thanks to Dennis Kuo and Brian Lee for excellent research assistance.

References

Broda, C and D Weinstein (2007). Defining price stability in Japan: A view from America. NBER Working Paper No. 13255, July.

De Grauwe, P (2006). Enlargement of the Euro Area: On monetary and political union. *CES ifo Forum*, 7(4), 3–10.

Financial Times, 30 March 2007.

Goyal, R and R McKinnon (2003). Japan's negative risk premium in interest rates: The liquidity trap and fall in bank lending. *The World Economy*, 26, 339–363.

Hayashi, Y (2007). Japan Inc comes back home (12 June). *Wall Street Journal*.

Lett, E and J Banister (2006). Labor costs of manufacturing employees in China: An update to 2003–2004. *Monthly Labor Review*, 129(11), 40–45.

Lindbeck, A (1979). *Inflation and Unemployment in Open Economies*. Amsterdam: North Holland.

McKinnon, R (2005). *Exchange Rates under the East Asian Dollar Standard: Living with Conflicted Virtue*. Cambridge, MA: MIT Press.

McKinnon, R (2007). Why China should keep its dollar peg. *International Finance*, 10(1), 43–70.

McKinnon, R and K Ohno (1997). *Dollar and Yen: Resolving Economic Conflict between the United States and Japan*. Cambridge, MA: MIT Press.

McKinnon, R and G Schnabl (2006). China's exchange rate and international adjustment in wages, prices, and interest rates: Japan deja vu? CES ifo, Working Paper No. 1720, May.

Qiao, H (2007). Exchange rates and trade balances under the dollar standard. To appear in *Journal of Policy Modelling*.

Taylor, J (2007). *Global Financial Warriors*. New York: WW Norton.

The Economist, 10 February 2007.

MANAGING FLEXIBILITY: JAPANESE EXCHANGE RATE POLICY, 1971–2007

SHINJI TAKAGI

Professor of Economics, Graduate School of Economics
Osaka University, 1-7 Machikaneyama
Toyonaka, Osaka 560-0043, Japan
takagi@econ.osaka-u.ac.jp

The paper reviews Japan's exchange rate policy from the end of the Bretton Woods era to the present. The Japanese authorities used various tools to manage the yen–dollar exchange rate over much of this period. The most dominant was official foreign exchange intervention, which in most instances took the form of "leaning against the wind". Capital controls were also used but, with full capital account convertibility, ceased to exist as an instrument of exchange rate policy by the mid-1980s. Following the post-Plaza appreciation of the yen, the authorities eased monetary policy to arrest the appreciating pressure. The possible role of exchange rate policy in the great asset inflation that followed, however, remains unanswered. More recently, exchange rate policy during the period of prolonged stagnation and fragile recovery was made subordinate to the overall stance of macroeconomic policy. In this regard, particularly striking in terms of scale and frequency was the "great intervention" of 2003–2004. Equally striking has been the total absence of official intervention since. It would require a renewed substantial volatility of the yen to know whether this indeed marks a permanent shift in Japan's exchange rate policy.

Keywords: Japanese exchange rate policy; exchange rate management; Japanese economic policy.

1. Introduction

This paper reviews Japan's exchange rate policy from the end of the Bretton Woods era in 1971 to the present. Although the Japanese authorities have maintained a flexible exchange rate regime that is free of capital controls and market intervention since the spring of 2004, over much of the post-Bretton Woods era, they used capital controls, market intervention and possibly other measures to manage the Japanese yen exchange rate. The use of these measures was sometimes active and extensive; at other times, it was more limited and restrained. A major purpose of this paper is to illuminate the policy context in which the authorities used these measures as instruments of managing the otherwise flexible exchange rate regime.

A review of Japan's post-Bretton Woods experience allows us to gain insight into the workings of a flexible exchange rate regime in a large economy, and to understand the challenges faced by its policymakers in managing what turned out to be a widely fluctuating exchange rate. The Japanese yen, which remained unchanged at 360 yen per US dollar throughout the Bretton Woods era, followed a sustained appreciating trend that lasted for more than 20 years (Figures 1 and 2). Although there were periodic reversals of this trend, there were also four bouts of spectacular rise — 1971–1973 (when the yen appreciated from

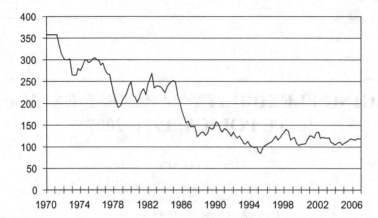

Figure 1. The Yen/Dollar Exchange Rate, Q1 1970–Q1 2007 (yen per dollar; end of period)
Source: IMF, Internation Financial Statistics.

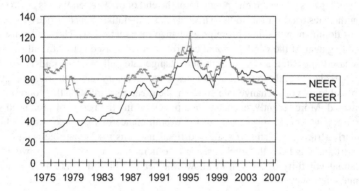

Figure 2. The Yen's Nominal and Real Effective Exchange Rates, Q1 1975–Q1 2007 (Year 2000 = 100; an increase indicates appreciation)
Source: IMF, International Financial Statistics.

360 to 254 against the dollar); 1976–1978 (from over 300 to less than 180); 1985–1987 (from 260 to almost 120); and 1992–1995 (from more than 130 to less than 80).[1] In sharp contrast, from 1995 to 2007, the yen vacillated between 100 and 140 per US dollar, while displaying trend depreciation in real effective terms.

At the outset, two qualifications must clearly be stated. First, for the purposes of this paper, we define exchange rate policy narrowly as consisting of policy measures that are specifically designed to influence exchange rates in a particular direction.[2] Exchange rates

---

[1]The yen reached a record 79.75 per US dollar briefly on 19 April 1995.

[2]This narrow definition corresponds to how "action to influence an exchange rate" is defined in a decision of the IMF Executive Board. The "Guidelines for the Management of Floating Exchange Rates", adopted on 13 June 1974, state that such action "includes, besides exchange market intervention, other policies that exercise a temporary effect on the balance of payments and hence on exchange rates, and that have been adopted for that purpose" and mention, among others, "official borrowing or lending, capital restrictions, separate capital exchange markets, various types of fiscal intervention, and also monetary or interest rate policies". On the other hand, no policies "adopted for demand management purposes" or "for purposes other than balance of payments purposes" are regarded as action to influence the exchange rate. See Executive Board Decision No. 4232-(74/67), *Selected Decisions of the International Monetary Fund*.

are influenced by many factors, which are mostly economic but may include political or even psychological ones. Thus, if we define exchange rate policy broadly to include any policy measure that ends up influencing exchange rates in one way or another, it means that we can discuss the topic only within a broad general equilibrium framework of the Japanese and world economies. This is not what we do.

Second, the paper does not purport rigorously to analyze the impact of Japanese exchange rate policy, let alone its effectiveness in bringing about desired or intended outcomes. Exchange rates are just one of many factors that influence the macroeconomic outcome of an economy. Thus, it is not possible to evaluate the impact or effectiveness of exchange rate policy without fully specifying how exchange rates interact with all other relevant macroeconomic variables. The aim of our exercise must remain rather modest. We may make qualified judgment on the impact or effectiveness of policy actions, but without offering rigorous supporting evidence.

As it turns out, the Japanese authorities have almost exclusively used, as instruments of exchange rate policy, capital controls and related measures (until they fully liberalized the capital account in the mid-1980s) and foreign exchange market intervention. Although both of these types of policy action fall in the jurisdiction of the Ministry of Finance, the role of the Bank of Japan cannot be ignored. Especially in the case of market intervention, the Bank not only acts as the Ministry's agent in conducting actual operations, but also determines its economic outcome through decisions on how much to sterilize. For this reason, unless explicitly stated otherwise, we use the term *monetary authorities* as referring to the combined Ministry of Finance and Bank of Japan.

For ease of presentation, the discussion of exchange rate policy in the rest of the paper is organized chronologically. Section 2 covers most of the 1970s, a period of transition from a fixed to a flexible exchange rate regime. Section 3 takes us from the late 1970s to the mid-1980s, a period when Japan gradually liberalized its capital account. Section 4 discusses Japan's policy actions during the major episode of international policy coordination and its aftermath, from the mid-1980s through the early 1990s. Section 5 focuses on the large-scale market intervention of the 1990s and early 2000s. Section 6 attempts a broad characterization of Japan's exchange rate policy during the post-Bretton Woods era. Section 7 presents concluding remarks. Finally, Appendix A explains the methodology used to estimate the amount of intervention when official data are not available; and Appendix B gives a short summary of principal measures related to the capital control regime.

2. Learning to Float: The Early to Late 1970s

2.1. *From Bretton Woods to Smithsonian*

The Bretton Woods system of adjustable pegs came to an abrupt end on 15 August 1971, when the United States suspended the gold convertibility of the dollar and, as a result, the world's major currencies started to float against each other. Initially, Japan defended the Bretton Woods parity of 360 yen to a dollar through massive market intervention. The attempt was futile in preserving the peg, but effective in allowing the private sector to unwind its long position in US dollars. It is not possible to know exactly how much the authorities intervened in the market at that time because the intervention data are not available before April 1991.[3] However, a rough measure of *net* intervention, estimated from changes in foreign exchange reserves, indicates that the intervention was massive indeed, likely in the neighborhood of $5 billion (Figure 3).[4]

The yen joined the other floating currencies on 28 August 1971, when the authorities gave up defending the Bretton Woods parity. A few months of floating was then followed by an agreement among the Group of Ten (G-10) countries to restore a system of adjustable pegs. The agreement, reached at the Smithsonian Institution in Washington on 18 December 1971, stipulated the yen's new central rate to be 308 per US dollar, representing an appreciation of 16.88%. The adjustment made under the Smithsonian Agreement, however, did not prove durable, and speculative pressure surfaced again. The authorities responded by imposing or tightening controls on inflows.

For example, in 1972, the authorities tightened controls on the receipt of advances on contracted exports, limited the non-resident purchases of Japanese securities to the amount of non-resident sales, and imposed high reserve requirements on increases in non-resident free yen deposits,[5] thus effectively lowering the yen interest rates banks could offer to non-residents (the last measure was a precursor to what Chile would introduce some 20 years later). At the same time, controls on capital outflows were eased to mitigate appreciating pressure (see Appendix B for some of these measures). These and other measures proved

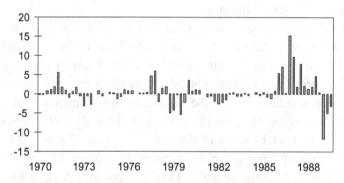

Figure 3. Japanese Foreign Exchange Market Intervention, Q2 1970–Q4 1989 (in billions of US dollars; a positive number indicates purchases of dollars)
Sources: IMF, International Financial Statistics; author's estimate.

---

[3]In fiscal year 2000, the Ministry of Finance began to release monthly intervention data at the end of each month and daily intervention data on a quarterly basis. At that time, the data going back to fiscal year 1991 were also made public.

[4]From the end of July to August 1971, the balance of foreign exchange reserves increased by $4.5 billion; in addition, there may have been use of "hidden reserves," as widely believed (Green, 1990). See Appendix A for the methodology used to estimate the amount of intervention through the end of the 1980s.

[5]Marginal reserve requirements were set at 25% in June 1972 and raised to 50% in July. They were then reduced to 10% in December 1973 and eliminated in September 1974 (Fukao, 1990).

insufficient and, on 14 February 1973, the authorities permanently abandoned all attempts to preserve the Smithsonian central rate and allowed the yen to float.

2.2. *Foreign exchange market intervention*

Following the initial appreciation of nearly 10%, the Japanese yen began to depreciate as speculative capital began to flow out of the country. The initial stance of the authorities was therefore to support the yen. They controlled the exchange rate within a narrow band around the presumed central rate of 265 yen to the dollar by selling dollars in the market (Komiya and Suda, 1991; Fukao, 1990).[6] The authorities abandoned this policy in the middle of October 1973, when the yen reacted sharply to the quadrupling of oil prices (the first oil shock). With an overheating of the Japanese economy and the revaluation of the yen, a deficit had already emerged in the current account. The oil shock worsened the situation, and strong selling pressure on the yen developed. The yen–dollar exchange rate reached 320 in January 1974, and the authorities sporadically sold dollars in the market (Quirk, 1977; Komiya and Suda, 1991). The yen stabilized at around 300 to the dollar in the latter half of 1974 and remained relatively stable throughout 1975.

The stance of intervention changed in the direction of moderating the appreciation of the yen through purchases of dollars (often on a large scale) in early 1976, when the yen began to show signs of strengthening. Following the meeting of the Group of Seven (G-7) countries held in San Juan in June 1976, however, the Japanese authorities scaled down the amount of intervention and generally limited intervention to smoothing operations. As the yen began to strengthen in 1977, market intervention was undertaken to purchase dollars; the authorities intervened heavily when the appreciation was particularly sharp in late 1977 and early 1978 (Figure 3).

Green (1990) calls this the first episode, since the floating of the yen, of prolonged and intensive intervention in the market. This was done in the context of an accelerating rise of the yen, which crossed the rate of 250 to the dollar for the first time. According to Komiya and Suda (1991), the volume of intervention in November 1977 and in March 1978 was estimated to be about 32% and 44%, respectively, of the volume of foreign exchange trading in Tokyo. From November 1978, the Bank of Japan joined the central banks of the United States, the Federal Republic of Germany and Switzerland in coordinated intervention by selling yen. As the yen began to depreciate with the second oil shock in 1979, intervention reversed its earlier pattern with large sales of dollars.

2.3. *Use of capital controls*[7]

The Japanese authorities continued to use capital controls as an instrument of exchange rate policy (Komiya and Suda, 1991; Takagi, 1991). With a weak yen, particularly following the

---

[6]The volume of intervention during the 7-month period from March to September 1973 was estimated to be about 50% of the total volume of foreign exchange trading in Tokyo (Komiya and Suda, 1991).

[7]The history of capital controls in Japan is more extensively reviewed in Fukao (1990), Komiya and Suda (1991) and Koo (1993). A selective summary is provided in Appendix B.

first oil shock, the authorities first abolished controls on capital inflows and then tightened controls on outflows. At the end of 1973, for example, they abolished the zero net increase requirement on inward securities investment, and lowered the reserve requirements with respect to increases in non-resident free yen deposits. In November and December 1973, they eased controls on the non-resident purchases of Japanese stocks and bonds, respectively; in August 1974, they fully liberalized purchases of Japanese government securities by non-residents. As a measure to discourage capital outflows, the authorities placed restrictions on the acquisition of short-term foreign securities by Japanese institutional investors and foreign currency deposits by residents (Komiya and Suda, 1991; Fukao, 1990).

Once the strength of the yen became evident in 1977, the Japanese authorities began to implement measures to encourage capital outflows and to discourage inflows (Fukao, 1990). To encourage outflows, for example, they liberalized residents' purchases of unlisted foreign bonds in April 1977, and removed the ceiling on residents' foreign currency deposits and the restrictions on residents' acquisitions of foreign securities in June 1977. To discourage inflows, in November 1977, they set a 50% reserve requirement (increased to 100% in March 1978) on net increases in non-residents' free yen accounts[8] and effectively disallowed non-residents to purchase short-term government securities. In March 1978, the authorities further restricted acquisitions of Japanese securities by non-residents.

3. Liberalizing the Capital Account: The Late 1970s to the Mid-1980s

3.1. *Liberalization and the revised foreign exchange law*

From late 1978, the yen began to show a sustained depreciation against the US dollar that would last, except for a brief period in 1980, until the beginning of 1985. Japan's current account surpluses began to shrink because of the high yen and an expansion of the Japanese economy. With the large increase in crude oil prices (the second oil shock) in 1979, the current account balance fell into a large deficit in 1979 and 1980. In view of depreciation pressure, the general stance of the authorities during much of this period was to support the yen. The intervention was reportedly massive in the spring and fall of 1979 (Ohta, 1982). In the spring of 1980, the Bank of Japan joined the central banks of other industrial countries in coordinated intervention to sell dollars.

With the depreciation of the yen, the stance of the authorities toward capital controls was again reversed. In fact, all capital inflow controls that had been taken in the high yen period were abolished during 1979, making it possible for non-residents to hold all types of Japanese securities. For example, in February 1979, the authorities lifted the earlier restrictions on the acquisition by non-residents of Japanese securities and non-resident free yen accounts. In May 1979, the government fully liberalized the participation of non-residents in the short-term *gensaki* (bond repurchase) market.[9] In March 1980, the authorities allowed

---

[8]In June 1977, the reserve requirements of 25% were introduced. In addition, in November, the marginal reserve requirements of 50% were instituted and, in March 1978, raised to 100%. The marginal requirements were reduced to 50% in January 1979 and then eliminated in February.

[9]It was around this time that deviations from short-term covered interest parity declined sharply between Tokyo and the London offshore market (Otani and Tiwari, 1981).

Japanese banks to raise funds in London and transfer them to their head offices and removed the interest ceiling on non-resident free yen accounts.

These and other liberalization measures were implemented within the framework of the 1949 Foreign Exchange and Foreign Trade Control Law, which in principle prohibited all cross-border capital transactions except by administrative fiat. The February 1979 measure (to totally liberalize the non-resident purchases of Japanese securities) and the May 1979 measure (to grant non-residents full access to the *gensaki* market) constituted the culmination of the series of *ad hoc* liberalization measures taken over the years. In view of the difference that had emerged between the existing prohibitive law and the liberalized practice, the need to simplify procedures led to a major revision of the Foreign Exchange Law in December 1980, which in principle allowed all external transactions to be freely conducted, unless specifically prohibited (Takagi, 1988a).

3.2. *Further liberalization and its reversal*

The revised Foreign Exchange Control Law allowed non-financial institutions and wealthy individuals to acquire high-yielding foreign financial assets almost freely,[10] but there remained prudential regulations on the foreign securities investment of financial institutions and institutional investors. In the early 1980s, the authorities also decided to liberalize some of these prudential regulations. In particular, they expanded the scope of financial institutions authorized to invest in foreign securities to cover trust banks and the Postal Life Insurance System, subject to a prudential limit (previously, only investment trusts and insurance companies had been authorized).

As the trend depreciation of the yen became evident in April 1982, however, the authorities reacted by implementing temporary measures to restrict net foreign investments by institutional investors (Fukao, 1990). In April 1982, for example, life insurance companies were requested to limit "voluntarily" net purchases of foreign bonds to 10% of the net increase in assets. Pension trusts, the Postal Life Insurance System and non-life insurance companies were likewise requested to comply with similar "voluntary" restrictions. The Japanese authorities emphasized that these and other temporary restrictions only represented "voluntary compliance" by financial institutions.

In the meantime, the Japanese authorities intervened in the market from time to time, this time to support the yen (Figure 3). The Bank of Japan also tightened monetary conditions in early 1982 — pushing the call money rate from 6.5% in mid-March to 7.1% in mid-April. Although monetary policy was soon eased,[11] concern over possible foreign exchange impact held back the Bank of Japan from making even a small reduction in the discount rate in late 1982 and in 1983 (Frankel, 1984; Green, 1990). On balance, the measures implemented to

---

[10]With respect to non-financial institutions and individuals, only two restrictions remained: (i) they must make all foreign exchange transactions through authorized foreign exchange banks; and (ii) as a corollary, they could not hold bank deposits in foreign countries. As a compensation for the second restriction, they were instead authorized to hold foreign currency deposits with domestic financial institutions without limit.

[11]This high interest rate policy was eased in late August and completely terminated in late November, in view of domestic considerations (Komiya and Suda, 1991).

strengthen the yen proved insufficient to offset the outburst of pent-up demand for foreign securities,[12] given the much higher level of US interest rates and the liberalization of capital outflows (see below for additional measures).

3.3. *Liberalization under Japan-US agreement*

Japan's expanding current account surpluses became a topic of major controversy in the world, with some economists, especially in the United States, arguing that a weak yen was the principal contributing factor (e.g., Bergsten, 1982). With pressure from the business community, the US government approached the Japanese counterpart in the fall of 1983 and, in November, the two parties agreed to set up an *ad hoc* Yen/Dollar Working Group to address the yen's presumed weakness. The US position, based on what Frankel (1984) calls "questionable economic logic", held that the yen was undervalued because: (i) Japan was not attractive to international investors, and (ii) the currency was not attractive to international users. The Japanese side did not necessarily agree with such an assessment, but went along because the alternatives (such as further trade concessions) were far worse.

The report of the Yen/Dollar Working Group was released in May 1984, setting forth specific measures to liberalize Japanese barriers against the inflow and outflow of capital, "internationalize" the yen and deregulate domestic capital markets (Frankel, 1984). In a nut-shell, notable capital account and financial liberalization measures included: the relaxation of the eligibility of non-resident firms to issue yen-denominated (samurai) bonds in Japan and their terms; the elimination of the so-called "real demand rule", whereby a forward exchange contract needed to correspond to a bona fide transaction (April 1984); the relaxation of the conditions for euro–yen issues by residents (April 1984); and the relaxation of the conditions for euro–yen issues by non-residents (December 1984). Many of these and other measures tended to encourage capital outflows from Japan, so that the net likely impact of the yen–dollar agreement was, contrary to the intentions of the US government, to weaken the yen further.[13]

4. From Plaza to Louvre and Beyond: 1985 Through the Early 1990s

4.1. *From Plaza to Louvre*

The yen began to appreciate moderately in early 1985, rising from over 260 to the dollar in February to less than 240 in September. The appreciation, however, accelerated sharply following the agreement of the Group of Five (G-5) countries in September. The crux of the agreement, reached over the weekend of 21–22 September at the Plaza Hotel in New York City, was to correct the overvaluation of the dollar. The communiqué, dated 22 September

---

[12]High-yielding foreign assets were so popular that, by 1984, they reached the prudential limit of insurance companies (Koo, 1993).

[13]Koo (1993) provides another perspective on the likely impact of the yen–dollar agreement. By pushing the Japanese government to deregulate the domestic financial markets, the US agenda made it difficult for the Japanese authorities to invoke moral suasion to restrain Japanese investors from buying assets abroad, thereby strengthening the hand of institutional investors who were demanding additional deregulation of foreign investments.

1985, in part read: "[The Ministers and Governors] believe that ... some further orderly appreciation of the main non-dollar currencies against the dollar is desirable. They stand ready to cooperate more closely to encourage this when to do so would be helpful."

By the time the Japanese market reopened on Tuesday, 24 September after a 3-day holiday weekend, the yen had already appreciated by more than 10 yen to a dollar from foreign market trading. The Bank of Japan intervened heavily (reportedly by selling $1.3 billion) but the yen instead depreciated slightly during the course of the day. The yen began to appreciate again on the following day, continuing the trend to reach 212 in early October (Figure 4). Based on these observations, and the fact that the appreciation during this period almost entirely occurred in the New York market, Ito (1987) emphasizes not the intervention itself, but the announcement effect of the G-5 process as a critical factor. He argues that the "surprise" was the very fact that the Federal Reserve intervened in the market at all, reversing the US policy of benign neglect.

The yen appeared to stabilize at 214–218 to a dollar in October. Considering that the appreciation thus far achieved was not sufficient, on 24 October, the Bank of Japan jacked up short-term interest rates by well over 100 basis points overnight (the call money rate would increase from 6.2% to 8.5% in mid-December). The yen's appreciation restarted on the following day and continued for some time (Figure 4): it rose from 216.7 to the dollar on 24 October to 214.8 on 25 October, and further to 200 in late November. Ito (1987) notes that most of the yen appreciation during this period occurred in the Tokyo market, suggesting that it was the change in Japanese monetary policy that triggered and sustained the appreciation.

In 1986, the weak domestic economy, resulting from the deflationary impact of the recent sharp appreciation, was becoming a major concern. Coordinated interest rate cuts were arranged to stimulate domestic demand without disrupting the newly achieved configuration of exchange rates. The Bank of Japan lowered the discount rate from 5% to 4.5% in late January and to 4% in March, in coordination with the Federal Reserve and the Bundesbank; it cut the rate further to 3.5% in April, this time in harmony with the Federal Reserve alone. Following a series of discount rate cuts by the Federal Reserve during the summer of 1986, the Bank of Japan further reduced the discount rate to 3% in November 1986 in order to prevent a further appreciation of the yen (Funabashi, 1988).

With sufficient appreciation of the yen secured, the authorities attempted to achieve exchange rate stability, though without much success. Following the further appreciation in

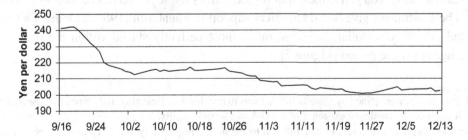

Figure 4. The Yen/Dollar Exchange Rate, 16 September–13 December 1985
Source: Datastream (London closing rates).

March 1986, the authorities intervened heavily in the foreign exchange market by purchasing dollars — this lasted until the summer. With no sign of appreciation pressure abating, the Japanese Minister of Finance met with the US Secretary of the Treasury in Washington in late October 1986 to conclude the first "Baker–Miyazawa" Agreement, whereby the Minister pledged to expand domestic demand and imports in exchange for a US statement that the dollar had fallen far enough. When the dollar began to fall again, in January 1987, Mr. Miyazawa flew again to Washington to conclude a second agreement (Funabashi, 1988; Koo, 1993).

4.2. *Policy coordination under the Louvre Accord*

It was under these circumstances that, in February 1987, the authorities of the G-6 countries[14] met at the Louvre in Paris to agree that the US dollar had fallen far enough and to express their readiness to "cooperate closely" to help stabilize exchange rates "around current levels". In particular, the communiqué announced on 22 February stated: "The Ministers and Governors agreed that the substantial exchange rate changes since the Plaza Agreement will increasingly contribute to reducing external imbalances and have now brought their currencies within ranges broadly consistent with underlying economic fundamentals … Further substantial exchange rate shifts … could damage growth and adjustment prospects".

The operational details of the Louvre Accord were not disclosed, but some argue that the G-6 governments established a target zone for the yen–dollar (as well as deutsche mark–dollar) exchange rate. Funabashi (1988), based on extensive interviews with senior G-5 policymakers, suggests that the central rate established for the yen was 153.5 per US dollar, with a margin of 5% on either side. He further suggests that, at a G-5 meeting held in Washington on 7 April, Japan agreed to rebase the yen's central rate to 146 per dollar, the previous day's closing rate, with a 5% margin. This rate is said to have been binding from 7 April to 18 October.

Esaka (2000), based on the methodology proposed by Lewis (1995), assigned the numbers 0, −1 and +1, respectively, to no intervention, dollar-selling intervention and dollar-purchasing intervention (based on information obtained from Japanese press reports) and estimated a multinominal logit model of intervention under the Louvre Accord. His key finding is that the probability of dollar-purchasing intervention became equal to the probability of dollar-selling intervention at 151.91 yen to the dollar, while the probability of intervention was minimized at 150.08 yen to the dollar for the entire sample period (23 February–18 October).[15] These estimates give broad empirical support to Funabashi (1988)'s claim of a target zone. Indeed, the yen–dollar exchange rate almost perfectly stayed within the presumed target ranges over the period (Figure 5).

---

[14]The G-5 countries were joined by Canada in what was to become a G-7 meeting. Italy boycotted the meeting because it opposed the continued existence of the G-5 as a separate entity.

[15]The implied target levels were 149 and 148 yen to the dollar, respectively, for 7 April–18 October. Lewis (1995), using a similar methodology, found that the implied target level for the yen (corresponding to the second measure) was 150.4 to the dollar for the entire period.

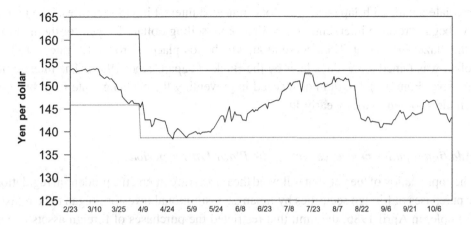

Figure 5. The Yen/Dollar Exchange Rate, 23 February–16 October 1987
Sources: *Nihon Keizai Shinbun*; Funabashi (1988).

To keep the exchange rate within the agreed ranges, the Japanese authorities took various measures, often in coordination with their US (and German) counterparts. According to press reports, the Bank of Japan intervened in the market on 37 days (out of 169 days) between 22 February and 18 October; moreover, the intensity of intervention increased as the exchange rate deviated more from the presumed central rate (Lewis, 1995).[16] In particular, when the yen reached the presumed floor of 138.7 yen per dollar in early May, the Bank of Japan reportedly joined the Federal Reserve in purchasing dollars on a massive scale. The generally massive size of intervention during 1987 is evident in Figure 3.[17]

Coordinated policy actions in support of exchange rate stability could not be sustained. When, after recovering to the 150-yen level, the dollar began to depreciate again, the Federal Reserve, in early September, raised the discount rate to defend the dollar. In view of possible inflationary pressure, however, the Bank of Japan was compelled to allow short-term interest rates to rise by as much as 5% towards the end of the month.[18] It was then evident that the Louvre Accord was breaking down. The dollar began to depreciate even more, falling from 140 yen in October to 120 yen in December. When the G-7 countries met again around Christmas to proclaim that the dollar had fallen far enough, the markets no longer believed the credibility of G-5 policy coordination.[19]

During 1988, the yen–dollar exchange rate remained relatively stable. The Bank of Japan reportedly intervened in times of the perceived weakness of the dollar in support of the dollar (e.g., in January, April and November of 1988), and in times of the perceived strength of the dollar in support of the yen (e.g., in June and September of 1988). In 1989, the yen began

---

[16]Esaka (2000) noted that no intervention by the Bank of Japan (but not the Federal Reserve) was reported in the press when the exchange rate depreciated from the central rate.

[17]Another large scale dollar-purchase intervention was reported from immediately after the stock market crash of October 1987 through December 1987, but this was outside the framework of the Louvre Accord.

[18]Germany also began to raise interest rates.

[19]Esaka (2000) estimated the expected rate of devaluation to be significantly negative during most of the Louvre period to conclude that the target zone for the yen was not very credible in the first place.

to depreciate again, with Japanese investors' renewed interest in US securities. The Federal Reserve began "reverse intervention" on 30 March, selling dollars for yen for the first time since the Plaza Agreement. The intervention, which took place at around the rate of 133 yen per dollar, was joined a few days later by the Bank of Japan (Koo, 1993). The intervention was massive (Figure 3), but did not succeed in preventing the exchange rate from breaking through the 150-yen mark by early June.

4.3. *Additional policy measures during the Plaza-Louvre period*

With the appreciation of the yen that followed the Plaza Agreement, the prudential regulations on the purchases of foreign securities by Japanese institutional investors began to be relaxed. For example, in April 1986, the limit that restricted the purchases of foreign assets in each month to 20% of new investments was raised to 40%; the limit was then abolished all together in August 1986, when the similar flow restrictions were suspended for other types of institutional investors.

The stock restrictions were also relaxed. In March and April 1986, the ceiling on foreign securities investments by insurance companies and trust banks (for pension trust accounts) was raised from 10% to 25% of total assets; the ceiling was further raised to 30% in August 1986. Trust banks were authorized to invest in foreign bonds (for loan trust accounts) up to 1% of total assets in February 1986 and up to 3% in June 1986 (and further to 5% in February 1989). In April 1987, the Trust Fund Bureau of the Ministry of Finance was authorized to invest in foreign securities for the first time, up to 10% of total assets. In June 1987, the ceiling for the Postal Life Insurance System was increased from 10% to 20% of total assets.

For all intents and purposes, Japan had a fully open capital account by this time, and capital controls — prudential or otherwise — had ceased to exist as an instrument of exchange rate policy. True, there were still prudential regulations, but, with substantial relaxations, they were no longer binding on the behavior of institutional investors (Fukao and Okina, 1989). As a result, in May 1987, when the yen–dollar exchange rate hit the presumed floor under the Louvre Accord, the Ministry of Finance had no recourse to capital controls, except reportedly to harass foreign exchange banks by requiring every conceivable kind of data on their foreign exchange dealings (Koo, 1993).

With fewer options to influence the exchange rate, the authorities began to use conventional macroeconomic policy tools more actively.[20] For example, the Bank of Japan lowered the discount rate five times in just over a year, pushing it down to 2.5% on 20 February 1987. Following the Louvre Accord, the Bank of Japan further eased monetary conditions: the call money rate, for example, fell from 3.9% in mid-March to 3.1% in mid-May. Monetary policy remained generally easy during the period of relative strength of the yen in 1987 and 1988. The policy of easy money was only reversed in response to the sharp depreciation

---

[20]The expansionary macroeconomic policies of the immediate post-Plaza years were also meant to stimulate domestic demand in light of the deflationary impact of the rising yen, and to reduce the current account surplus without strengthening the yen further.

of the yen in 1989, when the Bank raised the discount rate to 3.25% in May and further to 3.75% in October.

De Andrade and Divino (2005) confirm the key role exchange rate considerations played in the determination of monetary policy stance. By regressing the call rate on deviations from purchasing power parity (a proxy for real exchange rate misalignment), the output gap and inflation, they show that the interest rate was countercyclical to the real exchange rate, thus concluding that the Bank of Japan targeted exchange rate stability. Movements in the exchange rate were shown to explain those in the interest rate remarkably well from the mid-1980s to mid-1990s, especially from August 1985 to May 1987. The unfortunate consequence of the easy monetary policy designed to stabilize the yen, coupled with an expansionary fiscal policy designed to expand domestic demand and to reduce current account surpluses, was to create an unprecedented period of asset price inflation through 1990.

5. The Lost Decade and Fragile Recovery: From the Mid-1990s Through 2004

5.1. *The macroeconomic environment*

In 1991, with a bursting of the bubble economy,[21] economic growth decelerated and, in 1992, the Japanese economy entered a prolonged period of stagnation. Annual growth over the next decade averaged less than 1%, compared with over 4% during the previous decade. Growth appeared to pick up in 1996, only to fall back. In 1998, severe recession set in, with negative growth in 1998 and 1999. Although annual economic growth finally exceeded 2% in 2003 and 2004, the recovery was fragile at best. The recession was compounded by sustained deflationary pressure; annual CPI inflation averaged less than 1% over the lost decade. The moderate recovery of 2003–2004 did not end the deflation, with the average CPI inflation of −0.4% for 2003–2006. In terms of corporate goods prices, the price level was 13% lower in 2003 than in 1991.

To stimulate domestic demand and to fend off deflationary pressure, the authorities eased both fiscal and monetary policies substantially. The general government balance, which was in small surpluses in the early 1990s, deteriorated sharply; it has been in deficit in every year since 1993 (with deficits exceeding 7% of GDP in virtually every year from 1999 to 2003). As a result, the balance of gross public debt rose from about 70% of GDP in the early 1990s to over 180% in 2005. As to monetary policy, the Bank of Japan lowered the discount rate in several steps from 4.5% in December 1991 to 0.5% in September 1995. With no additional room left to maneuver, in early 1999, it reduced short-term interest rates to virtually zero, a policy it continued to follow except for the period August 2000–March 2001.

The magnitude and intractableness of the economic problem required an extraordinary action. From March 2001 to March 2006, the Bank of Japan followed what became known as the quantitative easing monetary policy (QEMP). It consisted of three pillars: (i) the Bank supplied ample liquidity by using the current account balances (i.e., commercial bank deposits held at the central bank) as the main operating target; (ii) it publicly committed itself

---

[21] Stock prices peaked in December 1989 (and continued to decline until March 2003), while the peak of real estate prices was in 1991.

to maintaining ample liquidity until core CPI inflation became zero or higher on a sustained basis; and (iii) it increased the purchases of Japanese government bonds, if necessary, to inject liquidity (Oda and Ueda, 2007). Over the period of QEMP, the Bank of Japan steadily increased the targeted current account balances, from about 5 trillion yen in March 2001 to 30–35 trillion yen in March 2006.

Among the hardest hit by the prolonged stagnation of the economy was the banking sector. With slow growth, deflation and a collapse of asset prices, especially in the real estate market, the balance of bad loans held by banks rose sharply, putting a large number of banks in difficulty. When some large financial institutions failed in November 1997, Japan was on the verge of a banking crisis. In 1998, the Japanese government finally came up with a framework to close down weak banks and recapitalize solvent but undercapitalized ones with an injection of public funds amounting to 60 trillion yen. The sum of bad loans and cumulative write-offs, which was estimated at 10% of GDP in 1998, continued to rise for some time (Hoshi, 2001), but a subsequent wave of nationalization and consolidation gradually restored health to the banking sector.

5.2. *The big bang and its impact on the yen*

Prolonged stagnation weakened the shackles of vested interests, allowing the Prime Minister to announce a comprehensive deregulation of Japan's financial markets in November 1996. With macroeconomic policies obviously not working, it was thought, structural reforms, including in the financial sector, would help revitalize the Japanese economy. Called the financial "big bang", a term borrowed from the 1980s deregulation of the London financial markets, the plan sought to make Japan's financial markets and institutions more competitive and efficient ("fair, free and global", to use the government's slogan) by eliminating existing barriers and impediments.

While the big bang involved reforms in all areas of the financial system and would take several years to complete, the first set of measures involved the elimination of the last two remaining foreign exchange market regulations on 1 April 1998. First, non-financial institutions were allowed to deal directly in foreign exchange transactions without the inter-mediation of authorized foreign exchange banks. Second, Japanese residents were allowed to open and maintain foreign currency accounts with financial institutions located in foreign countries. The 1980 Foreign Exchange Law was revised to shift the legal basis of control from prior approval or application to *ex post* reporting requirements, if any.

In the week of this action, the yen depreciated against the dollar from about 130 to 135. The Bank of Japan intervened during the following week to support the yen, selling over $20 billion (or buying 2.8 trillion yen) on 9–10 April. From the third week of April, however, the yen began to depreciate again until it peaked at over 145 in the second week of June. It is not clear if the subsequent fall of the yen was necessarily due to the big bang reforms. The lasting impact of the big bang appears to lie in the working of the foreign exchange market. Both the bid-ask spreads of deal quotes and exchange rate volatility declined after the big bang, with little impact on the volume of trading, suggesting that competition and efficiency increased in the market (Ito and Melvin, 1999).

5.3. *Intervention as a tool of macroeconomic policy*

With interest rates near zero, the authorities lost the option to stimulate the economy by further reducing the nominal interest rates. In such an environment, a deflationary shock could even raise real interest rates and deepen the recession. In the international policy circles, there was active discussion of the possibility of using yen depreciation as a means of ending the deflationary pressure (McCallum, 2000; Svensson, 2001). Such a view amounted to making exchange rate policy as a tool of monetary policy in the absence of an effective monetary policy instrument.[22]

The Japanese authorities did not pursue such a radical approach, but continued to intervene in the market, often on a massive scale. Because the Japanese government has released detailed intervention data going back to April 1991, we have a reasonably accurate view of exactly what the authorities did (Figure 6). In the early 1990s, the authorities intervened frequently on a modest scale. The tactic changed on 21 June 1995 to infrequent but large-scale intervention (Ito and Yabu, 2007).[23] This lasted until 14 January 2003, when intervention became both frequent and large-scale.[24] Since March 2004, when this intervention tactic ended, the Japanese monetary authorities have refrained from intervening in the foreign exchange market altogether.

The last episode of intervention — the "great intervention" (Taylor, 2006) — was conducted when the economy remained weak and uncertain but began to show signs of fragile recovery. The amount of intervention from January 2003 to March 2004 — 35 trillion yen of dollar sales — amounted to 7% of annual GDP and exceeded the corresponding period's

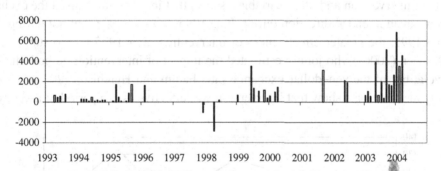

Figure 6. Japan's Monthly Foreign Exchange Market Intervention, 1993–2004 (in billions of yen; a positive number indicates purchases of US dollars)
Source: Japanese Ministry of Finance.

---

[22]Coenen and Wieland (2003) discuss, in a macroeconomic model consisting of the US, the Euro Area and Japan, the impact of yen depreciation.

[23]According to Ito (2003), on this day, a new Director-General of the Ministry of Finance International Bureau took office and convinced the Minister and Vice Minister of Finance that frequent small-scale intervention was taken as given by market participants and that, to have impact, intervention needed to be more decisive and to have an element of surprise. The first intervention under the new strategy took place on 28 June.

[24]On 15 January 2003, a new Vice Minister of Finance took office, with a different intervention philosophy (Ito, 2005). Lack of announcement was another notable feature of the intervention during the 2003–2004 period.

current account surplus of about 21 billion yen. Both in 2003 and 2004, the purchases of foreign assets by the public sector were so large that the private sector recorded a surplus in the capital account despite the economy's large current account surplus. The great intervention was at least initially welcomed by the authorities of other industrial countries, especially the United States, as an instrument of supporting Japan's fragile recovery through further monetary easing (Taylor, 2006).

For the period as a whole, official intervention appeared to be overwhelmingly in the direction of selling yen for dollars (Figure 6). On a closer look, for the period April 1991–December 2002, there were 32 days of yen-purchasing intervention and 182 days of yen-selling intervention. The intensity of intervention to sell yen rose towards the end of each appreciation cycle, that is, in 1995 and in 1999–2000 (Figure 7). On the other hand, towards the end of the yen's depreciation cycle in 1998 (when the prospects for Japan's banking sector were bleak indeed), there was large-scale intervention to buy yen.[25]

The pattern of intervention during the 2003–2004 period was entirely different. Although intervention intensified as the yen appreciated further, its frequency and scale remained high through 16 March 2004, the last day the authorities intervened in the foreign exchange market. Ito (2005) shows that the pattern of intervention during this period could be explained remarkably well by the net long position of currency futures at the Chicago Mercantile Exchange, an indicator of speculative pressure against the yen.

Given the availability of daily intervention data, and especially the exceptional magnitude of the intervention from 1995, a number of empirical studies have investigated the effectiveness of intervention during this period. Ito (2003), regressing daily exchange rate changes over intervention and other variables, shows that intervention caused the exchange rate to move in an intended direction during June 1995–January 2003, but not during April 1991–June 1995; the greater effectiveness of intervention after 1995 is also suggested by Kim and Sheen (2006), who jointly estimated the impact of intervention on both the level and the volatility of the yen–dollar exchange rate. Fatum and Hutchison (2006), using an event study methodology, show that intervention was effective over a period of 2–3 days up

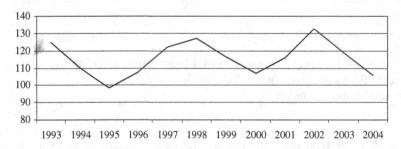

Figure 7. The Yen/Dollar Exchange Rate, January 1993–December 2004 (yen per dollar; end of period)
Source: IMF, International Financial Statistics.

---

[25]These observations are consistent with the empirical findings of Frenkel, Pierdzioch and Stadtmann (2004) that interventions intensified as the exchange rate deviated further from an "implicit" target in either direction.

to possibly 15 days during April 1991–December 2000, especially when it was coordinated with the Federal Reserve.

For the more controversial 2003–2004 period, Ito (2005) shows, in a similar regression analysis to Ito (2003), that the intervention was effective in changing the daily exchange rate in a desired direction, but not as effective as it was during the 1995–2002 period, attributing part of the result to the largely unannounced and predictable nature of the intervention. Fatum and Hutchison (2005), using the event study methodology of Fatum and Hutchison (2006), find that intervention had no significant impact on the exchange rate during 2003, and that it was even counterproductive during the first quarter of 2004, with the exchange rate moving in the opposite direction of what was intended. The weaker effectiveness of intervention for this period can be understood in the context of a trend appreciation of the yen, which moved from 119 in January 2003 to 104 to the dollar in March 2004.

6. Characterizing Japan's Exchange Rate Policy

From the end of the fixed exchange rate regime in the early 1970s, the Japanese monetary authorities in principle allowed the yen to be determined by demand and supply conditions in the foreign exchange market. At times, however, they attempted to influence the exchange rate in a certain direction by official market intervention, use of capital controls and, on a few occasions, interest rate policy. It appears that, conducting exchange rate policy, the authorities paid almost exclusive attention to the exchange rate of the yen against the US dollar. From January 1993 to March 2004, for example, the authorities intervened in the foreign exchange market 341 times; of this total, intervention was conducted against non-dollar currencies only 24 times.[26]

Until the beginning of the 1990s, the Japanese authorities followed an intervention policy of "leaning against the wind", in an effort to moderate market pressure without necessarily targeting a particular level for the exchange rate. For the period of 1973–1989, Takagi (1991) estimated the intervention reaction function of the Japanese monetary authorities by regressing the value of intervention (as a percent of foreign exchange reserves) on a logarithmic change in the quarterly average yen–dollar exchange rate and a set of other explanatory variables. He also included slope dummies to see if the pattern of intervention was different across sub-periods as well as if it was symmetric with respect to depreciation and appreciation. His results show that the coefficient of the exchange rate variable was negative throughout the period and statistically significant for the sub-periods of 1978–1985 and 1985–1989, indicating that the intervention was indeed the leaning-against-the-wind type (Table 1).

Leaning against the wind does not mean that the authorities resisted every exchange rate movement. The authorities sometimes did not react to significant reversals of prevailing trends, as was the case during the Louvre period. Because the yen exchange rate generally moved in alternating appreciation and depreciation phases, intervention often appeared

---

[26]Specifically, the authorities intervened to buy deutsche marks once and euros 18 times; on five occasions, they sold dollars for Indonesian rupiah during the Indonesian crisis in 1997.

Table 1. The Intervention Reaction Function of Japanese
Monetary Authorities, 1973–1989[a]

	Coefficients of Exchange Rate Movement	
	(1)	(2)
1973:2–1978:2	−0.64 (1.14)	−0.55 (0.97)
1978:3–1985:3	−1.17 (3.46)**	
Depreciation		−1.96 (3.41)**
Appreciation		−0.49 (0.94)
1985:4–1989:2	−0.92 (2.66)**	
Depreciation		−1.05 (1.11)
Appreciation		−0.78 (1.90)*

[a]Quarterly data; the dependent variable is the value of intervention
as a percent of foreign exchange reserves; the explanatory variable
is a logarithmic change in the quarterly average yen–dollar nominal
exchange rate; figures in parentheses are t-values; * (**) indicates that
the statistic is significant at 5% (1%).
Source: Takagi (1991, Tables 1–2).

asymmetric. Takagi (1991) shows that intervention was statistically significant only with respect to depreciation during 1978–1985, while it was statistically significant only with respect to appreciation during the post-Plaza period of 1985–1989. This was a reflection of the fact that the former was a period of trend depreciation against the dollar and the latter a period of sustained yen appreciation. Yet, intervention was consistently on both sides, reflecting the near random walk nature of high-frequency exchange rate changes (Takagi, 1988b);[27] it was also symmetric, as indicated by the negative coefficient of the exchange rate variable in either direction. For the period as a whole, given the leaning-against-the wind intervention policy, the steady rise of foreign exchange reserves was a natural outcome of the secular, long-term appreciation of the yen from 1971 through the 1980s and beyond (Figure 8).

From the beginning of the floating period to the early 1980s, the authorities also resorted to use of capital controls as a tool of exchange rate policy. Because use of capital controls lacked the flexibility of market intervention, its purpose was to counter the yen's broader trend movement. In the early part of the post-Bretton Woods era, capital controls may well have had their intended effect on the exchange rate, given the limited volume of cross-border capital flows. By the same token, official market intervention may also have had some impact. The ability of the authorities to influence the movement of the exchange rate during this period is indicated by the sharp appreciation of the yen in 1977–1978, which may have occurred because the monetary authorities — the only agents capable of purchasing

---

[27]The mean of daily exchange rate changes from 1975 to 1986 was virtually zero. The distribution was fat-tailed (with a large kurtosis) and thus indicative of infrequent but large changes (Takagi, 1988b).

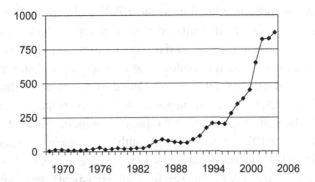

Figure 8. Japan's Foreign Exchange Reserves, 1970–2006 (end of year; in billions of US dollars)
Source: IMF, International Financial Statistics.

foreign assets freely — did not finance the current account surpluses, given their rather passive intervention strategy (Fukao, 1990).

As capital flows were increasingly liberalized over time, the authorities lost a major tool of exchange rate policy. As the foreign exchange market deepened and as more wealth was committed to the market, tolerance for risk also increased, allowing a larger balance of payments imbalance to be accommodated without pressure on the exchange rate (Fukao and Okina, 1989). With the pent-up demand for foreign assets, the result in the first half of the 1980s was a massive outflow of long-term capital that far exceeded the current account surplus. The authorities had little permanent impact on the trend depreciation of the yen during this period. But once the demand was satiated, there was little the authorities could do to stop the secular appreciation of the yen. Much has been said about the efficacy of the Plaza Agreement of 1985. The truth is that the yen had already begun to appreciate against the US dollar in early 1985. Given the massive current account deficits of the United States, the major realignment of the exchange rates of major currencies in the latter part of the 1980s might have happened in any case, with or without the Plaza Agreement.

Exchange rate policy during the "lost decade" of the 1990s and the period of fragile recovery that subsequently followed is a different story entirely. With the zero nominal interest rate floor on monetary policy and the limit to fiscal policy coming from the substantial accumulation of public debt, exchange rate policy was assigned the task of accommodating the overall macroeconomic policy stance. It was to resist sharp appreciation — to mitigate deflationary pressure and to support export growth. Sterilized or not, intervention was a sustainable policy because the Japanese government was earning higher interest income on an increasing amount of foreign securities than paying out interest on their domestic debt counterparts. That is to say, Japanese intervention carried no quasi-fiscal cost, unlike the case in most emerging and developing countries.[28]

Recent empirical work suggests that intervention, sterilized or not, affects short-run exchange rate dynamics, including volatility (see, for example, Dominguez, 1998; Beine,

---

[28]Ito (2005) estimates the amount of net interest income to be about 5.4 trillion yen from 1991 to 2004, disregarding the compounding of interest income.

2004). In the case of Japanese intervention in the 1990s and early 2000s, empirical work based on official data has indicated that intervention occasionally had an intended effect on the direction of exchange rate change on a daily or possibly weekly basis. Going beyond the short-term, however, it is difficult to believe that intervention had substantial and lasting impact on the exchange rate, unless it was accompanied by a permanent change in economic fundamentals. It is in this respect that how much of the foreign exchange market intervention was sterilized by the Bank of Japan remains a topic of continuing interest.

For the earlier period of 1973–1989, when the authorities pursued a leaning-against-the-wind policy, Takagi (1991) estimates that the reaction of the monetary base to a change in foreign exchange reserves (a proxy of intervention) was statistically not significant, meaning that intervention was almost fully sterilized (Table 2). If the sample period is divided into three sub-periods, however, it was found that the coefficient of intervention was negative and statistically significant during 1972–1978 (when the stance of monetary policy was tight), but positive and statistically significant during 1985–1989 (when the stance was easy). During this latter period, the estimate of 0.5 suggests that a half of the intervention was sterilized on a quarterly basis.

How much of the "great intervention" of 2003–2004 was sterilized? Ito (2005) argues that the intervention provided an opportunity for unsterilized intervention, while Fatum and Hutchison (2005) contend that the great intervention did not lead to more rapid base money creation than otherwise would have been the case. In considering this issue, we must keep in mind that the Bank of Japan had a target range for the banking sector's current account balances (CABs), which it raised in five steps from 15–20 trillion yen in October 2002 to 30–35 trillion yen in January 2004. On a daily basis, a close look shows that the Bank of Japan fully accommodated or fully sterilized the reserve change arising from intervention with almost equal probability (Table 3). The central bank's apparent reluctance to fully accommodate the resulting reserve flow when the intervention was especially large may mean that it did not wish to allow the CAB target to be exceeded by a large margin on a

Table 2. The Reaction of Base Money to a Change in
Foreign Exchange Reserves, 1973–1989[a]

	Coefficients of Intervention	
	(1)	(2)
1973:2–1989:2	0.16 (1.58)	
1973:2–1978:2		−0.62 (2.12)*
1978:3–1985:3		0.15 (1.41)
1985:4–1989:2		0.50 (2.31)*

[a]Quarterly data; the dependent variable is a change in base money; the explanatory variable is a change in the balance of central bank credit to the Foreign Exchange Fund Special Account; figures in parentheses are t-values; * indicates that the statistic is significant at 5%.
Source: Takagi (1991, Table 3).

Table 3. The Settlement Day Reaction of Base Money to Intervention Episodes, 15 January 2003–16 March 2004[a]

	Fully Sterilized	Partially Sterilized	Fully Accommodated	Total
Greater than 500 billion yen	—	14	1	15
Greater than 300 billion yen but less than 499 billion yen	8	2	7	17
Less than 299 billion yen	39	8	40	87
Total number of intervention episodes	46	24	48	119[b]

[a]Based on the comparison of the size of intervention (at time t) to the subsequent change in Bank of Japan current account balances from $t + 1$ to $t + 2$ (when the settlement takes place).
[b]Excludes six intervention episodes that took place when the Japanese market was closed for trading.

daily basis. At the same time, it did not fully sterilize the reserve flow when the intervention involved more than 500 billion yen.

On a monthly or quarterly basis, however, the Bank of Japan was trying to supply adequate liquidity to the market, by targeting an ever-increasing range for the current account balances. In one sense, the central bank was using official intervention by the Ministry of Finance as an instrument of achieving this target. Alternatively, we can also view the steady rise in the CAB target as a reflection of the central bank stance to create additional room for intervention to remain unsterilized.[29] In terms of the medium-term growth of base money, Watanabe and Yabu (2007) estimate that the central bank sterilized about 60% of the reserve inflows resulting from the great intervention. We may conclude that foreign exchange policy during this period was subordinate to the overall stance of macroeconomic policy designed to support the fragile recovery.

7. Conclusion

During the flexible exchange rate period of the past 35 years, the Japanese monetary author-ities used official market intervention, capital controls and interest rate actions from time to time, in order to manage the yen–dollar exchange rate. Official intervention was the most dominant tool of exchange rate management through much of this period. Judging from the largely symmetrical nature of the official intervention, it appears that the overriding motive was to smooth exchange rate fluctuations, although the motive during some sub-periods (such as 1986–1988 and 2003–2004) was more likely to prevent further or any apprecia-tion. Use of capital controls appeared effective initially but, with a trend toward full capital account convertibility, they lost effectiveness over time and ceased to exist as an instrument of exchange rate policy by the time of the Plaza Agreement in 1985.

---

[29]These views are consistent with the fact that, following the end of the great intervention in early 2004, the CAB target of 30–35 trillion yen was not raised again.

Following the post-Plaza appreciation of the yen, the Japanese monetary authorities, lacking capital controls as an instrument and being frustrated at the apparent failure of official intervention to stop the tide of appreciation, resorted to easy monetary policy in order to arrest the appreciating pressure and to stimulate the domestic demand weakened by the currency appreciation. What triggered the long-term real appreciation of the yen in the first place from the mid-1980s through the end of the decade? Would the appreciation have taken place in any case with or without the Plaza Agreement? Was it then a mistake to use monetary policy to manipulate the exchange rate, if the real exchange rate was responding to fundamental economic factors? The ultimate cause of the great asset inflation that followed, and the possible role exchange rate policy played in the process, remains unanswered.

The paradigm extensively reviewed in this paper may now have changed. As noted, the authorities have not intervened in the foreign exchange market since March 2004. Even in August 2007, when the yen appreciated sharply against the US dollar (from 120 yen to a dollar to 114 within a matter of several days), the authorities remained unengaged. Part of the lack of official presence in the market may have something to do with the sustained weakness of the yen from 2004 to 2007. Some observers have noted that the yen remained weak because investors were taking advantage of low Japanese interest rates to borrow in yen for investment in foreign currencies. In this view, the temporary strengthening of the yen in August 2007 was attributed to the unwinding of this so-called "yen carry-trade" position. It will require a substantial trend appreciation of the yen to know whether March 2004 indeed marked a permanent shift in Japan's exchange rate policy regime.

Acknowledgments

The author thanks Charles Adams and Yip Sau Leung, the editor of this volume, for useful comments on an earlier draft. Remaining errors, if any, are his own.

Appendix A. Estimating the Amount of Foreign Exchange Market Intervention in Japan, 1970–1989

The Japanese government only began to release detailed intervention data in FY 2000, retroactive to FY 1991. To obtain some idea of the magnitude of intervention prior to 1991, we have estimated the quarterly time series of *net* intervention from the quarterly changes in Japan's foreign exchange reserves, as follows:

$$I_t = RES_t - RES_{t-1} - TBR_t[(RES_t + RES_{t-1})/2],$$

where I_t is the amount of intervention (in dollars) during period t, RES_t is the dollar value of foreign exchange reserves at the end of period t, and TBR_t is the average US Treasury bill rate during period t. Here, intervention is expressed in dollars in order to avoid attributing exchange-rate-induced valuation changes to the actions of the authorities.

This methodology embodies the idea that a proxy of *net* intervention can be obtained by calculating changes in the end-of-period balance of official foreign exchange reserves adjusted for estimated interest earnings during the period. This understates the true amount of *gross* intervention if the authorities were engaged in both selling and purchasing foreign exchange in the same quarter. Moreover, it does not account for the use of "hidden reserves" in the conduct of intervention in the 1970s, as widely believed (Green, 1990).

Appendix B. A Chronology of Selected Measures Related to the Long-Term Capital Control Regime in Japan, 1970–1989[30]

(a) Outflows

April 1970	Investment trusts authorized to purchase foreign securities up to $100 million.
January 1971	Insurance companies authorized to purchase listed foreign securities up to $100 million.
July 1971	Securities companies authorized to purchase listed foreign securities on behalf of individual investors; ceiling on the purchases of foreign securities by investment trusts and insurance companies abolished.
February 1972	Trust banks authorized to purchase listed foreign securities.
March 1972	Major foreign exchange banks authorized to purchase listed foreign securities.
May 1972	Purchases of unlisted foreign securities by residents liberalized; over-the-counter sales of foreign securities by domestic securities companies authorized.
October 1972	Medium- and long-term loans subject to blanket approval.
January 1974	Foreign exchange banks, securities companies, insurance companies and investment trusts requested voluntarily to refrain from increasing the net value of foreign securities investments; medium- and long-term loans no longer subject to blanket approval (now subject to item-by-item approval).
August 1974	Medium- and long-term loans prohibited in principle.
June 1975	The voluntary restriction on foreign securities investments lifted except for foreign exchange banks.
June 1976	Purchases of foreign securities by residents subject to automatic approval.
November 1976	Regulation on medium- and long-term loans relaxed.
March 1977	The voluntary restriction on foreign securities investments lifted for foreign exchange banks.
April 1977	Purchases of unlisted bonds liberalized.

---

[30] Adapted from Takagi (1994), which relied on various issues of Japanese Ministry of Finance, *Annual Report of the International Finance Bureau* and *Zaisei Kinyu Tokei Geppo*; Fukao (1990); Komiya and Suda (1991); and Koo (1993).

July 1978	Foreign currency-denominated medium- and long-term loans by major foreign exchange banks subject to blanket approval.
October 1980	Yen-denominated medium- and long-term loans liberalized.
December 1980	Purchases of securities liberalized; medium- and long-term loans subject only to notification (with the exemption of major foreign exchange banks).
April 1982	Life insurance companies requested voluntarily to limit net purchases of foreign bonds to about 10% of the net increase in assets.
May 1983	The Postal Life Insurance System authorized to purchase foreign securities up to 10% of total assets.
November 1983	Controls introduced on increases in the foreign currency assets of pension trusts.
April 1984	Yen-denominated foreign loans by banks liberalized.
April 1985	Medium- and long-term euro–yen lending to non-residents liberalized by overseas branches of Japanese banks.
February 1986	Trust banks authorized to invest in foreign bonds up to 1% of total assets (for loan trust accounts).
March/April 1986	Regulations on foreign securities investments by life and non-life insurance companies and trust banks (for pension trust accounts) relaxed from 10% to 25% of total assets.
April 1986	Acquisition of foreign currency assets by life insurance companies and pension trusts limited to 40% of the increase in total assets (until August 1986).
June 1986	Regulations on investment in foreign bonds for the loan trust accounts of trust banks relaxed from 1% to 3% of total assets.
August 1986	The voluntary restriction on purchases of foreign bonds relaxed for life insurance companies and pension trusts from 25% to 30% of total assets.
April 1987	The Trust Fund Bureau of the Ministry of Finance authorized to invest in foreign securities up to 10% of total assets.
June 1987	The investment limit on foreign securities for the Postal Life Insurance System increased from 10% to 20% of total assets.
February 1989	Investment limit on foreign bonds for the loan trust accounts of trust banks further relaxed from 3% to 5% of total assets.

(b) Inflows

July 1971	Securities companies authorized to sell listed foreign securities on behalf of individual investors.
November 1973	Regulation on the purchases of Japanese stocks by non-residents abolished.
December 1973	Regulation on the purchases of Japanese secondary bonds by non-residents abolished (except for unlisted bonds with remaining maturities of less than one year).

August 1974	Purchases of Japanese primary bonds by non-residents liberalized; the regulation regarding remaining maturity length abolished.
June 1977	Purchases of Japanese stocks and bonds by non-residents subject to automatic approval.
March 1978	Purchases, by foreign investors, of yen-denominated domestic bonds with remaining maturities of less than five years and one month prohibited.
January/February 1979	The restriction stated above eased and then abolished.
December 1980	Purchases of securities through designated securities companies liberalized.
July 1984	System of designated securities companies abolished.
May 1989	Voluntary restraint on medium- and long-term euro–yen loans to residents abolished.

References

Beine, M (2004). Conditional covariances and direct central bank interventions in the foreign exchange markets. *Journal of Banking and Finance*, 28, 1385–1411.

Bergsten, CF (1982). What to do about the US-Japan economic conflict. *Foreign Affairs*, Summer, 1059–1075.

Coenen, G and V Wieland (2003). The zero-interest-rate bound and the role of the exchange rate for monetary policy in Japan. *Journal of Monetary Economics*, 50, 1071–1101.

De Andrade, JP and JA Divino (2005). Monetary policy of the Bank of Japan — Inflation target versus exchange rate target. *Japan and the World Economy*, 17, 189–208.

Dominguez, KM (1998). Central bank intervention and exchange rate volatility. *Journal of International Economics*, 17, 161–190.

Esaka, T (2000). The Louvre Accord and central bank intervention: Was there a target zone? *Japan and the World Economy*, 12, 107–126.

Fatum, R and M Hutchison (2005). Foreign exchange intervention and monetary policy in Japan, 2003–2004. *International Economics and Economic Policy*, 2, 241–260.

Fatum, R and M Hutchison (2006). Effectiveness of official daily foreign exchange market intervention operations in Japan. *Journal of International Money and Finance*, 25, 199–219.

Frankel, JA (1984). The yen/dollar agreement: Liberalizing Japanese capital markets. Policy Analyses in International Economics No. 9, Institute for International Economics.

Frenkel, M, C Pierdzioch and G Stadtmann (2004). On the determinants of "small" and "large" foreign exchange market interventions: The case of the Japanese interventions in the 1990s. *Review of Financial Economics*, 13, 231–243.

Fukao, M (1990). Liberalization of Japan's foreign exchange controls and structural changes in the balance of payments. *Bank of Japan Monetary and Economic Studies*, 8, 101–165.

Fukao, M and K Okina (1989). Internationalization of financial markets and balance of payments imbalances: A Japanese perspective. *Carnegie-Rochester Conference Series on Public Policy*, 30, 167–220.

Funabashi, Y (1988). *Managing the Dollar: From the Plaza to the Louvre*. Washington: Institute for International Economics.

Green, DJ (1990). Exchange rate policy and intervention in Japan. *Journal of Asian Economics*, 1, 249–271.

Hoshi, T (2001). What happened to Japanese banks? *Bank of Japan Monetary and Economic Studies*, 19, 1–29.

Ito, T (1987). The intradaily exchange rate dynamics and monetary policies after the Group of Five agreement. *Journal of the Japanese and International Economies*, 1, 275–298.

Ito, T (2003). Is foreign exchange intervention effective? The Japanese experience in the 1990s. In *Monetary History, Exchange Rates and Financial Markets*, Vol. 2, P Mizen (ed.), pp. 126–153. Cheltenham, UK: Edward Elgar.

Ito, T (2005). Interventions and Japanese economic recovery. *International Economics and Economic Policy*, 2, 219–239.

Ito, T and M Melvin (1999). Japan's big bang and the transformation of financial markets. NBER Working Paper No. 7247.

Ito, T and T Yabu (2007). What promotes Japan to intervene in the forex market? A new approach to a reaction function. *Journal of International Money and Finance*, 26, 193–212.

Japanese Ministry of Finance, *Annual Report of the International Finance Bureau* (in Japanese), annual issues.

Japanese Ministry of Finance, *Zaisei Kinyu Tokei Geppo* (in Japanese), monthly issues.

Kim, S-J and J Sheen (2006). Interventions in the yen–dollar spot market: A story of price, volatility and volume. *Journal of Banking and Finance*, 30, 3191–3214.

Komiya, R and M Suda (1991). *Japan's Foreign Exchange Policy, 1971–1982*. Sydney: Allen and Unwin.

Koo, RC (1993). International capital flows and an open economy: The Japanese experience. In *Japanese Capital Markets: New Developments in Regulations and Institutions*, S. Takagi (ed.), pp. 78–129. Oxford: Blackwell.

Lewis, KK (1995). Occasional interventions to target zones. *American Economic Review*, 85, 691–715.

McCallum, BT (2000). Theoretical analysis regarding a zero lower bound on nominal interest rates. *Journal of Money, Credit and Banking*, 32, 870–904.

Oda, N and K Ueda (2007). The effects of the Bank of Japan's zero interest rate commitment and quantitative monetary easing on the yield curve: A macro-finance approach. *Japanese Economic Review*, 58, 303–328.

Ohta, T (1982). Exchange-rate management and the conduct of monetary policy. In *Central Bank Views on Monetary Targeting*, P Meed (ed.), pp. 126–131. New York: Federal Reserve Bank of New York.

Otani, I and S Tiwari (1981). Capital controls and interest rate parity: The Japanese experience, 1978–1981. *International Monetary Fund Staff Papers*, 28, 793–815.

Quirk, PJ (1977). Exchange rate policy in Japan: Leaning against the wind. *IMF Staff Papers*, 24, 642–664.

Svensson, LEO (2001). The zero bound in an open-economy: A foolproof way of escaping from a liquidity trap. *Bank of Japan Monetary and Economic Studies*, 19, 277–312.

Takagi, S (1988a). Recent developments in Japan's bond and money markets. *Journal of the Japanese and International Economies*, 2, 63–91.

Takagi, S (1988b). On the statistical properties of floating exchange rates: A reassessment of recent experience and literature. *Bank of Japan Monetary and Economic Studies*, 6, 61–91.

Takagi, S (1991). Foreign exchange market intervention and domestic monetary control in Japan, 1973–1989. *Japan and the World Economy*, 3, 147–180.

Takagi, S (1994). Structural changes in Japanese long-term capital flows. In *The Structure of the Japanese Economy*, M Okabe (ed.), pp. 435–458. London: Macmillan.

Taylor, JB (2006). Lessons from the recovery from the "lost decade" in Japan: The case of the great intervention and monetary injection. Paper presented at a conference held at the Cabinet Office, Government of Japan.

Watanabe, T and T Yabu (2007). The great intervention and massive money injection: The Japanese experience, 2003–2004. Institute of Economic Research, Hitotsubashi University.

CHINA'S EXCHANGE RATE SYSTEM REFORM*

PAUL S. L. YIP

Division of Economics, School of Humanities and Social Sciences
Nanyang Technological University, Nanyang Avenue, Singapore 639798
aslyip@ntu.edu.sg

This paper first documents the rationales behind the transitional exchange rate system reform adopted by China on 21 July 2005. It then outlines the theory behind the medium- and long-term exchange rate arrangements that could be adopted. Thereafter, the paper provides recommendations on supplementary packages that could increase the chance of a successful reform, and increase China's immunity and resilience against financial crises in the future. Finally, the paper discusses the market and economic developments after the transitional reform, and highlights that failure to check the stock market bubble and rampant property inflation could turn the initial success of the reform to an eventual failure and bring disasters to China in the longer future.

Keywords: Exchange rate system; financial crisis; Asia; China.

1. Introduction

This paper first documents the rationales behind the transitional exchange rate system reform adopted by China on 21 July 2005. Whether or not one agrees with the reform, it was one of the biggest experiments on the choice of exchange rate systems and the exit from a peg in recent decades. Thus, documentation of the considerations and rationales behind the reform is important. If the reform proves to be successful, the experiment will provide valuable lessons to those economies adopting a pegged exchange rate system. It will also provide important evidences on propositions from international macroeconomic theory. If the reform turns out to be unsuccessful, the experiment will provide insights on what could have gone wrong and what could contribute to a failure of reform, especially on the inconsistencies among major economic characteristics and system settings. It is also hoped that the documentation could provide basic background information for future developments of rigorous economic modeling on China's exit strategies from the peg, which could further stimulate more generalized theories, and hopefully a literature, on exit strategies in the future.

The paper also outlines medium- and long-term exchange rate arrangements that could be adopted by the Chinese government. Documentation of the plan and the rationales behind it could invite healthy debate on appropriate medium- and long-term exchange rate arrangements for China. If the debate results in conclusions supportive of the plan, the Chinese

---

*A former version of this paper was presented at China's State Administration of Foreign Exchange.

government would be more confident in taking the step forward. If the debate turns out with better suggestions or even strong arguments against the plan, the Chinese government would be able to avoid unnecessary mistakes. Besides, the eventual implementation of the original or revised plan would provide important insights and evidences on international macroeconomic theory.

The structure of the paper is organized as follows. Section 2 briefly reviews the advantages and disadvantages of various proposals before the transitional reform implemented on 21 July 2005. Section 3 discusses the set of proposals that was eventually adopted by the Chinese government. On top of the transitional arrangements, there were also detailed proposals on the medium- to long-term arrangements and supplementary measures that could increase the chance of a successful reform. Section 4 first reviews the transitional reform implemented in 2005 and the immediate market response. It then reviews the proposed measures to deal with the moderate speculative inflows. Section 5 discusses the developments of asset inflation and the general price inflation since 2006 and 2007. It then highlights that excessive and unchecked asset and CPI inflation, instead of exchange rate appreciation, could be the more likely cause of a crisis, and hence, an eventual failure of the whole exchange rate system reform in the longer future. Section 6 concludes.

2. Debate Before the Reform

As summarized in Zhang (2004), Chinese economists were debating on variants of a few sets of options on the exchange rate system before the reform in 2005. The first set of options was to keep the peg, with some suggesting additional measures to mitigate the appreciation pressure on the renminbi, the Chinese currency.[1] Because of the existence of capital control in China, speculative funds could only flow into China through illegal channels or abuse of legal channels.[2] As a result, speculative inflows were still well within the sterilization capacity of the People's Bank of China, the Chinese central bank (e.g., see Garton and Chang, 2005). That is, if China wants to maintain the peg in the forthcoming years and at the same time control her money supply, she can achieve the two targets with large enough

---

[1] Among the academia in the western world, Mundell (2004) was the one very much in favor of keeping the peg. McKinnon (2005, 2006) also highlighted the costs of moving away from the peg, and emphasized the role of differential wage growth between China and the US as the major adjusting variable. Among the Chinese economists who preferred keeping the peg, some believed that it would be important to have additional measures to mitigate the appreciation pressure on the renminbi. One such measure is the encouragement of regulated outflows of capital through the introduction of the scheme of Qualified Domestic Institutional Investors (QDII). While this could help in the longer future, the Chinese government should implement the scheme with great caution as it would involve a relaxation of regulations which could result in erratic outflows at a time the Chinese government dislikes. That is, during the favorable period, the Chinese authority might have overrelaxed the regulation so as to encourage sufficient capital outflows to offset the appreciation pressure. But when the atmosphere or market expectation changed from a favorable one to an unfavorable one, there could be a sudden surge in capital outflows under the overrelaxed regulation. Based on this concern, the author has recommended that the Chinese government should be prepared to cut the annual approved amount of QDII investment when market expectation suddenly changes from a favorable one to an unfavorable one.

[2] One good example of illegal channels is through underground money changers. Examples of abuse of legal channels are overinvoicing of exports by exporters, and abuse of FDI channel to bring in funds driven by speculative motives.

issuance of government bonds. However, as noted by Eichengreen (2004) and Frankel (2005), the ability of the Chinese central bank to keep up the sterilization of this scale indefinitely is questionable.[3] Eichengreen and Frankel also highlighted that it is advisable to exit a peg when times are good and the currency is strong, than to wait until times are bad and the currency is under attack. No doubt, the Chinese authority was aware that she might not be able to maintain the peg forever. Moreover, there was substantial external political pressure, especially from the US, for an exit from the peg. Thus, as long as the exit would not involve too heavy a cost, the Chinese government would be interested in viable proposals, although the proposals could be quite far from what the US was asking for.

The second set of options was a major revision (say, 15%–25%) or medium revisions (say, 5%) of China's exchange rate.[4] The rationale behind the major revision is a once-and-for-all unanticipated jump in exchange rate to the equilibrium level to avoid the possibility of a "one-way bet" for speculative inflows. Nevertheless, as will be explained in the subsequent section, major revaluation of this magnitude would cause coordination failures, and hence enormous and relatively persistent economic costs to China. Besides, even under the case of relatively modest price elasticities of exports and imports, the effect of such major revaluation to China's economic growth and unemployment could be too huge for China to bear. In particular, given that the unemployment situation in China was not as good as the high economic growth rates implied, major revaluation could push the unemployment rate to politically and socially unbearable levels.[5] Furthermore, as noted by Eichengreen (2004), there are difficulties in deciding the right amount of revaluation, and there would be serious costs if the authority gets it wrong.

For the case of medium revaluation(s), the initial revaluation would reward speculators that had bet for a revaluation. The realized revaluation would encourage far greater speculative inflows through the excited expectation of further revaluation(s) or appreciation(s). If the then greater speculative inflows were too big (e.g., exceeded the sterilization capacity of the central bank), the associate monetary growth pressure would sooner or later force the central bank to accept further appreciations or revaluations. By then, there could be a development of herding behavior which would eventually push the Chinese currency well beyond the equilibrium level,[6] and seed a potential financial crisis or major correction in the distant

---

[3]As shown by Cheung, Chinn and Fujii (2003), Chinese capital control is declining in magnitude although it continues to bite. Thus, the required scale of sterilization would be bigger in the future.

[4]In this set of proposals, the Chinese authority could choose variants among a new peg, a managed float, a pure floating or even the two-stage reform recommended by Goldstein (2004).

[5]Although real economic growth rates in China were in the impressive range of 8%–10%, there were enormous amounts of disguised unemployment and surplus labor. Thus, the employment situation in China was not as good as that implied by the high economic growth rates. Moreover, because of the huge size and great diversity within China, it is never an easy job to maintain the political and social stability there. Thus, even if there were just a slowdown of economic growth to, say, 3%–4%, the associate rise in unemployment could be large enough to invoke social instability, which might substantially weaken the leadership of the political leaders and hence invoke political instability.

[6]Along with the appreciations, it is likely that the greater speculative inflows would cause excessive monetary growth and hence, higher inflation. For the effects of herding behavior, see Frankel and Froot (1986, 1987) and the related literature.

future. Even if the greater speculative inflows were within the central bank's sterilization capacity, it would substantially increase the sterilization burden of the central bank. Thus, it is not advisable for the Chinese government to accept any medium-size revaluations or appreciations that exceed the transaction costs and risk premium of speculative inflows.

The third set of options was the adoption of an exchange rate band, which could be adjustable or fixed, and with medium band (say, ±3% or 5%) or wide band (say, ±10% or 15%). Proponents here normally favored an adjustable band, believing that such a band could be adjusted with changes in market fundamentals. No matter whether the band is adjustable or fixed, this set of options would encounter the same problem as those in the second set of options during the initial phase. Given the market's belief of a substantial undervaluation of the renminbi,[7] the adoption of a medium or wide exchange rate band would only result in an immediate appreciation of the renminbi to the upper edge of the band. Thus, the realized large appreciation in the wide band design would imply high economic costs for China. On the other hand, the realized medium appreciation in the medium band design would reward speculators and attract increased speculative inflows.

In addition to the above three sets of options, there was a proposal to peg the renminbi against a basket of currencies. Whether it is *vis-à-vis* the US dollar or a basket of currencies, the author is of the view that there are other pertinent dimensions needed to be considered. The whole reform should involve well-specified decisions on each relevant dimension or characteristic of the system. That is, in addition to the decision of focusing on a basket of currencies or the US dollar, one still has to make decisions on other dimensions such as: (i) whether the exchange rate should be fixed, adjustable or highly flexible; (ii) whether there should be a major revision, or a few medium revisions, in the level of exchange rate; and (iii) whether there should be a narrow, medium or wide exchange rate band. As we will see in Section 3, the actual reform task is a more sophisticated exercise which requires right decisions in all the relevant and interrelated dimensions. From this angle, the shift of focus to a basket of currencies is at most one important dimension of the whole reform.

3. The Proposals

In view of the limitations of the above proposed reforms on China's exchange rate system, the author had written a series of reform proposals[8] that could be classified into the following three areas of reforms: (a) the appropriate transitional arrangements; (b) the medium- to

---

[7]There was a debate on whether the renminbi was undervalued, and if so, by how much (see, for example, Frankel, 2005; Goldstein, 2004; Funke and Rahn, 2005; Chang and Shao, 2004; Cheung *et al.*, 2007). However, on the expectation side, the market did widely believe the renminbi was substantially undervalued. As market expectation was the major cause of the flows of speculative funds into China, this paper will focus on the effect of such market belief while leaving the estimation on the valuation of the renminbi for the ongoing debate.

[8]The proposals were sent to the appropriate authorities in China. They were also published in major Chinese newspapers in Hong Kong (*Hong Kong Economic Journal*) and Singapore (*Lianhe Zaobao*) between November 2004 and July 2005, followed by further post-reform comments and follow-up proposals between August 2005 and September 2007. Yip (2005) also contains a chapter that provides a summary discussion of these proposals.

long-term arrangements; and (c) supplementary package of policies that could increase the chance of a successful reform as well as China's immunity and resilience against financial crises in the future. As we will see, the reforms implemented by the Chinese authority closely resembled these proposals, which had far more sophisticated dimensions than previous proposals in the debate.

3.1. *Transitional arrangements*

3.1.1. *Gradual appreciation, no widening of band or big jump in exchange rate*

The first part of the proposals highlighted that any widening of the exchange rate band at the initial stage is not advisable. Given the market's belief of a substantial undervaluation of the renminbi (see footnote 7), a widening of the band would only result in an immediate appreciation of the renminbi to the upper edge of the band, which would in turn induce more inflows of speculative funds, thus creating greater pressure for appreciation. Neither should there be any major or medium jump in the exchange rate. Instead, the Chinese government should, at the initial stage, engineer a very gradual appreciation of, say, 2% per annum, with the precondition that speculative funds could not profit after the deduction of the transaction costs and risk premium of the (illegal) inflows.[9] If necessary, the Chinese government could raise the effort of inspection and penalty so as to increase the transaction costs and risk of this type of speculation.

Once the above gradual appreciation is sustained for a few years, the Chinese government could further refine its exchange rate policy based on the changing economic conditions. For example, it could raise the appreciation rate to, say 3% if there was a rise in global inflation. It could also resort to depreciation in the case of extreme economic adversity. If there was no major change in the economic conditions, it could maintain the 2% appreciation target. These actions would gradually convince the market that the renminbi is no longer fixed *vis-à-vis* the US dollar, but could appreciate or depreciate against the US dollar or a basket of currencies. This in turn would lay the foundation for China to move towards its preferred exchange rate system in the longer term.

The benefit of a very gradual appreciation is that it can maintain a relatively low exchange value of renminbi for a reasonably long period, thus ensuring a strong economic growth and employment until the medium future.[10] The cost is, of course, less favorable terms of trade.

---

[9]Because of the capital control, the transaction costs and risk of speculating for an appreciation of the renminbi are reasonably high (i.e., higher than 2%). Thus, the 2% target is just a tentative suggestion which also takes care of the psychological effect. The Chinese government can make its judgment in striking a balance between the psychological effect and its estimate of the speculators' transaction costs and risk premium. Nevertheless, it should also be highlighted that, even when there is no appreciation of the renminbi, the speculators' gain in property and share price can be more than the transaction costs and risk premium. Thus, curbing of asset inflation would also play an important role in discouraging speculative inflows of funds (see Sections 3.3.2 and 5 for details).

[10]As explained in footnote 5, the employment situation in China was not as good as that implied by the high economic growth rates of 8%–10%. A major revaluation or appreciation could push the unemployment rate to politically and socially unbearable levels.

But given Chinese policymakers' strong preference for the former to the latter, the gradual appreciation would be the obvious choice.

3.1.2. *A basket of currencies with special care to the exchange rate against the US dollar at the early stage*

The next part of the proposals was on whether the gradual appreciation should be monitored against a basket of currencies or against the US dollar during the transitional reform. While it recommended the Chinese government to declare a shift of the monitoring target towards a basket of currencies, it also highlighted the importance of maintaining at most a moderate appreciation against the US dollar at the early stage (the first year) of the transitional period. This was because the renminbi was fixed against the US dollar before the reform. To avoid any profit from speculation, proper control on the appreciation of the renminbi against the US dollar was necessary. However, at the second stage (e.g., the later years) of the transitional arrangements, China should gradually bring market attention from just the rate against the US dollar back to that against a basket of currencies through speeches by officials. By then, the economy would be better equipped to deal with nominal swings in individual currencies.[11] Again, Singapore's successful experience in this aspect was also used to support the argument.

3.1.3. *A narrow exchange rate band at the early stage*

The proposals also highlighted that any exchange rate band at the early stage should be as narrow as possible, mainly because market confidence at this stage would be of utmost importance. A widening of the band without any specific purpose would only weaken confidence and invite unnecessary speculation. However, once the gradual appreciation has been in practice for a few years, the Chinese government could consider a gradual expansion of the adjustable exchange rate band, and prepare herself for the next stage of the reform.

3.2. *Medium- to long-term arrangements*

3.2.1. *The debating process before the medium-term recommendation*

For the medium and long run, the related part of the proposals first noted that a fixed exchange rate system might not be the best choice for China.[12] It also highlighted that the phenomena

---

[11]For example, suppose there is a 10% appreciation of the euro against all other currencies, and the weight of euro in China's basket of currencies is 25%. If China keeps her nominal effective exchange rate unchanged, the renminbi would depreciate against the euro by 7.5% and appreciate against other currencies by 2.5%. The effect of the latter two would offset each other, leaving China's price competitiveness unchanged with the nominal swing of euro. By automatically offsetting the effect of nominal swings in individual currency with a basket of currencies, the monetary authority's task would be greatly simplified, as the authority would only have to adjust her nominal effective exchange rate with changes in the real sector.

[12]See Yip (2005) for a summary of the disadvantages of the fixed exchange rate system.

of herding behavior and exchange rate overshooting could result in undesirable outcomes if China were to adopt a pure floating regime.[13] Instead, it recommended more detailed studies of some interesting and desirable features in:

(a) the monitoring band system in Singapore; and
(b) a floating exchange rate system with occasional interventions similar to, but more frequent than, that of the US system.[14]

A spur of interest in Singapore's exchange rate system

The recommendation had resulted in a spur of official interest in Singapore's exchange rate system, and senior officials were sent to Singapore for further understandings of the system in March 2005. In May 2005, there was news that the Chinese authority might adopt an exchange rate system similar to that of Singapore. Under this system, the renminbi would be monitored against a basket of currencies, with an exchange rate band within which the renminbi would be allowed to fluctuate. However, the exact band width and the weight of each currency in the basket would not be disclosed. The aim was to maintain a certain degree of confidentiality to increase the level of speculation difficulty against the monetary authority. Along with this, the Chinese government could adjust the exchange rate band with changes in China's internal economic conditions and global trade environments.

In response to the above proposed design, the author wrote an article expressing his appreciation and concern on the design.[15] In particular, he emphasized that there were significant differences between Singapore and China. A mere adoption of Singapore's exchange rate system without due regard to these differences could be disastrous. More importantly, long-term arrangements should not dilute or distract the importance of the transitional arrangements. Even if the design were perfect in the long-term, problems or mistakes in the transitional arrangements could result in failure of the whole reform.

The article first elaborated on the advantages of the proposed design, and then discussed its relative importance in the whole reform. It elaborated that the non-disclosure of the currency basket weights and band width had increased the market's information costs and uncertainty in going against the Monetary Authority of Singapore (MAS). Although institutional investors and speculators could roughly estimate the basket weights from

---

[13]Frankel and Froot (1986, 1987) explained that herding behavior in the foreign exchange market could lead to huge cycles in foreign exchange rate. The development of exchange rate overshooting models (e.g., Dornbusch, 1976; Kouri, 1976; Calvo and Rodriguez, 1977; Dornbusch and Fischer, 1980; Rodriguez, 1980; Buiter and Miller, 1981, 1982; Mussa, 1982) also revealed that exchange rate had turned out to be far more volatile than that assumed by proponents of flexible exchange rate system in the late 1960s or early 1970s (e.g., Johnson, 1969; Friedman, 1969).

[14]As explained in Yip (2005), the main purpose of the occasional interventions is to discourage herding behavior when deemed necessary.

[15]The article was sent to the related authorities. It was also published in major Chinese newspapers in Hong Kong (i.e., *Hong Kong Economic Journal* on 19 May 2005) and Singapore (i.e., *Lianhe Zaobao* on 7 June 2005).

Singapore's trade statistics so that the information cost was rather small for them, for the general public this information cost was large and even insurmountable for many people. Meanwhile, MAS's non-disclosure of the band width and flexibility in revising the internal band target would increase the public's uncertainty in joining the speculation during normal circumstances. Even if institutional speculators attempted to mobilize the general public through market reports or rumors, the above information costs and risks to the general public would make it difficult to mobilize the general public under normal circumstances.

The risk of an immediate adoption of the Singapore system

However, the situation would be different if the Singapore dollar or renminbi was believed to be substantially undervalued or overvalued. Under this scenario, the general public's expected return from joining the speculation would easily overcome the hurdle due to the above information costs and uncertainty. Worse still, as long as the general public believed that the return would be greater, they would join the speculation without any need to pay for the information costs. Thus, the information costs and uncertainty for joining the speculation would fall substantially under this extreme condition.

In fact, this is the major difference between Singapore and China that needs to be addressed. As Singapore has adopted the adjustable band system for many years, her current exchange rate is unlikely to be far away from the equilibrium level. As a result, the above mentioned information costs and uncertainty for the general public would be sufficient to discourage speculators from mobilizing the general public to speculate against the monetary authority. However, China has adopted the fixed exchange rate system for many years. Market participants widely believed that her exchange rate level was substantially undervalued. As a result, the expected gain from betting for renminbi appreciation would be substantial, thus implying the above mentioned information costs and uncertainty would not be able to exert its influence under this extreme condition.

In other words, as the starting levels of exchange rate were different, a mere adoption of Singapore's exchange rate system in China would not be able to stop the renminbi from making substantial appreciation. Once there is a substantial appreciation, the Chinese government's credibility in this aspect would disappear. Under this circumstance, the proposed exchange rate band system would not be able to function properly. Worse still, because of herding behavior and the inclination of extrapolating past trend in the foreign exchange market, the renminbi could eventually overappreciate, thus laying the seed for economic contraction or even a financial crisis in the future.

Thus, the advantages of the long-term design would not be sufficient to guarantee a successful reform. Appropriate transitional arrangements could sometimes be more important than long-term arrangements. It would also be dangerous for China to let the long-term design dilute the focus on the transitional arrangements and the whole reform.

After expressing the above concern, the article reiterated that the focus of the transitional arrangements should be a target of 1%–2% annual appreciation of the renminbi during the early stage of the transitional period. In particular, China should not accept any appreciation that is greater than the transaction costs and risk premium of speculation so as to avoid increased inflows of speculative funds. Neither should China allow any wide or medium exchange rate band, whether disclosed or undisclosed. Otherwise, market forces would push the exchange rate to the upper edge of the band, and hence attract enormous speculative inflows. In other words, during the transitional period, the one that could help the exit from a fixed exchange rate system would still be a variant of a fixed exchange rate system. The only difference is that the former would permanently stay at a fixed level of exchange rate (i.e., 8.28 renminbi per US dollar), while the latter would set the appreciation target to 1%–2% per annum (with moderate variations along the appreciating path). Nevertheless, this small step would change the market expectation of a permanently fixed exchange rate. The small change would in fact be a big step in the whole exchange rate system reform.

Finally, the article clarified that the author's previous proposals did not recommend a mere adoption of Singapore's exchange rate system even in the long run. In fact, the difference in the degree of openness might imply a very different choice in the long run. For example, as a small open economy with high capital mobility, Singapore has found it more suitable to have an exchange rate targeting while giving up her independent control on money supply (see MAS, 1982/1983; Teh and Shanmugaratnam, 1992; Yip, 2003). On the other hand, China is a large economy where internal demand could be more important than external demand. As a result, there are advantages for China to have independent control of her money supply. Thus, it was still debatable which long-term exchange rate arrangements would be most suitable to China.

A safe and reversible roadmap of reform

After the above warnings, the proposed design was shelved, or at least held up, for a while. In early July 2005, the author proposed the following roadmap of reform with particular emphasis on the *safety* and *reversibility* of the reform:

Step 1: Implement the transitional arrangement discussed in Section 3.1. If everything works well for some years, proceed to Step 2. In case of unexpected adverse developments, stay unchanged or go back to the fixed exchange rate system.

Step 2: Gradually widen the exchange rate band to achieve an exchange rate band system similar to that in Singapore.[16] If everything works well for some years, consider the advantages and disadvantages of proceeding to Step 3. In case of unexpected adverse developments, stay unchanged with the new arrangement or go back to the system in Step 1.

Step 3: Gradually widen the exchange rate band in Step 2 towards infinity and proceed towards a floating system with more occasional interventions than that in the US. If everything works well, stay with this new system. In case of unexpected adverse developments, go back to the system in Step 2.

---

[16]Note that the exchange rate band system in this step could be different from the Singapore system in aspects other than the exchange rate band.

The transitional arrangement was chosen as the first step because it was the alternative that was most similar to the original fixed exchange rate system. It was the *safest choice* because the only recommended change was a shift from a horizontal path of exchange rate against time to an upward sloping path (i.e., it did not recommend a major or medium jump in exchange rate or widening of exchange rate band at the early stage). On the other hand, as explained earlier, a reasonably large or medium jump in exchange rate or widening of band would attract increased speculative inflows, thus creating substantial upward pressure on the renminbi and raising the chance of a reform failure. Because of its similarities with the original fixed exchange rate system, the transitional arrangement was also the *most easily reversible choice*. For example, in case of unexpected adverse developments, it would be easier and less costly for the Chinese authority to retreat to a viable system (i.e., the original fixed exchange rate system) by announcing a change in the expected upward path of exchange rate back to a horizontal one.

The exchange rate band system in Step 2 was recommended because it is a viable system (i.e., exists in Singapore) with crucial features somewhere between the systems in Steps 1 and 3 (i.e., its similarities with the system in Step 1 is much greater than that between the systems in Step 1 and Step 3). If the system in Step 1 works well for some years, the only major change towards Step 2 would be a gradual widening of the exchange rate band. Compared with the system in Step 3, it is also much more reversible to the system in Step 1 (which would be a viable system if the authority had chosen to move from Step 1 to Step 2). For example, in case of unexpected adverse developments, the Chinese authority could easily retreat to a viable system by narrowing the exchange rate band back to that in Step 1.

In view of external political pressure[17] for some changes away from the fixed exchange rate system at that time, the paper noted that the implementation of Step 1 and then Step 2 would each take at least a few years. This will give researchers sufficient time to sort out the appropriate long-term direction of the exchange rate system reform (see the recommendation discussed in Section 3.2.2). If it is found that the system in Step 3 is the appropriate one for the long run, the Chinese authority can proceed to Step 3 by gradually widening the exchange rate band in Step 2 towards infinity. On the other hand, if it is found that the system in Step 3 is not appropriate for China in the long run, the Chinese authority can stick with the system in Step 2 or move towards a modified system that would be the most appropriate system for China in the long run.

To further convince the Chinese authority to adopt the above view and proposal, the article drew an analogy between the proposal and the Chinese traditional wisdom of military strategy. According to the traditional military wisdom, moving an army forward or retreating an army is never a simple forward or backward movement of the army. Detailed plans on

---

[17] Senior officials had reflected that they were not that constrained by external political pressure if they believed a certain change is risky or undesirable. However, as China might have made implicit agreements in the first half of 2005 for some exchange rate system reform later in the year, there seemed to be a pressure for some changes at that time.

how to move the army forward or backward step-by-step, and group-by-group, are important. This analogy seemed to have raised the authority's trust on the viability of the proposal. On 21 July 2005, a first-stage reform package was announced, although the long run choice of China's exchange rate system was yet to be sorted out.

3.2.2. *The medium-term recommendation*

To address the above question on the longer-term direction of the reform, the author finally solved the problem by publishing a recommendation on 12 September 2005 (i.e., almost two months after the reform on 21 July 2005).[18] The article first used the doctrine of Impossible Trinity (e.g., see Krugman and Obstfeld, 2007) to highlight that an economy could only achieve any two goals of the following three: (a) free mobility of capital; (b) stability in exchange rate; and (c) independence in monetary policy. It also used the examples of Hong Kong, Singapore and the US to illustrate the issue. For example, with free capital mobility and a fixed exchange rate implicit in its currency board system, Hong Kong has given up the choice of using independent monetary policy to finetune her output (i.e., her quantity of money supply is determined by market demand,[19] and her interest rate has to follow the US rate under normal circumstances, no matter whether she likes it or not). Another example is Singapore. As capital is also freely mobile, Singapore has to choose between an independent exchange rate policy and an independent monetary policy. As a small open economy, Singapore has chosen to target her exchange rate.[20] For the US, capital mobility is also high. Meanwhile, the importance of her huge domestic market has dictated the use of independent monetary (interest rate) policy for the finetuning of her internal balance.[21] As a result, the US government has chosen to let her exchange rate be determined by market forces (i.e., a flexible exchange rate system).

After elaborating on the doctrine of Impossible Trinity, the article recommended China to opt for an independent monetary policy and independent control of the renminbi along a gradually appreciating path, while maintaining her current level of capital control. This is so because China, similar to the US, is a large economy in which the huge domestic market is crucial to her output determination. Thus, an independent monetary policy is important. Meanwhile, as the renminbi has been widely believed by market participants to be substantially undervalued, a release of the current control on the exchange value of the

---

[18]The recommendation was published in the *Hong Kong Economic Journal* on 12 September 2005 and the *Lianhe Zaobao* (Singapore) on 20 October 2005.

[19]With a currency board system, Hong Kong's money supply is demand-determined.

[20]As highlighted in Yip (2005), Singapore has opted for the use of exchange rate policy to influence her internal balance while leaving the external balance as a residual balance. It first explained that the net Central Provident Fund (CPF) contribution in Singapore had resulted in persistent and huge current account (and balance of payment) surplus by ensuring Singaporean residents spend less than what they earn. It then noted that the Singapore government was not particularly concerned with the variations in the external balance because the variation is only between a bigger surplus and a smaller surplus.

[21]As a large economy, the US's interest rate decision would also influence the world interest rate. This implies an additional advantage for the US to opt for an independent interest rate policy.

renminbi would result in substantial appreciation, which could result in severe recession in the Chinese and neighborhood economies.[22] In the worst scenario, this could in turn affect the political status of the leaders and hence, the stability of China. Once the political stability is endangered, it could result in endless turmoil. Thus, avoiding the sharp appreciation of the renminbi and the possibility of political instability are of utmost importance.

If China prefers maintaining an independent monetary policy and avoiding sharp appreciation of the renminbi, she has no choice but to maintain the current degree of capital control. Failure to do so would destroy or weaken her ability in achieving the first two objectives.[23] The capital control would of course imply costs such as efficiency loss. However, as there were substantial problems in China's financial system, such as the huge amount of non-performing bank loans and extensive moral hazard activities, further liberalization of the capital control would provide a more lax environment for more extensive moral hazard activities. Furthermore, capital control could be the last defense against the outbreak of financial crises in China in the longer future.[24] Removing the control before a proper clearing of the non-performing bank loans and proper establishment of internal control against the extensive moral hazard activities might not be a wise choice. On the other hand, if China could maintain her current degree of capital control, she could still continue to grow at the currently fast growth rate.

In short, if China cannot clear the problems of huge non-performing bank loans and extensive moral hazard activities, she is not qualified to enjoy the benefit of free capital mobility. Rushing for liberalization without the right environment would only destroy the growth prospects of China. On the other hand, with a reasonable degree of capital control, China could still grow at a relatively fast and stable pace.

Although China has not officially announced the medium- to long-term direction of reform, feedback from senior officials suggests that the Chinese authority has found the above arguments convincing. Baring out unexpected developments in the future, China would probably opt for independent control of her money supply and good monitoring of

---

[22]If the renminbi were substantially undervalued, it could be dangerous to lift the control and let the market forces search for the equilibrium value of exchange rate. In particular, the economic outcomes of a gradual appreciation to the equilibrium value could be very different from a substantial appreciation towards the "equilibrium". In the former case, the economic structure and market behavior will have sufficient time to make the required adjustments. On the other hand, a large appreciation in a short period could on one hand cause immediate destructions (say, on exports), and on the other hand fail to achieve the substituting expansion (say, on import-substituting production or high value-added exports). In addition, a precondition for market forces to work is the absence of coordination failure so that market (e.g., price and demand) signals could be transmitted through each sub-market of the economic chains. If agents in one particular part of a chain failed because of a sharp appreciation, agents in the subsequent part of the chain would not receive the right market signals. In such a case, the market will not work in the way it is hoped for. In fact, failure of the shock therapy in the Russian economic reform is one good example of the coordination failure.

[23]As there are capital flows through the illegal channels or abuse of legal channels, China will normally need the help of sterilization to achieve the two objectives. As long as there are sufficient controls on these capital flows so that they lie within the central bank's sterilization capacity, China will be able to monitor her exchange rate and money supply.

[24]Even if there were a plunge in asset price, an effective control would ensure that the money fly-away from the related asset will still stay in the economy, thus alleviating the impacts of the plunge in the asset price.

her exchange rate along a gradually appreciating path in the medium future (say, the next ten years). By then, if the problems of huge non-performing bank loans and extensive moral hazard activities are cleared, China can consider the costs and benefits of moving towards a flexible exchange rate system with occasional interventions.

3.3. *Supplementary package*

In addition to the transitional and medium- to long-term arrangements, the series of proposals also stressed the role of supplementary measures in (a) increasing the chance of a successful reform; and (b) increasing China's *immunity* and *resilience* against potential crises in the future.

3.3.1. *Banking reform*

Firstly, the proposals highlighted the importance of reforms in the banking sector in achieving the above two goals. By highlighting that the outbreak of the Asian financial crisis in 1997–1998 was very much related to the non-performing loans in Thailand and other Asian economies, the proposals pointed out that the huge amount of non-performing loans in China could be a source of problems in the future. The banking sector is a particularly important sector because the related flows of funds are analogous to blood flows in the human body. If an event (e.g., bank run) causes a malfunctioning of the heart (banking sector) such that the blood (funds) cannot flow to various parts of the body (industries), the person will die. On the other hand, the loss of another industry is analogous to the loss of an arm or a leg; the person (economy) can still survive, albeit in more unpleasant ways. Thus, clearing the non-performing bank loans to make sure that the banking sector will function properly, and free of bank runs or speculative attacks, is of utmost importance. In view of this, the author proposed to allow foreign banks to own a sufficient stake of domestic banks so as to improve internal control and reduce moral hazard activities in the banking industry.[25] The author also recommended the recruitment of less corruption-inclined chief and senior bank executives from foreign countries so as to facilitate the establishment of proper internal control within domestic banks.[26]

3.3.2. *Control of asset inflation*

The series of proposals also highlighted the importance of controlling asset inflation. It first noted that what eventually matters is the real exchange rate appreciation, which could

---

[25]When the author made the proposal, he thought that this could only alleviate the problem, mainly because the amount of non-performing bank loans in the four major state-owned commercial banks were too huge to be absorbed by major banks in the international market. He believed that foreign banks would only be interested in, and capable of, acquiring small and medium-size domestic banks (i.e., buy the right of doing banking business in China by absorbing the non-performing loans). However, the subsequent development was much better than originally anticipated, mainly because the possibility of Initial Public Offerings (IPOs) of the "reformed" domestic banks had offered potential profit as well as exit for these foreign investors.

[26]This could even change the mode of operation.

be done by a nominal exchange rate appreciation, a surge in domestic inflation, or both. For example, even if the Chinese authority manages to keep a gradual appreciation of the renminbi, sustained and rapid asset inflation could still push domestic rentals, wages and prices to uncompetitive levels and seed the possibility of a financial crisis in the distant future. The proposals also highlighted the importance of curbing any potential rampant asset inflation era at the early stage, i.e., before the asset inflation is incorporated in people's expectation. Otherwise, the expectation would cause changes in people's behavior, which would in turn fuel the asset inflation.

For example, as documented in Yip (2005) on Southeast Asia's experience of the asset inflation era before the financial crisis in 1997, the formation of the expected asset inflation had caused a surge in people's asset demand and their gearing in asset investment. In the property market, the expected property inflation had induced many existing property owners to shift to bigger properties or invest in additional properties. For those without a property, their relatives' and friends' investment gains had created enormous peer pressure and temptation for them to consider investing in properties. Even for those who were originally not inclined to get rich through property investment or those who did not have a strong need to own a property, the persistent rise in property price eventually pressurized many of them to join the herd for property investments. As a result, the demand for property surged with the expected property inflation. Similarly, the expected share price inflation had caused a substantial rise in the demand for shares.

In addition, Yip's (2005) book noted that the expected rise in asset prices had induced (i) the public to reduce their cash to deposit ratios; and (ii) the banks to reduce their desired excess reserve to deposit ratios. Thus, the change in behavior would increase the money multiplier, which would cause a surge in money supply even if the central bank managed to control the monetary base. Worse still, with expected asset inflation, banks and enterprises had strong incentives to borrow foreign currency loans and convert them into domestic currency for domestic usage.[27] This in turn raised the money supply through a rise in monetary base. Thus, all these changes in behavior arising from the expectation of asset inflation tend to offset any government's curbing measures and fuel the asset inflation. Hence, two conclusions can be drawn from the above discussion:

(i) It is always better to curb any potential rampant asset inflation era at the early stage, i.e., before the asset inflation is built into people's expectation.
(ii) If an expectation of rampant asset inflation has been formed or established, the government has to raise the curbing measures substantially before the asset inflation can be

---

[27]In the case of a solid expectation of high asset inflation, the impact of this could be beyond the sterilization capacity of the central bank. In such cases, banks and loan officers would be under enormous competition and performance pressure to increase their loan growth. For example, suppose a Chief Executive Officer (CEO) sees a surge in another bank's loan growth from 20% to 25%. To justify his survival and "value" as perceived by the Board of Directors, he has to raise his bank's loan growth to 25% or more, even though he knows that this is done at the cost of a much higher credit risk. Similarly, when a loan officer sees some of his colleagues being rewarded or promoted because of the achievement of higher loan growth during the asset inflation period, he will be under performance and peer pressure to increase his own loan growth even though he knows that some of the borrowers could be overleveraging in their investments.

properly controlled. That is, in addition to the original amount of curbing, extra curbing is required to offset the effect of the above changes in economic behaviors induced by the expected asset inflation.

In fact, because of the failure to recognize the above changes in economic behaviors induced by asset inflation, most market participants and Asian central banks had mistakenly believed that the curbing measures were not effective. Because of this misjudgment, the related central banks did not recognize that they could, and should, raise the curbing measures to offset the impacts of the changes in economic behaviors on asset inflation. Meanwhile, market participants continued, or even escalated, their asset investment. As a result, there were far from sufficient curbing measures, giving people the wrong impression that the curbing measures could only have minor and short-lived effects on the asset inflation. In Section 5, we will discuss the application of the above discussion on China's curbing of asset inflation in 2006 and 2007.

3.3.3. *Variable wage component*

Thirdly, the proposals recommended the Chinese government to establish the Singapore-type of variable wage component (VWC) in the current wage structure.[28] This could be done by allocating a certain percentage (e.g., 80%) of subsequent wage increments into the variable wage component until the latter forms 25%–30% of employees' total wage bill. During the normal period, the employees will receive the full amount of the variable wage component. In fact, the variable wage component could only be reduced through proper government procedures during the crisis period (e.g., proposed by the national wage board and approved by the premier).[29] For example, suppose sustained asset inflation and exchange rate appreciation over the next ten years have made China's wage and currency no longer competitive, and there is a speculative attack on renminbi thereafter.[30] In response to this speculative attack, the Chinese government can announce, say, a 10% nation-wide reduction in wage through a cut in the variable wage component. Such a reduction in wage, along with the depreciation of the renminbi triggered by the speculative attack, will help restore China's competitiveness and hence increase her resilience from the crisis. In addition, if speculators know in advance that the Chinese government has this powerful policy weapon (i.e., the VWC) that could influence the equilibrium level of China's exchange rate, their inclination of engineering a speculative attack could be greatly reduced. At the very least,

---

[28]The government could encourage the private sector to follow their initiated changes for government and semi-government bodies. Alternatively, she could pass a law requesting every employer to allocate a certain percentage of subsequent wage increment into the variable wage component until the latter reaches the target ratio of the total wage bill. The author is in favor of the second alternative.

[29]If private employers want to maintain another variable wage component as a buffer against firm-specific shocks or moderate business cycles, they could set up another variable wage component (e.g., variable bonus component) that could be varied by the employers.

[30]Note that the greatest danger to China's exchange rate system reform is not now, but in the longer future (e.g., when sustained asset inflation and exchange rate appreciation allows speculative attack to trigger a financial crisis, especially when the non-performing bank loans remain substantial).

a wage cut can reduce the required downward adjustment (and hence the instability) of renminbi. Because of this, speculators will not dare to push the Chinese currency too far as an announced wage cut amid a medium-size depreciation can seriously hurt these speculators. Thus, China's immunity against a potential crisis would be increased. In addition, the chance of a reform failure, in terms of an eventual collapse of exchange rate in the longer future, would be reduced. Unfortunately, as the establishment of a variable wage component is outside the authority of the central bank, reforms along this direction have not yet been seriously explored.

3.3.4. *Capital control*

Finally, the proposals reiterated the importance of maintaining a sufficient degree of capital control (i.e., inconvertibility of capital account) until (i) the problems of non-performing bank loans and extensive moral hazard activities are cleared, and (ii) the real exchange rate has gradually adjusted to levels reasonably close to its equilibrium level. That is, removing capital control should be the last step of the reform.

4. The Transitional Reform and the Immediate Market Response

4.1. *The reform announced in July 2005*

On 21 July 2005, the People's Bank of China finally announced a reform whose timing was unanticipated by the market. In the reform,

  (i) the renminbi was revalued against the US dollar by 2.1% (i.e., from 8.28 renminbi per US dollar to 8.11 renminbi per US dollar);
 (ii) the renminbi-US dollar rate would only be allowed to fluctuate within a very narrow band of ±0.3% around the closing rate of the previous working day;[31] and
(iii) the renminbi would be monitored against an undisclosed basket of currencies instead of against the US dollar.

The interesting point here is that the renminbi was only revalued by 2.1% instead of a medium revision (e.g., 5%) expected by some market participants. As explained in Section 3.1.1, the main reason behind this more moderate appreciation was the concern of increased inflows of speculative funds if there was a medium-size revaluation. That is, if the realized revaluation were greater than the transaction costs and risk premium of the speculation, it would attract more (illegal) inflows of speculative funds. A major revision was also ruled out because of its potential harmful impact on the unemployment problem as well as the economic growth of the Chinese economy. On the other hand, the 2.1% appreciation was made to deal with external political pressure for the renminbi appreciation: according to feedback from senior officials, China did have a bargaining power to resist external pressure for exchange rate appreciation. However, if the change was within the acceptable limit, the

---

[31] The band against other major currencies such as the euro or yen was 1.5%, which was subsequently widened to 3% from 25 September 2005.

Chinese government would not mind making the concession if it could allow the other government to better deal with the internal political pressure on the same issue. Thus, the 2.1% revaluation could be regarded as a good compromise between internal and external needs.

Another interesting point is related to (ii), i.e., a narrow exchange rate band against the US dollar. As explained in Section 3.1.3, a widening of exchange rate band at the early stage of the reform without any specific purpose would only weaken confidence and invite unnecessary speculation. Thus, the measure was meant to avoid unnecessary speculation or other complications at the early stage of the transitional period.[32]

4.2. *Market response during the first year of the reform*

After the announcement on 21 July 2005, the immediate market response was more moderate than originally expected. No doubt, the People's Bank of China's professional performance on the administrative aspect contributed to the better than expected result. More importantly, there was sufficient debate and discussion before the reform, thus resulting in the correct choice of a very moderate appreciation at the first stage of the reform and avoidance of inappropriate choices, such as a medium-size revaluation or a medium-size exchange rate band. As a result, many market participants found that the transitional reform had its own logic, viability and credibility. Supplemented by the government's reputation and the likelihood that the transaction costs and risk premium[33] of the (illegal) speculation could be greater than the expected gain from the gradual appreciation, many market participants had chosen to believe the Chinese government and gave up the choice of joining the speculation.

Of course, there were also some speculators who still believed in a chance of further sharp appreciation(s) or revaluation(s) in the future. Furthermore, those who had connections with potentially profitable targets (such as domestic property) and underground money changers

---

[32]Although the mean of the exchange rate band against the US dollar could vary so that the movements of the Chinese currency over a reasonable period of time could be quite different from that of the US dollar, it should be noted that the narrow exchange rate band *vis-à-vis* the US dollar would also mean that short-term movements of the Chinese currency could not deviate too much from the US dollar. In fact, should there be a sharp enough short-term rise or fall in the US dollar so that there is a conflict between announcements (ii) and (iii), announcement (ii) would be a more binding constraint on the short-term movements of the renminbi. However, this kind of conflict might not be observable or could be overcome because: (a) The widening of exchange rate band between the renminbi and other foreign currencies (e.g., the euro and yen) from 1.5% to 3% since 25 September 2005 had substantially reduced the likelihood of a conflict between the two announcements. Together with the adjustable means of the bands (for the renminbi *vis-à-vis* the US dollar rate as well as the renminbi *vis-à-vis* other foreign currency rates), this would mean that there has to be a very sharp rise or fall in the US dollar before such conflict could arise; (b) The non-disclosure of the weights of each currency in the currency basket had made the conflict less observable; and (c) In the extreme case of a very sharp rise or fall in the US dollar (say, one year after the reform in July 2005), the Chinese government would be justified to relax the exchange rate band between the renminbi and the US dollar. Bearing in mind that announcement (ii) is only a transitional arrangement which could be relaxed at the later stage of the transitional period, the author agreed that it was worthwhile to include announcement (iii) in the 2005 reform.

[33]For normal investors in foreign countries, the transaction costs would include the inconvenience costs and time costs in understanding the regulations, market practice and culture in China. The unfamiliarity with the Chinese market and regulations would also mean a very high risk premium for these investors. Thus, the transaction costs and risk premium for these normal investors were rather high.

(lower transaction costs) had chosen to join the speculation. As a result, there were still some inflows of speculative funds through illegal channels or abuse of legal channels. Nevertheless, the amount of inflows during the first year seemed to be within the sterilization capacity of the central bank.

4.3. *Two important characteristics that contribute to the success*

Unlike the prediction of Goldstein (2004) who believed the "go-slow approach" would create a "one-way bet" for speculators and thereby increase speculation on the renminbi appreciation, the transitional exchange rate system reform explicitly took into account an important economic characteristic in China: speculative inflows into China, whether through illegal channels or abuse of legal channels, were in principle illegal by nature. The illegal nature in turn implied non-negligible transaction costs and risk premium for the speculative inflows, which further resulted in a corridor, or range of exchange rate appreciation through which the exchange rate system reform could go through. Beyond this corridor, speculators would profit from the speculation which could in turn attract increased speculative inflows. However, within this corridor, the gain from appreciation would be less than the transaction costs and risk premium. More importantly, the illegal nature of the speculative inflows also implied that China would be well-justified to widen the corridor through greater effort of inspection and heavier penalty when deemed necessary. As a result, many market analysts and participants found that the transitional reform had its own logic, viability and credibility.[34] Comments by these analysts in the second half of 2005 had in turn induced more market participants believing in the viability and credibility of the transitional reform.

Another important characteristic of the transitional reform was that it tried to work on market expectation. By portraying a logically viable reform, it managed to bring the market expectation towards its target path. This had in turn convinced many potential investors that the gain from appreciation could be lower than the associate transaction costs and risk premium.

4.4. *Measures to deal with speculative inflows*

Despite the relative success of the reform in the first year, there were moderate inflows of speculative funds through illegal channels or abuse of legal channels. If not curbed or sterilized, this could result in excessive monetary growth and asset inflation. Thus, in addition to sterilization, the author made further proposals to deal with the speculative inflows. These proposals were important not only because they could reduce the required amount of

---

[34]For example, many commercial bank economists, such as those in Hong Kong, had bought the argument and were (a) projecting a very gradual appreciation; and (b) indicating that the potential gain from the appreciation could be more than offset by the lower renminbi deposit rates in Hong Kong. Even for those foreign investment banks which need to attract business by exaggerating the potential appreciation, many of them had gradually reduced their projected appreciation so as to ensure their forecast would not be too far away from the realized appreciation.

sterilization, but also because they could sustain the success of the reform.[35] The proposals first noted that the number of participants who chose not to join the speculation (i.e., the believers) should be far greater than those who chose to join (i.e., the non-believers). Otherwise, the size of the speculative inflows would exceed the limit that the central bank of China could deal with. Thus, the Chinese government should by all means keep the trust of these believers by honoring this implicit promise of at most a very gradual appreciation in the next few years. Failure to honor the implicit promise would invite the believers to think otherwise, which could result in enormous inflows and hence, disastrous outcomes. Once the Chinese government manages to do so, the next step is to convert the non-believers into believers through subsequent result of very gradual appreciation as well as enhanced publicity of the government's intention.

The proposals then suggested measures along the following two directions:

(a) policies that could reduce the incentives of speculative inflows; and
(b) measures that could offset the impacts of the speculative inflows on domestic monetary growth.

4.4.1. *Measures that discourage speculative inflows*

Raise the transaction costs and risk premium of speculative inflows

Along the first direction, one viable way is to increase the transaction costs and risk premium of the (illegal) speculative inflows. For example, if part of the inflows was conducted through underground money changers, the Chinese government could raise the effort of inspection and penalty against these money changers. The proposals did recognize that it would be impossible to eliminate all the underground money changers. However, the aim of the proposals was not the elimination of these money changers, but a rise in the transaction costs and risk premium of speculative inflows, at least at the transitional stage of the reform. Again, the proposals borrowed the Chinese military wisdom by highlighting the importance of publicizing the government intention and successful arrests of some underground money changers. In the next few months, there were a few successful arrests of underground money changers, which seemed to have helped curb speculative inflows through underground money changers at that time.

Control the investment returns of speculative inflows

To reduce the incentives of speculative inflows, it is also important to contain the expected investment returns of these inflows in the domestic market. As some of the speculative funds were invested in the property market in China, it is important to avoid a *sharp* and *sustained* rise in property price during the transitional reform. Note that what we need to avoid here is sharp and sustained asset inflation. Gradual property inflation comparable to international

---

[35]For example, if there were other considerations that constrained the central bank from issuing too many government bonds for sterilization, or there were some other reasons that caused a bigger surge in speculative inflows beyond the central bank's sterilization capacity in the future, the following suggested measures would mitigate the burden of sterilization.

rates after risk adjustment, or a large once-and-for-all rise in property price, will have relatively little effect on speculative inflows. The proposals also highlighted the importance of avoiding a sharp and sustained rise in share price during the transitional reform.[36]

In view of an emerging sign of asset inflation from mid-2006, the author had recommended to curb the asset inflation at the early stage. Unfortunately, as will be discussed in Section 5, because of the Chinese government's negligence on the risk and consequences of an established expectation of asset inflation, there was an eventual development of a stock market bubble and rampant property inflation since late 2006.

Further works on market expectation

To further discourage speculative inflows, the Chinese government could work on market expectation through enhanced publicity of the government's intention and viability of the reform. In addition to official clarifications, informal channels such as comments by market analysts with good relations with the government or spreading of those views in the market would help a lot.

4.4.2. *Measures that offset the impacts of speculative inflows*

In addition to the discouragement of speculative inflows, the proposals also highlighted the importance of offsetting the impacts of the speculative inflows on money supply. It first explained that the problem created by the speculative inflows was not the associate rise in foreign reserves as highlighted in the media, but the associate rise in money supply which could imply asset and CPI inflation pressure. Thus, the key here should not be the spending away of the precious foreign reserves, but the mopping up of excess money supply which may or may not involve a reduction in foreign reserves.[37]

One way to mop up the excess money supply is to increase outward foreign investments and purchases of productive assets. Examples of the former include investments in oil fields in Africa and South America, mines in resource-abundant countries and high-technology companies in developed economies. Examples of the latter include purchases of airplanes to support the expansion of Chinese airlines. Here, the proposals stress the importance for the Chinese government to avoid financing state-owned enterprises' investments and purchases through a direct transfer of government's foreign reserves to the related enterprises. Instead, all enterprises should first raise the funds from the domestic market and then convert them to the foreign currencies through the foreign exchange market. Otherwise, the investments and purchases would not help mop up the excess money supply. To convince the policymakers, the proposals quoted the successful experience of Singapore, which had substantially expanded her foreign outward investments after the Asian financial crisis. The foreign investments and the implied capital outflows had helped to keep the Singapore dollar low, which had in turn facilitated Singapore's recovery during the post-Asian financial crisis period.

---

[36]In addition to the avoidance of sustained and excessive returns in the property and share market, it is also important to keep a reasonable differential between domestic deposit rate and foreign borrowing rate so that the expected exchange rate appreciation gain of speculative inflows will not exceed the sum of the differential and the risk premium.

[37]For example, sterilization will reduce money supply without any reduction in foreign reserves.

Another possible way is to use the rise in foreign reserves originated from the speculative inflows to purchase foreign bonds and securities, and then securitize these foreign currency assets in the domestic financial market. The sales of these securitized assets to Chinese residents would help mop up the excess money supply. To avoid any government exchange rate risk on the securitization, the interest and principal repayments could be specified in the related foreign currencies.[38] The advantage of this is that the Chinese government would have very good control on the amount of securitization. If there were huge amount of speculative inflows, the Chinese government could keep the monetary base unchanged by an equivalent increase in the amount of securitization. As the domestic demand for such securitized assets in China is likely to be huge, the Chinese government would be able to use this method to offset huge amount of speculative inflows. On the other hand, if there was a reversal of speculative flows, the Chinese government could freeze the securitization or even redeem the securitized assets, which would in turn offset the effect of the flow reversal on money supply.

In the keynote speech paper for a policy conference organized by China's State Administration of Foreign Exchange in October 2006, the author had further recommended the Chinese government to gradually scale up outward foreign investment and use it as a long-term solution against the monetary growth pressure arising from the trade surplus, net FDI inflows and speculative inflows. While China's foreign reserves could be considered as huge, the paper also highlighted that the amount of foreign assets held by China's private sector are extremely low. Thus, outward foreign investment will serve not only as a good long-term solution against the monetary growth pressure, but also as a good way to increase China's private and public holdings of foreign assets until it reaches a level and ratio that is consistent with China's major economic power status in the future. The paper also pointed out that the above measures will take a long time to reach its full scale and become an effective tool to offset the effect of the three types of inflows. During the interim period, the issuance of government bonds should still be the main tool to mop up the excess money supply. In particular, the Chinese government should completely sterilize all the inflows to avoid unnecessary asset and CPI inflation.

The paper and the earlier recommendations were very well received by the Chinese government. For example, in 2005–2006, the Chinese government had used two one-off purchases of the US planes to mitigate the US pressure for renminbi appreciation. In 2007, the China Investment Corporate Limited, similar to the Government Investment Corporation in Singapore, was formally established with the dual task of (i) issuing long-term bonds to mop up the excess money supply in the economy; and (ii) using the proceeds to purchase foreign reserves from the government for her, and China's, overseas investment purposes. Unfortunately, as will be discussed in Section 5, there was insufficient sterilization before the long-term solution could reach its expected scale. Such negligence has in turn resulted in unnecessary asset inflation in 2006 and 2007.

---

[38]To increase her ability to deal with abrupt reversal of capital flows and the associate reduction in domestic money supply, the Chinese government could add a clause in the securitized assets that she could redeem the securities with domestic currencies at a reasonable penalty interest rate when deemed necessary.

5. Excessive Asset Inflation: The More Likely Cause of a Failed Reform

In Section 3.3.2, we have explained that even if the Chinese authority managed to keep a gradual appreciation of the renminbi, sustained and rapid asset inflation could still push the rentals, wages and domestic prices to uncompetitive levels and seed the possibility of an economic crisis in the distant future. It also highlights that:

(a) it is always better to curb any potential rampant asset inflation era (or asset bubble) at the early stage; and

(b) if an expectation of rampant asset inflation has been formed, much greater curbing measures are needed before the asset inflation could be properly controlled.

In fact, despite the relative success of the transitional reform, the author had, from November 2005 onwards, written a series of articles warning the Chinese government that excessive and unchecked asset inflation, instead of exchange rate appreciation, could be the more likely cause of a crisis and hence, an eventual failure of the whole exchange rate system reform in the longer future.[39]

Unfortunately, as was the case in the crisis-hit economies during the more than ten years asset inflation era before the Asian financial crisis, the Chinese government had underestimated the consequences of asset price inertia and expected asset inflation built up at the early stage of a rapid asset inflation era. Below, we will review the sequence of events in the form that it can illustrate the mistakes are in fact avoidable. It is hoped that readers in the future will learn from this history so that such type of asset inflation could, and should, be avoided.

5.1. *The formation of a stock market bubble*

5.1.1. *Asset inflation: Inertia, expectation and changes in economic behaviors*

On 5 June 2006, the author published an article warning that China's stock market could be in the early stages of a rampant bull run (the Shanghai Composite Index at that time was still below 1,700, see Figure 1). It first noted that Chinese share prices had accumulated *an upward inertia* from its trough in mid-2005[40] (e.g., the Shanghai Composite Index at end

---

[39]The first article was published in the *Hong Kong Economic Journal* on 16 November 2005 and in the *Lianhe Zaobao* on 24 November 2005. This was followed by a series of articles between May 2006 and September 2007.

[40]Before the rebound in 2005–2006, a significant portion of the majority shares held by the "legal entities" were not allowed to be traded in the market. This had created severe incentive problems. For example, controlling executives could not benefit from the improvement of the company's performance as they were not allowed to sell the shares even if the price rises with the improved performance. On the other hand, senior executives had the incentive to exploit the company at the cost of the shareholders, thus resulting in quite a number of scandals. After a number of big scandals, the Chinese government finally decided to introduce a detailed reform that removed the restriction. As the reform would mean a much larger supply of shares in the market, it had resulted in a few years of bear stock market until the trough in mid-2005. The stock market reform does have a significant contribution in redirecting firm managers' efforts towards profit maximization of the firm. Nevertheless, as we will see, the rebound plus the government's negligence on the consequence of an established upward inertia had resulted in a stock market bubble thereafter.

May 2006 was 62% higher than its trough in 2005). It then used the experience of the US and Hong Kong to highlight the possibility that a sustained upward inertia, if unchecked, could result in an *expectation of asset inflation* in the stock market, which could in turn push the share price into an automatic path towards a huge bubble.[41] To stop the formation of such asset inflation expectation in the stock market, the article proposed to use the prosecution of those listed companies with fake accounting reports to (i) improve the foundation of China's stock market for more healthy developments in the future; and (ii) contain the rise in share prices and guide the share market to rise along a more gradual and sustainable path.

Unfortunately, it was too early for the Chinese government to appreciate the importance of such a warning and share the author's early anticipation of a potential stock market bubble. From November 2006 onwards, the inertia in the rise in share prices had finally resulted in an expectation of further rise in share prices, which had in turn caused sharper rises in share prices thereafter (see Figure 1). By the end of December 2006, the Shanghai Composite Index rose to 2,675, which was 63% higher than that on the end of May 2006, and 165% higher than the trough in mid-2005. During a keynote speech in a policy conference organized in Beijing by the State Administration of Foreign Exchange in late December 2006, the author took the opportunity to warn of the possibility of a stock market bubble. This had in turn resulted in an internal report in the same authority and three articles published in the

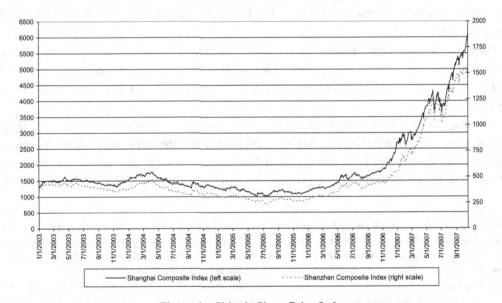

Figure 1. China's Share Price Index

---

[41] Since the trough arising from the political incidence in China in 4 June 1989, Hong Kong share and property prices had rebounded and accumulated an upward inertia, which had further pushed the asset prices into a bubble path until the bubble burst in 1997. Similarly, the Dow Jones Industrial Index had accumulated an upward inertia during its rebound from the trough of 1739 in October 1987 to 3169 at end 1991. During the subsequent years, this inertia had in turn pushed the index further up to the peak of 11,722 in January 2000 before the index fell to the trough of 7,286 in October 2002.

Hong Kong Economic Journal. The latter was also summarized by a publication of the Xinhua News Agency, China's official news agency.

In these publications, the author urged the Chinese government to curb the rising trend of the stock market. Otherwise, the Shanghai A-Share Index would go beyond 3,000, 4,000 and then 5,000 points. By then, the only remaining question would be at which point (i.e., 5,000, 7,000 or 9,000 points) the bubble would burst.[42] Besides, the further the index rose, the greater would be the pain after the bursting. To convince the Chinese authority, the articles first highlighted that the expectation of asset inflation in the stock market was already firmly established by late 2006. Worse still, such expectation was beginning to cause some *changes in economic behaviors*, which would fuel the share prices and push China's stock market into an automatic path towards a huge bubble. For example, more and more individuals and enterprises had started to invest in the stock market. Existing stock market participants had also started to increase their investments in the stock market by increasing their borrowings and/or using funds originally meant for other purposes.[43] Sooner or later, individuals and enterprises would reduce their desired cash to deposit ratios, while banks would reduce their desired excess reserve to deposit ratios. Both of these would increase the money multiplier, which would increase money supply even if there were no change in monetary base. Worse still, the rise in share (and property) prices would, through the change in people's economic behaviors, induce more inflows of funds through illegal channels or abuse of legal channels, thus fueling the rise in share (and property) prices.

In addition to the above changes in economic behaviors, the articles also pointed out the possibility of a few forthcoming *vicious cycles*, such as that between property price inflation and share price hike; and that between the stock market boom and rising consumption and investment.[44]

Finally, the articles also highlighted that, along with the surge in share price, *herding behavior* would gradually develop, which would further fuel the stock market towards a huge bubble. Once the herding behavior is established, more and more fund managers would be attracted, or forced by performance pressure, to join the herd by speculating for further rise

---

[42] As the anticipation was too forward-looking for the readers at that time to believe, the statement that the index could go beyond 5,000 points was deleted from the above mentioned internal report by the officer in charge. Neither was it included in the Xinhua News Agency's publication. However, it was published in the *Hong Kong Economic Journal.* Whatever the case, seven months later, the index did rise beyond 5,000 points.

[43] As many individual investors were investing most of their savings originally meant for future housing, marriage, education, retirement and other important purposes, the amount of additional funds was enormous. Nevertheless, the additional funds due to enterprises could be even bigger, when funds were diverted out, legally or illegally, from the working capital, savings and assets of private enterprises and public organizations. Thus, the ongoing injection of these additional funds into the stock market had resulted in persistent surges in the share prices.

[44] For example, rise in share price would increase share investors' demand for housing, while rise in property prices would increase listed property firms' profits, and allow property owners to use the properties as collaterals to borrow more money from the banks for greater investment in the stock market. Meanwhile, there could be a vicious cycle between the stock market boom and rising consumption and investment through the wealth effect and Tobin's q-effect (e.g., the rising share prices will increase individual consumption and firms' investment, which would in turn push the listed companies' profit further up).

in share prices, even if some of them are aware of the risk of an eventual bursting. Similarly, bank managers and chief executives would be attracted, or forced by performance pressure, to increase loans to the stock (and property) market, even if they are aware that some of the loans are not that secure and the lending boom is not sustainable. Once the stock market has entered the middle stage of the bubble with herding behavior, more and more funds and people would be attracted to join the stock market, leading to further surges in share prices. At this stage, standard curbing measures such as moderate rise in interest rate will not be sufficient to stop the share price from rising. However, when the stock market enters the final stage of the bubble during which close to 100% of the potential participants and funds has already joined the market, the rise in share prices will slow down and eventually stop. At this time, even a very mild change can trigger a fall in share price, a herding behavior in the downward direction, and a reversal of the above vicious cycles and changes in economic behaviors until the share prices plunge to a level well below the normal equilibrium level.

5.1.2. *The corrections in 2007 and the subsequent surges*

The above warnings had attracted the attention of the Chinese government. From late January 2006 onwards, quite a number of senior Chinese officials had come out in an orderly manner to warn Chinese shareholders on the risk of share speculation. These had in turn caused a 10.9% correction in the Shanghai Composite Index (i.e., it fell from 3,097 on 30 January 2007 to 2,612 on 5 February 2007). Nevertheless, in an internal correspondence with an authority,[45] the author warned that this type of stock market boom (with an established upward inertia and expectation) is usually very stubborn. To prevent the stock market from resuming its surge after the moderate correction, the Chinese government should prepare a series of curbing measures so that they could be pushed out in an orderly manner in case of early sign of resumption of the upward momentum, such as a medium or major rebound. Unfortunately, no further curbing measures were planned. As a result, the index rebounded sharply in the next 11 days (i.e., by 14.8% to 2,998 on 16 January 2007, the eve before the long Chinese New Year holiday). After the holiday, the index shot further up to 3,041 in the first working day (i.e., 26 February 2007). However, concerns that there could be further curbing measures during the major national political meetings in March had thereafter caused an 8.4% correction of the index to 2,785 on 5 March 2007. Further to this correction, the author recommended the maintenance of market's perceived risk of further curbing measures so as to keep the index within a range for at least one year. Once the upward momentum and the associated expectation were properly halted, the Chinese government could then allow the share prices to rise at the normal and sustainable speed.

However, because of reasons only known to the author at a later stage (see later discussion), the recommendation did not seem to have any effect on the Chinese government. Recognizing that further persuasion along this line would only result in negative

---

[45]The main points were later included in my article published in the *Hong Kong Economic Journal* on 2 February 2006.

consequences, and bearing in mind the need to concentrate efforts to persuade the Hong Kong Exchange to suspend the announced introduction of the renminbi futures market,[46] the author had decided to temporarily suspend further persuasion on the stock market intervention until the share price rose to levels that would alarm the State Council to reconsider the risk and harm of an unchecked share price hike. During the above inaction period, the author eventually recognized that a government research institute and some think-tanks had submitted reports and recommendations to the State Council stating that it was not easy to have the current stock market boom. The State Council should use this golden opportunity to push for further developments of China's stock market. As shown in Figure 1, the misleading reports and recommendations had contributed to the extreme sharp rise in the Shanghai Composite Index between 5 March and 29 May in 2007 [i.e., in less than three months, it rose by 56%, or 1,550 points, from 2,785 to 4,335, with an average price-earning (PE) ratio around 50]. Worse still, huge amount of individual investors were speculating heavily in penny stocks and shares with extremely poor fundamentals, thus resulting in huge bubbles in the latter.

In the later stages of the share price hike (i.e., between 22 April and 23 May in 2007), the author judged that it was time to write a series of articles to convince the Chinese government on how misleading the above reports and recommendations were. The articles first noted that the stock market and economic boom as well as the greater amount of funds raised from the stock market were achieved through rises in share prices to higher and higher levels.[47] If share prices continued to rise at such rampant speed, then a collapse of the stock market would only be a matter of time. By then, China would pay heavily for the mistake. The articles then explained that the net economic losses during the subsequent bust period would be much greater than the net gains during the boom period.

With the rise in share prices seeming to be out of control at the later stages (i.e., huge amount of funds were flowing into the stock market, and share prices continued to rise even if the Chinese central bank raised the interest rate and banks' reserve ratio requirement), there were worries even among government officials that the Chinese government would not be able to contain the share price hike. To remove the worry and clarify the confusion, the second part of the article series explained that, theoretically, there existed strong enough curbing measures that could stop the share price hike. For example, if the banks' required reserve ratio was raised to 100%, the money supply would be reduced to the amount of currency issued. By then, there would be insufficient liquidity in the economy. While China would not be so silly as to raise the ratio to 100%, the discussion suggested that there existed a high enough banks' required reserve ratio that could reverse the situation of excess liquidity

---

[46]Through a series of press articles and television interviews as well as letters and personal visits to the related Chinese authorities in Beijing, the Hong Kong Exchange and the Hong Kong government between December 2006 and May 2007, the author managed to convince the related authorities that the renminbi futures market could destroy the capital control and hence the exchange rate arrangements at that time. In May 2007, the Hong Kong Exchange finally suspended the introduction of the renminbi futures market. Nevertheless, during the lobby, the author had paid heavily in terms of personal health.

[47]Similarly, the economic boom was achieved by a higher inflation rate.

(i.e., excess money supply) into a situation of just enough, or a slight shortage of, liquidity. Meanwhile, the Chinese government could always keep the monetary base unchanged by using the additional foreign reserves, whether arising from trade surplus, net FDI inflows or speculative inflows, to back up an equivalent amount of domestic bond issuance by the Ministry of Finance on behalf of the forthcoming China Investment Corporate Limited (CIC). So, the question was not whether the Chinese government *could* reverse the excess liquidity condition and stop the share price hike or not, but whether the Chinese government would be *willing* to stop the hike, or be *skillful enough* to stop the hike in a less costly way.

Thereafter, the article series proposed a list of effective curbing measures. To search for the right dose of curbing measures and hence achieve a correction at a reasonably low cost, the series also suggested to implement the measures one after another. For more powerful measures such as using a significant part of the foreign reserves to back up the CIC bond issuance, which would imply a very strong effect at the beginning through anticipation of further changes in the future, the government could separate the initial impacts into two parts by first indicating the intended policy to the market before a formal implementation at the second stage. Thus, the indication of intention would first affect the market through the market's expectation of such a possibility. With the formal implementation at the second stage, the remaining impacts would take place as the expected probability of the policy would by that time rise from less than one to 100%.

After meeting with China's central bank governor in an international meeting in late May 2007, China's premier Wen Jiabao finally announced that the Chinese government would be determined, and able, to maintain financial stability in China. On 30 May 2007, China's Ministry of Finance announced a rise in the stock market stamp duty from 0.1% to 0.3%. As stamp duty was traditionally used to curb stock market bubbles in China and the rise in stamp duty was historically followed by a significant plunge in China's stock market, the announcement, together with the high and vulnerable share price level at that time, had caused a significant correction of the Shanghai Composite Index. For example, it fell 6.5% from a local peak of 4,335 on 29 May 2007 to 4,053 on 30 May, and then to an intra-day trough of around 3,200 on 5 June, before it closed at 3,767 on the same day. Thereafter, the index fluctuated around the range of 3,700–4,200 for the next seven weeks. While believing that the index was still on the high side, the author had at the end of May 2007 recommended to reduce the stock market bubble through a few steps, first by keeping the index below the psychological barriers of 4,200 and 4,335 (i.e., the local maximum achieved on 29 May 2007) with appropriate curbing measures; then by pushing the index further down to the range of 3,800–4,000 in the month after, and further to the range of 3,600–3,800 or 3,600–4,000 in the next 1–6 months. The aims of the 3-step recommendation were: (a) to minimize the economic costs of adjustment by avoiding sharp plunges which could affect the normal running of the economy; and (b) to keep the losses and pains of share investors within bearable levels.

Unfortunately again, because of misleading recommendations by at least two groups of research officials or think-tanks, the State Council did not recognize the importance of keeping the psychological barriers,[48] not to mention the need to bring the index down to less risky levels. Meanwhile, the Chinese supervisory body had approved too many new mutual funds which were becoming extremely popular after the corrections since 30 May 2007.[49] Because of these two mistakes, the mutual funds, now with huge amounts of inflows of funds from individual investors, were able to push the index beyond the psychological barriers in an extremely tactful way.[50] As a result, the index shot up from 3,616 on 5 July 2007 to 5,321 on 3 September 2007 (i.e., by 1,705 points, or 47%, in less than two months).

5.1.3. *China's last chance to stop the stock market bubble?*

Upset with the above developments and the potential risk, the author had decided to make his final warning to the Chinese government in early September 2007. In the final warning article,[51] the author first noted that the average PE ratios in the Shanghai and Shenzhen stock markets had already reached 59 and 69, respectively. If share prices continued to rise at the current pace and momentum, the Chinese government would very soon reach the "dead position" defined in the Chinese military strategy literature. That is, the Chinese government would be "kidnapped" by the very high share price level in the sense that she would no longer dare to implement any curbing measures as this could easily trigger the bursting of the bubble. Even if the government chooses to do nothing, a relatively minor shock some time in the future could be sufficient to trigger the bursting.

The article then did the following cost and benefit analysis for the Chinese leaders: first, if the Chinese government managed to use sufficient curbing measures to stop the share prices from rising further (or better still, push it lower to less vulnerable levels), China would continue to have a bright prospect of eventually becoming a major world economic power. This would be so even if the curbing measures resulted in a fall of GDP growth from the overheated rate of 11.9% to a more sustainable rate of 10% or even a slowdown rate of 9%, simply because 9%–10% would still be very high compared with the world average. By then, the current Chinese leaders would not disappoint the trust of the Chinese people and their predecessors including Deng Xiaoping. On the other hand, if share prices were allowed to rise at the current pace, then a bursting of the bubble and a complete destruction of the related leaders' historical status would just be a matter of time. Besides, the more it

---

[48]From the news in the media well after the changes, there were some think-tanks recommending the government to give up any target on the share index. Another group of officials recommended to keep the stock market boom to allow more central government enterprises to complete their reform and transformation through IPOs in the stock market. Unfortunately, these recommendations were made without recognizing that (i) the stock market was already at very high and unsustainable levels, and (ii) the stock market could easily resume its dangerous upward momentum.

[49]Before the correction on 30 May 2007, there was a significant portion of individual investors speculating in penny stocks or shares with extremely poor market fundamentals. As the mutual was less hurt by the correction due to their focus on blue chips, mutual funds became very popular thereafter.

[50]The mutual funds as a whole had persistently used the following strategy to push the index up from less than 3,700 to more than 5,300: first pushed the index beyond a whole number barrier (e.g., 3,800, 4,000, 4,200), then took a very brief rest and then pushed the index beyond the next whole number barrier.

[51]The article was directed to the related Chinese authorities through the author's personal communication channels in early September. It was also published in the *Hong Kong Economic Journal* on 6 September 2007.

rose before the bursting, the worse would be the subsequent plunge and economic crisis. If the recession were severe enough, it could even trigger political and social turmoil, which would be extremely dangerous for countries like China. As the chance of a bursting of a bubble in a particular period would depend on (i) how high the share price level is, and (ii) whether there is a large enough shock to trigger a bursting, nobody can accurately predict when the bursting will occur. However, what is sure is that, the greater the rise in the share (and property) prices, the greater will be the probability of a bursting. Until the very end, share prices can rise to such a high level that even relatively minor shocks can trigger a collapse.

The article then classified the potential bursting into two types. The first type is one in which there is a large enough triggering shock at the early stage. As the cumulated rise in share price before the bursting is still smaller than that of the second type, the bursting would result in only severe economic recession, but not severe political and social instability. Of course, such bursting would still imply enormous economic pain to a huge number of Chinese citizens. In addition to the harm done to hundred millions of share investors and their innocent family members, it would hurt an even greater number of innocent people. For example, many firms may become bankrupt because they cannot collect the account receivables from those firm owners who follow the stock market speculating herds.[52] Thus, employees of the innocent firms and their family members would also suffer. Even for those firms who are not affected by this, the reduction in aggregate demand arising from the economic recession would still force them to make massive retrenchments. Furthermore, the collapse of the stock market will, to a certain extent, result in a plunge in the already high property price, thus substantially increasing the amount of banks' non-performing loans and the number of "property slaves", a very popular nickname in China for those property owners who suffer heavily from the high mortgage repayment burden arising from the high property price. In short, the bursting will affect not only hundred millions of share investors and their family members, but a much greater number of innocent people through direct business and economic relations, indirect multiplier effects and domino effects, such as the triggering of a collapse in property prices, the weakening of the banks' ability and incentive[53] to finance firms' normal business, etc. With such deep and extensive damages, the related Chinese leader's reputation and historical status would be completely destroyed.

However, perhaps the most disastrous outcome is the second type of bursting in which the bubble has the chance to grow into a huge one before the bursting. In this case, the economic damages would be large enough to cause the resignation of the premier and severely weaken the central government's authority of ruling. By then, there could be struggles for political power among factions within the Communist Party, thus resulting in political instability or

---

[52]Note, this had to some extent happened in some crisis-hit economies during the Asian financial crisis in 1997–1998.

[53]Because the adverse selection and moral hazard problems would have become more severe (e.g., much greater risk and difficulty in identifying the right borrowers and monitoring their behavior), the already hurt banks during that time will usually choose to close their umbrella (i.e., do not lend or lend a much smaller amount whenever in doubt).

even military confrontation. Meanwhile, the severe economic recession could also trigger Chinese people's suppressed hatred against corruption, the high degree of income inequality and other unreasonable phenomena, which could result in further social instability or turmoil. If other competing countries at that time try to systematically support the unrest and fuel the conflict, it is possible for China to be split into a few parts. By then, China would have been dragged into endless political and social instability. Economic stability would then be a luxury, not to mention the prospect of developing into a major world economic power.

To convince the Chinese leaders that the chance of the above two outcomes was not as slim as it first appeared, the article quoted the experience of the Asian financial crisis during which the political leaders and central bank governors in Indonesia, Thailand and Korea had all lost their power in the crisis or post-crisis periods. Finally, the article warned that, with the share prices already at the vulnerably high levels, the skill required to achieve a soft landing would be extremely high (i.e., it required fairly accurate choice in the types, doses, sequencing and timing of the curbing measures). Even a moderate misjudgment of the situation or the extent of the problem could be sufficient to result in either failure to stop the bubble or extremely costly plunges in share prices. For example, it is possible for the authority to underestimate the market's resistance to the curbing measures when share prices are rising, and the market's fragility to the cumulated curbing effect when share prices are starting to correct.

Soon after the submission of the warning article to the related Chinese authorities through the author's personal channel, the People's Bank of China, the State Administration of Foreign Exchange, the Ministry of Finance, the China Securities Regulatory Commission and other related government bodies announced a series of curbing measures. These measures include further rises in interest rates and banks' required reserve ratio; the Ministry of Finance's issuance of special government bonds on behalf of the newly set up China Investment Corporate Limited (i.e., to offset part of the monetary growth pressure arising from trade surplus, net FDI inflows and speculative inflows); the extension of the QDII scheme to allow for overseas share investment by Chinese residents through funds managed by securities firms or investment banks (i.e., to encourage controllable outflows to offset part of the inflows); a temporary suspension in the approvals of new mutual funds for domestic share investment; and the speeding up of IPOs by Hong Kong-listed Chinese enterprises in China's A-share market (i.e., to increase the supply of shares so as to absorb part of the excess liquidity in the share market and to pull down the average PE ratio in China's A-share market).[54]

---

[54]In addition to these measures, the basic infrastructure of the stock futures market was also made ready for the final approval by the top leaders. Without the stock futures market, share investment in China has been skewed to the purchase of shares in the upward direction as there is no major facility for share investors to bet for a fall in share price. The establishment of the stock futures market will allow share investors to bet for either a rise or fall in share price. Nevertheless, the author believes that the timing of such a set-up and the choice of a low gearing ratio at the initial stage is important. Otherwise, it could cause more problems than benefits. For example, with a vulnerably high share price level, some major fund managers could profit a lot with the following strategy: (i) first, quietly build up a huge short position in the stock futures market and accumulate huge amount of index component shares in the spot market at the normal price; and (ii) then trigger a panic sale of shares by shorting in the futures market and dumping shares in the spot market in a high profile. When the

Thereafter, the Central Propaganda Department published an article warning of the risk of share investment, suggesting that the Party leader instead of just the State Council could now be in charge of the problem. Yet, because of the established upward inertia and expectation, and more importantly, the resistance of the mutual funds,[55] the Shanghai Composite Index had only made a minor correction before it surged further up to 6,092 on 17 October 2007, with an average PE ratio of 71.

Fortunately, with persistent waves of curbing measures made by the Chinese government and some fund managers' gradual awareness of the risk of the unsustainable high share price level, the Shanghai Composite Index started to correct and reached 5,270 on 19 November 2007. In a follow-up proposal on the same day, the author highlighted that China's stock prices were still too high. The proposal then recommended the Chinese government to squeeze out part, but not all, the bubble content in the stock market by (a) allowing China's stock index to fall with the global stock market correction and the forthcoming US economic slowdown or recession triggered by the sub-prime credit woe; and (b) continuing her battle with the domestic CPI inflation (see the discussion in Section 5.3). If China could finetune her curbing measures and gradually squeeze the bubbles by small steps until the Shanghai Composite Index reached and stayed in a slightly overvalued, but not excessively overvalued, range for one or two years, the relatively high profit growth of China's listed companies could help to reduce the bubble content to more reasonable levels. By then, even if the stock index is still on the high side, it would no longer be able to trigger a severe economic recession and hence political and social instability. [Postscript: With further deterioration of the external economy, greater monetary austerity measures arising from rising domestic inflation, market's gradual realization of the overvaluation of Chinese shares, anticipation of weaker domestic economy and other bad news, the Shanghai Composite Index finally made significant corrections in 2008H1. By 24 June 2008, the index had reached the fairly safe level of 2803. Although future deteriorations of the external and domestic economies could trigger further corrections in the stock index, it is unlikely that these corrections are sufficient to cause the above-mentioned political and social instability. Thus, it could be said that China had at least managed to squeeze a stock market bubble in a not too abrupt and costly way, although there was room for improvement for a more gradual squeezing and

---

share prices plunge to low enough levels, they could profit the gains by buying back shares in the spot market and unwinding their short position in the futures market. Thus, wrong timing in the establishment of the stock futures market could be an event that triggers the bursting of China's stock market bubble. To avoid this and to provide Chinese share investors with a facility to hedge or bet for a fall in share price, the author believes it is better to start with an initial low gearing ratio of no more than 4 times (preferably 2 times). An initially low gearing ratio will also allow us to identify problems and correct mistakes at the early stage. For example, with a high gearing ratio, individual investors may easily become bankrupt if they underestimate the risk of, or become addicted to, gambling in the stock futures market. With a low gearing ratio at the initial stage, some of them may have a chance to learn from a painful, but not yet irreversible, mistake. When everything is going well, the Chinese authority can then gradually raise the gearing ratio to higher levels.

[55] A survey among the fund managers suggested that 80% of the fund managers at that time believed that Chinese share prices were overvalued. However, because of the influx of money into the funds, absence of any major short-selling facilities and performance pressure, many fund managers have no choice but to keep on bidding up share prices.

correction. The author believes that academics and policymakers in other economies could learn a lot from more detailed studies of China's success and minor mistakes in the whole process.]

5.2. *Property inflation*

Along with the rise in the share prices, the property prices also shot up in 2006 and 2007.[56] In May 2006, the author had written four articles on property inflation in China. The articles first emphasized that the Chinese government had to curb the rise in property inflation before the formation of an expectation of further rises in property prices. This is so because, as explained in Section 5.1, the expectation could cause changes in economic behaviors, the emergence of a few vicious cycles as well as the evolution of herding behaviors including panic demand and excessive speculative demand. All these will further fuel the property prices up to unsustainable levels. The articles then explained the consequences of rampant property inflation and recommended a series of curbing measures (e.g., a reduction of M2 growth to, or below, the 16% target through sufficient issuance of government bonds; a substantial increase in government supply of housing; an increase in the down payment percentage; having a maximum limit on the length of the mortgage period; an introduction of a progressive property tax; making local officials accountable for the rise in property prices in their cities or counties; compulsory information disclosures for developers and estate agents on the price and quantity of flats available for sale; prohibition of selling properties bit-by-bit through the so-called toothpaste squeezing strategy; greater penalties and charges on land or flat hoardings by developers). In June 2006, the government had introduced a series of property-specific curbing measures. Unfortunately, there was no major reduction in monetary growth and substantial increase in direct supply of government housing. Besides, developers and local officials also found various ways to circumvent some of the curbing measures. As a result, there was only a temporary slowdown in the property inflation.

In October–November 2006, the author published two important articles which were then widely cited in the media in China. The articles first pointed out that the often-used supply and demand analysis is the wrong model for China's property market (i.e., there are barriers of entry leading to significant asymmetries between the supply and demand sides). The articles then explained that, because of microeconomic distortions and macroeconomic considerations, sole reliance on the "market force" to determine the price and output in China's property market would result in extremely undesirable and inferior outcomes. The first microeconomic distortion is the highly unequal income and wealth distribution in China (i.e., between the general public and the rich who can invest in a lot of properties). The distortion is further fueled by the much higher purchasing power of overseas buyers from Hong Kong and other countries. As is well-known, for "direct" demand such as housing, the market can only do a good allocation if the income and wealth distribution is not too unequal. With highly unequal income and wealth distribution, it would be the demanders' wealth and

---

[56]Before the rise in share prices, property prices had already started to rise from 2005. However, most of the bubble in the property market was made in 2006 and 2007.

income instead of demanders' needs that determined where the limited supply of housing would go to. Thus, normal Chinese citizens' basic housing needs cannot be satisfactorily met, simply because their income and wealth are much lower than the rich Chinese and overseas buyers.

The second distortion is due to the significant degree of asymmetries between sellers and buyers in China's property market. Whenever one draws the supply and demand curves, an implicit assumption of numerous price-taking sellers and buyers is already made. There is also an implicit assumption of no asymmetries between sellers and buyers. However, in China's property market, there are extensive asymmetries between the developers and individual home buyers.[57] In particular, there are asymmetries in information, market power and holding power, which have allowed the developers to use various tricks to achieve a higher price with enormous profits, and a quantity supplied which is much lower than the social optimal. For example, because of significant barriers of entry such as huge fixed cost for each estate development and required accumulative experience for a developer to become reasonably efficient,[58] developers in China do have significant market power in choosing a high price by squeezing the quantity supplied below the social optimal. In addition to the asymmetry in market power, property developers in China have also exploited the information asymmetry by concealing, or even underreporting, the number of units available for sale (with some developers or estate agents even exaggerating the latest transaction price). This has allowed them to sell the units bit-by-bit (nicknamed as the toothpaste squeezing strategy), thus giving the potential buyers the impression that there are only limited number of units available for sale. This strategy would on one hand create a panic demand, and on the other hand allow the developers to charge higher prices to extract a significant portion of consumer surplus. With the stronger holding power created by the substantial amount of abnormal profit earned from past sale, developers are able to hoard a lot of land and develop their land lot-by-lot (and each lot phase-by-phase). This has on one hand allowed them to adopt a prudent pace of property development (which would involve a huge cost of development), and on the other hand create a limited supply of housing, thus enabling the property prices to shoot up, which will in turn create panic demand and more speculative demand. With the high property prices, some potential home buyers had chosen to wait. However, with the developers' strong holding power and continuing rise in property prices, many of these home buyers eventually decided to buy the property at a subsequently higher price quoted by the developers. In short, with the asymmetries, developers in China were not

---

[57]What we are discussing here is the market for new housing. However, as the price in the secondary housing market tends to follow the primary market closely (especially during periods of rampant property inflation), the conclusion on the movements of property prices will still apply for the whole property market. That is, at least during periods of rampant property inflation, the price in the primary property market will influence the expectation in the secondary market, and hence pull up the property prices in the secondary market. Of course, price movements in the primary market will still to some extent be constrained by the price level in the secondary market in the short run. Nevertheless, given a sufficient time, it is possible that the prices in the primary market can pull the price in the secondary market very far away from its current level.

[58]With the huge profit from estate development, there were in fact quite a number of new entries. However, the number of entries is far from sufficient because of the barriers cited in the main text.

only able to charge prices well above the social optimal level, but were also able to extract a significant portion of consumer surplus. By hoarding the land, they have also created a shortage of housing supply as well as panic and speculative demand, which have contributed to the rampant property inflation.

On the macro side, the articles also pointed out that the persistently high monetary growth (approximately 18%) arising from insufficient sterilization of the inflows due to the huge trade surplus, net FDI inflows and speculative inflows, was another major contributing factor for the rampant property (and share price) inflation. If the government mistakenly allows the excessive monetary growth and the persistent property inflation to continue, it will very soon result in high and sustained rental, wage and general price inflation, whose inertia can bring China's wages and prices to highly uncompetitive levels in the longer future. To convince the Chinese leaders of such possibility and risk, the article cited the experience of Hong Kong which was also highly competitive in the 1980s. However, with the substantial earnings arising from the opening up of China and the fixed exchange rate in her currency board system, repatriation of part of the substantial earnings into Hong Kong's property and share market had caused excessive monetary growth as well as rampant and persistent asset inflation. These in turn resulted in persistently high general price inflation until the rentals, wages and prices in Hong Kong had reached highly uncompetitive levels before the financial crisis in 1997. As a result, the crisis was able to trigger a substantial plunge in property and share prices, as well as a prolonged recession of more than seven years.

To avoid the repetition of Hong Kong's experience in China, the articles then recommended the Chinese government to:

(a) completely sterilize the inflows through greater issuance of government bonds, the QDII and other measures;
(b) appropriately adopt the Singapore housing system with direct provision of large amount of government housing, whose selling price is quite profitable to the government and yet far more reasonable than the private property price.[59]

Unlike the low-cost public housing system in China whose quantity is insignificant due to incentive problems, the price in the suggested scheme should be high enough with a reasonably high profit to the government and a relatively high ceiling on the applicant's income so that middle-income citizens could also queue for the government supply.[60] The articles also noted that even an announcement of the scheme would help to constrain the property inflation in the private market by attracting potential candidates to wait, reducing panic demand and influencing the market expectation. If possible, the new supply should form at least 40%–50% of total new housing supply so that it is sufficient to pull the private property inflation down. The existence of a large enough government housing supply would

---

[59] As the price in the private property market is much higher than the development costs of the residential buildings and the associated infrastructure, there exists such a price with substantial profit to the government and yet reasonable to individual home buyers.

[60] Note that the poor Chinese citizens would be under the low-cost housing scheme whose rental or selling price could be at, or below, the break-even level.

also create sufficient competition for the developers in the private market. For example, private condominiums in Singapore have to provide swimming pools, fountains and other facilities to justify a higher price than that of the Housing Development Board's flats. Without the competition from the government sector, the private developers can, and will, gradually develop more ways to exploit the home buyers during a rampant property inflation period. For example, to support higher property prices, they can gradually but persistently reduce the flat size, which will sooner or later reduce people's "norm" of acceptable flat size. In fact, this was the case in Hong Kong, and is happening in China. Meanwhile, the Chinese government can put the substantial amount of profit into a fund to support the required medical reform, educational reform and low-cost housing scheme for the poor.

The proposal was well-received by the Chinese government, which explained why the article could be widely cited in the press, television and electronic media in China. Unfortunately, because of time lags in decision and ideology problems which had hindered the full adoption of the proposal, the amount of announced public housing supply had not reached a meaningful scale by mid-2007. As a result, private supply still dominated the property market and private property price was able to shoot up at its own pace to extremely high levels. For example, as reported in the author's other warning note in July 2007, the price of a representative medium-class flat in Shenzhen has shot up from around RMB12,000 per square meter in October 2006 to over RMB20,000 per square meter in June 2007, a price level that is far beyond the affordability of a family with two income earners of university education. In view of the rampant property inflation and the implied macroeconomic risk, the People's Bank of China had, from September 2007 onwards, announced additional and property-specific curbing measures. For example, for a mortgagee with more than one property, the minimum down payment was raised from 30% to 40%, and the mortgage rate was raised from 0.85 times to 1.1 times of the basic lending rate. Meanwhile, as commercial banks in Shenzhen also recognized the property price there was unsustainably high, some of them raised the down payment and cut their housing loans even before the central bank's announced measures. By 2007Q4, the number of property transactions in Shenzhen had plunged to an extremely low level, partly because the property price was perceived to be unsustainably high and partly because there was only very limited financing provided by the banks. [Postscript: Thereafter, with far greater number of public housing supply plans announced in early 2008, property prices in Shenzhen started to fall in 2008H1, with property markets in other cities also showing signs of weakness. The author believes the task of the Chinese government in 2008–2009 and thereafter is to (a) use the above public housing scheme to offset the negative output impact of less private housing construction during the downturn; and (b) ensure the excessively high private property price would correct to more affordable levels with not-too-abrupt plunges.]

Whatever, given the unequal income and wealth distribution, the extensive degree of asymmetries between the developers and home buyers, and the macroeconomic risks discussed above, the author is of the opinion that the real long-term solution for China's property market is a substantial increase in public housing supply similar to that of Singapore. If China continues to rely on the "market force" allocation, normal Chinese citizens' basic housing needs will not be properly met; developers will be able to exploit individual home buyers through various tricks; and China will run a higher risk that property prices will shoot to risky and vulnerably high levels. The latter can in turn cause rises in rentals, wages and prices to highly uncompetitive levels, before a crisis or recession triggers painful adjustments.

5.3. *The rise in CPI inflation*

As early as November 2005, the author had written a few articles[61] warning that excessive monetary growth and persistent asset inflation would eventually result in high rental, wage and price inflation, albeit with substantial lags. If left unattended, this would result in expectation of higher inflation. With the help of monetary accommodation, this could cause a higher inflation and hence persistently push China's rentals, wages and prices to highly uncompetitive levels in the longer future, which has in fact happened in Hong Kong. At the time of that article, there was not yet a clear sign of asset inflation. Unfortunately, subsequent developments in China in 2006 and 2007 seem to follow the early part of the above discussion. In view of this, many of the author's articles in 2006 and early 2007 have been urging the Chinese government to (i) keep the M2 growth at or below her 16% target; and (ii) use various measures to curb the asset inflation. Nevertheless, for reasons discussed in the previous sections, the Chinese government did not do a reasonably good job on both fronts. As a result, CPI inflation has started to rise from early 2007.

In view of the early signs of a rising CPI inflation, the author has, from April 2007 onwards, written a series of articles on CPI inflation in China. In the April 2007 article, the author warned the Chinese government not to underestimate the problems behind the moderate rise of inflation to 3.3% in March 2007. It pointed out that behind the moderate rise in inflation were in fact excessive monetary growth of around 18%, an overheated economy (i.e., 11.1% real GDP growth in 2007Q1) and rampant asset inflation. It then used the expectation-augmented Phillips Curve and the European and American inflation experience between the 1950s and 1980s to highlight that (i) the higher output growth in China was achieved at the cost of a higher actual and expected inflation; and (ii) China will have to pay back in terms of lower output growth if one day she finds it necessary to bring the expected and actual inflation back to previous levels. Policymakers without proper training on the expectation-augmented Phillips Curve may not be able to see this because it takes time for the actual and expected inflation to build up its inertia. That is, at the early stages of the overheating and excessive monetary growth, China's output growth can go beyond the sustainable level with relatively little inflation cost, mainly because of an initially low expected inflation of around 2%. However, people will sooner or later revise their expected inflation up with the moderate rise in actual inflation. Once the expected inflation is revised up, the short run Phillips Curve will shift up. If the government cannot recognize that the higher output growth is not sustainable in the long run, this will result in higher and higher actual and expected inflation, until one day she finds it necessary to bring the inflation rate

---

[61]The first article was published in Singapore's *Lianhe Zaobao* on 24 November 2005 and in the *Hong Kong Economic Journal* on 16 November 2005.

to lower levels. However, with an established inertia in the expected and actual inflation, this will require a reduction in money supply growth and hence, an output growth below the long run level.

Unfortunately, Chinese policymakers at that time did not seem to recognize that the 11.1% real GDP growth in 2007Q1 and the 11.9% real GDP growth in 2007Q2 were far from sustainable. Meanwhile, there was a sharp rise in food price, which helped to push the CPI inflation further up to 6.5% in August and October in 2007. While some officials and market participants had attributed the surge of inflation to a sharp rise in pork and meat prices arising from a disease in pig farming, the author warned in another two articles that the key here is not the triggering cause, but the effect of expectation and monetary growth on subsequent inflation. That is, once there is a triggering cause that raises the actual inflation, upward revision of expected inflation and monetary accommodation will sooner or later cause an upward revision of wage increment, and hence a self-sustainable wage-price spiral. Even if the rise in pork price (i.e., the triggering cause) is reversed in a later stage, the established wage-price spiral will be able to sustain an inflation rate well above the world average.

In fact, China's current inflation experience is very similar to that of the western world before and after the oil crisis shock in the 1970s. The only differences are that: (i) the triggering cause in China is a rise in food price instead of a rise in oil price; and (ii) the rise in food price in China, albeit high at around 20%, is still much lower than the rise in oil price in the 1970s. Before the triggering cause, there were already excessive monetary growth and a wrong choice of unemployment rate or GDP growth well above the level with no extra inflation pressure. With a smaller triggering cause, one can expect that the inflation to be encountered by China will be smaller (i.e., probably around the mid-single digit level). If China wants to stop the inflation from rising further, she must reduce the excessive monetary growth and accept that the 11.9% real GDP growth in 2007Q2 is much higher than the sustainable level with no extra inflation pressure.[62] Failure to do so would mean a very high dis-inflationary cost when one day she finds it necessary to bring the high inflation rate down to a more reasonable level. [Postscript: With subsequent surges in global oil and food prices as well as two natural disasters, China's CPI inflation surged further to the peak of 8.7% in February 2008 before it moderated to 7.7% in May 2008. Meanwhile, the PPI inflation persistently rose to 8.2% in May 2008. By mid-2008, it is not yet clear whether the Chinese government would be able to bring the inflation down to more reasonable levels.]

6. Conclusions and Remarks

China's exchange rate system reform in 2005 is at most the first phase of the transitional reform. While the reform appears to be relatively successful, there is still a long way for China to prove the success of the whole reform. For example, China is still at the beginning of the second phase of the transitional reform which involves (i) a gradual widening of the narrow

---

[62]A check of the output growth before and after the current inflation suggests that the current sustainable GDP growth with no extra inflation pressure could be between 10% and 10.5% (e.g., around 10.2%).

renminbi-US dollar exchange rate band; and (ii) efforts to shift the market attention from the renminbi-US dollar exchange rate to a nominal effective exchange rate band.[63] On 18 May 2007, China made the first step by widening the renminbi-US dollar exchange rate band from $\pm 0.3\%$ to $\pm 0.5\%$. Unfortunately, as discussed in Section 5, because of the government's negligence on the consequence of incomplete sterilization and excessive monetary growth, China is now occupied with her battle against asset inflation and CPI inflation. Until these are brought under control, the Chinese government may not find it sensible to continue with the second phase reform.

Another challenge of the whole exchange rate system reform is the choice of, and the path towards, the medium- and long-term exchange rate system. Based on the doctrine of Impossible Trinity, this paper has recommended a medium- to long-term arrangement for China. In this arrangement, China is recommended to maintain her current degree of capital control so that she can monitor the changes in her exchange rate and control her money supply.

Supplementary packages are also important to the success of the exchange rate system reform. In addition to the proper control of asset inflation, an establishment of a large enough variable wage component in employees' total wage bill can increase China's immunity and resilience against potential crisis in the future (see the detailed discussion in Section 3.3.3). After the relatively successful first phase banking reform in 2005–2006 (i.e., first government injection of capital, then inclusion of foreign strategic partners and then IPOs), efforts should now be made to improve the internal control of banks and reduce non-performing loans in the banking system. Among the two, the author believes the key is more on the establishment of internal control. If the internal control is properly installed so that new loans have a much lower chance of becoming non-performing, the current pace of money supply and credit growth will make the original amount of non-performing loans less important in the longer future. On the other hand, if the internal control is not properly installed so that new loans still have a high chance of becoming non-performing, the absorption of past non-performing loans by the government, foreign strategic partners and shareholders will not be able to keep China away from banking or financial crises in the longer future. Thus, from the point of view of the whole economy, the most important criterion of assessing the success of China's latest banking reform should be the establishment of the internal control instead of the amount of IPO oversubscription or the associate rise in share prices.

If banks' internal control is properly established and other necessary conditions are met (e.g., after the real effective exchange rate has gradually adjusted to a level not too far away from its equilibrium), the Chinese government can consider the costs and benefits of moving towards a flexible exchange rate system with occasional interventions, or a modified version of the monitoring band system. Before then, it might be better to maintain a certain degree of capital control which could serve as a last defense against potential financial crises and speculative attacks.

---

[63]Upon the request of China's State Administration of Foreign Exchange, the author had written a detailed proposal for the second phase transitional reform which was also published in the *Hong Kong Economic Journal* on 7 August 2006 and 18–19 May 2007.

Although it will be a long way for China to prove the success of the whole reform, the reform design is at least theoretically viable. Nevertheless, the author is of the opinion that the greatest risk to China and her exchange rate system reform is probably not mistakes in the reform design, but mistakes in implementation. In particular, failure to contain the stock market bubble, the rampant property inflation and the relatively high CPI inflation can result in disastrous outcomes in China.

Acknowledgments

A former version of this paper was presented at the State Administration of Foreign Exchange of the Chinese government in August 2006. The author would like to express his thanks to the valuable comments made by the participants in the seminar organized in Beijing. The author is also grateful to Professor Partha Sen, Professor Y. K. Tse, Dr. C. Y. Sin and Dr. W. M. Chia for their feedbacks and suggestions on the paper. The usual disclaimer applies.

References

Buiter, WH and MH Miller (1981). Monetary policy and international competitiveness: The problem of adjustment. *Oxford Economic Paper*, 33(Supplement), 143–175.
—— (1982). Real exchange rate overshooting and the output cost of bringing down inflation. *European Economic Review*, 18(2), 85–123.
Calvo, GA and CA Rodriguez (1977). A model of exchange rate determination under currency substitution and rational expectations. *Journal of Political Economy*, 85(3), 617–625.
Chang, GH and Q Shao (2004). How much is the Chinese currency undervalued? A quantity estimation. *China Economic Review*, 15(3), 366–371.
Cheung, YW, MD Chinn and E Fujii (2003). The Chinese economies in global context: The integration process and its determinants. NBER Working Paper No. 10047.
—— (2007). The overvaluation of renminbi undervaluation. *Journal of International Money and Finance*, 26(5), 762–785.
Dornbusch, R (1976). Expectations and exchange rate dynamics. *Journal of Political Economy*, 84(6), 1161–1176.
Dornbusch, R and S Fischer (1980). Exchange rates and the current account. *American Economic Review*, 70(5), 960–971.
Eichengreen, B (2004). Chinese currency controversies. Paper prepared for the Asian Economic Panel, Hong Kong, http://www.hiebs.hku.hk/aep/eichengreen.pdf.
Frankel, J (2005). On the renminbi: The choice between adjustment under a fixed exchange rate and adjustment under a flexible rate. NBER Working Paper No. 11274.
Frankel, JA and KA Froot (1986). The dollar as a speculative bubble: A tale of chartist and fundamentalist. NBER Working Paper No. 1534.
—— (1987). Using survey date to test standard propositions regarding exchange rate expectations. *American Economic Review*, 77(1), 133–153.
Friedman, M (1969). Round table on exchange rate policy. *American Economic Review*, 59(2), 364–366.
Funke, M and J Rahn (2005). Just how undervalued is the Chinese renminbi? *World Economy*, 28(4), 465–489.
Garton, P and J Chang (2005). The Chinese currency: How undervalued and how much does it matter. In *Australian Treasury, Economic Roundup*, pp. 83–109, http://www.treasury.gov.au/documents/1042/PDF/08_RMBundervaluation.pdf.

Goldstein, M (2004). Adjusting China's exchange rate policies. Revised version of a paper presented at the IMF Seminar on China's Foreign Exchange System, Dalian, 26–27 May, http://www.iie.com/research/topics/renminb-hot.htm.

Johnson, HG (1969). The case for flexible exchange rates. *Federal Reserve Bank of St. Louis Review*, 51(6), 12–24.

Kouri, PJK (1976). The exchange rate and the balance of payments in the short run and in the long run. *Scandinavian Journal of Economics*, 78(2), 280–304.

Krugman, P and M Obstfeld (2007). *International Economics: Theory and Policy*, 7th Ed. Singapore: Addison-Wesley.

MAS (1982/1983). Annual Report, Monetary Authority of Singapore.

McKinnon, R (2005). China's new exchange rate policy: Will China follow Japan into a liquidity trap? *Singapore Economic Review*, 50, 463–474.

—— (2006). China's exchange rate trap: Japan redux? American Economic Association Meetings, Boston, 7 January.

Mundell, R (2004). China's exchange rate: The case for the status quo. Paper presented at the IMF Seminar on China's Foreign Exchange System, Dalian, China, 26–27 May.

Mussa, M (1982). A model of exchange rate dynamics. *Journal of Political Economy*, 90(1), 74–104.

Rodriguez, CA (1980). The role of trade flows in exchange rate determination: A rational expectations approach. *Journal of Political Economy*, 88, 1148–1158.

Teh, KP and T Shanmugaratnam (1992). Exchange rate policy: Philosophy and conduct over the past decade. In *Public Policies in Singapore: Changes in the 1980s and the Future Signposts*, L Low and MH Toh (eds.), pp. 285–314. Singapore: Times Academic Press.

Yip, PSL (2003). A re-statement of Singapore's exchange rate and monetary policies. *Singapore Economic Review*, 48(2), 201–212.

—— (2005). Some proposals on China's exchange rate system reform. In *The Exchange Rate Systems in Hong Kong and Singapore: Currency Board vs Monitoring Band*, PSL Yip (ed.). Singapore: Prentice Hall.

Zhang, J (2004). The debate on China's exchange rate — Should or will it be revalued? Stanford University, Hoover Institution, Essays in Public Policy, No. 112.

THE FOG ENCIRCLING THE RENMINBI DEBATE

YIN-WONG CHEUNG

Department of Economics, E2
University of California, Santa Cruz
CA 95064, USA
cheung@ucsc.edu

MENZIE D. CHINN

University of Wisconsin, Madison and NBER, USA

EIJI FUJII

University of Tsukuba, Japan

We assess some recently advanced arguments for the claim that the RMB is undervalued. These arguments are those based on the direct valuation of the RMB, trade imbalances, the accumulation of foreign exchange reserves, and the degree of policy dependence. The extant evidence does not support a strong verdict regarding RMB undervaluation that meets the statistical standards of academic empirical studies. One interpretation is that the evaluation of the equilibrium RMB exchange rate is far more complicated than it appears. Another view is that the data are insufficiently informative. Some related policy concerns are also discussed.

Keywords: Exchange rate uncertainty; trade surplus; international reserves; policy dependence.

1. Introduction

Essentially a dormant topic in the international forum until 2003, China's foreign exchange policy is now the focus of attention. Since then, criticism of the Chinese currency regime has been mounting. Some countries, among which the US is the most vocal one, sternly accuse China of gaining unfair advantages by keeping its currency, the renminbi (RMB), undervalued, and as a result, running a huge trade surplus, thereby exacerbating global imbalances. Even though the exchange rate regime reform instituted by China in July 2005 was warmly, albeit cautiously, welcomed, it has not silenced the calls for further flexibility of China's exchange rate.

During the high profile two-day US–China Strategic Economic Dialogue that took place in Beijing in December 2006, the US delegation led by Treasury Secretary Paulson, as expected, reiterated concerns about the RMB's undervaluation and urged China to allow further RMB appreciation. Interestingly, in its semi-annual report to the Congress released a few days after the Dialogue, the US Treasury Department maintained its prior stance and refrained from officially labeling China as a currency manipulator.[1]

The theme of the current exercise is to review some reasons advanced in the recent literature to sustain the claim that RMB is undervalued. First, we assess the argument based on the direct valuation of RMB. Then, we assess the arguments related to trade surpluses, international reserves, and policy dependence. In Section 3, some policy implications are presented.

2. Assessment

For economists, a currency is undervalued when the rate at which it exchanges for foreign currency is higher than what economic fundamentals indicate it should. In this case, the allegation is that it takes more units (yuan) of the Chinese currency RMB to buy a single dollar than is deemed appropriate. The overarching issue is, of course, how to define the appropriate or, in economic jargon, the equilibrium value of RMB. A quick review of the current status of exchange rate economics offers a grim hope to determine an equilibrium exchange rate in an unambiguous manner.

Since Meese and Rogoff published their seminal piece (Meese and Rogoff, 1983) that amplifies the difficulties inherent to empirical exchange rate modeling in 1983, a voluminous collection of studies echoing their conclusion has accumulated. Cheung, Chinn and Garcia Pascual (2005) present some recent evidence on this issue.

Given the lack of a commonly agreed theoretical model, assertions about the equilibrium (and disequilibrium) level of an exchange rate should be interpreted with great caution. The quintessential problem is that "undervaluation" — or currency misalignment in general — is in the eye of the beholder. Whether one sees a misalignment depends upon what economic model one has in mind. A hasty decision on RMB policy based on ill-founded evidence can do more harm than benefit to China and to its trading partners, especially the developing economies in the region.

In the next two sections, we take up the RMB valuation issue, not with a mind to proving that RMB is or is not undervalued. Rather, we wish to highlight the uncertainty surrounding the issue, both in terms of figuring out the right model for addressing the issue and the actual calculation of the degree of undervaluation.

2.1. *Analyses based on exchange rate indexes*

At the heart of the debate over the right way of determining the appropriate exchange rate level are contrasting ideas of what constitutes an equilibrium exchange rate, what time frame

---

[1] See The Treasury Department (2006). Indeed, the Treasury's semi-annual report, "International Economic and Exchange Rate Policies", has not labeled any country as a currency manipulator, at least, in the last decade. Reflecting their dissatisfaction with the report, the Grassley–Baucus bill on "The United States Trade Enhancement Act of 2006" was introduced with the intention to revamp the procedure of identifying a currency with a fundamental misalignment and provide explicit sanctions. See Frankel and Wei (2007) for a discussion of the empirical determinants of Treasury decisions.

the equilibrium condition pertains to, and, not least, what econometric method to implement. Some shortcuts have been used so often that some forget that they are shortcuts.

Most of the extant studies fall into some familiar categories, either relying upon some form of relative purchasing power parity (PPP) or cost competitiveness calculation, the modeling of deviations from absolute PPP, or structural models. The Appendix offers a brief review of these different approaches.

The relative PPP comparisons are the easiest to make, in terms of numerical calculation. On the other hand, relative PPP is uninformative about how a country's actual exchange rate stands *relative to others.*

To highlight the drawbacks of this oft-used relative PPP approach, we examine briefly what this methodology says about the RMB. While the exchange rate between the Chinese yuan and the US dollar is the usual focal point, trade-weighted exchange rates provide better measures of relative prices. As a matter of principle, trade-weighted rates are to be preferred to bilateral rates since the reliance on the latter can lead to misleading inferences about overall competitiveness. Figure 1 depicts the IMF's trade-weighted effective RMB exchange rate index from January 1986 to February 2007, and a fitted linear trend. The index is expressed so lower values mean a stronger Chinese currency. In line with expectations, in the years since the East Asian crisis, the RMB has experienced a downward decline in value.

In the early warning system literature that developed in the wake of the financial crises of the 1990s, a typical measure of currency misalignment was the deviation from a deterministic trend. The linear trend in Figure 1 suggests that, during the new millennium, RMB is undervalued for some very brief periods. Indeed, such a measure yields a 5.5% RMB overvaluation in February 2007.

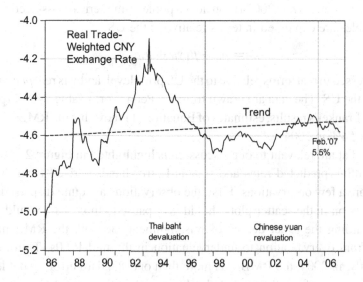

Figure 1. Log Trade-Weighted Real Chinese Yuan (CNY) Exchange Rate, 1986M01–2007M02, and Linear Time Trend
Source: IMF, *International Financial Statistics*, and authors' calculations.

Of course, a quick glance at the data indicates that a simple trend is much too simplistic a characterization. For instance, suppose instead that one assumed that the relevant period was 1990 onward; then a different degree of misalignment would be the determination. The observation essentially echoes those reported in Cheung *et al.* (2007a), which shows that the deviation from a deterministic trend approach can yield either an over- or under-valuation estimate depending on the choices of exchange rates and sample periods. We also noted that using the bilateral China–US real exchange rate gives similar ambiguous results on RMB misalignments.

The fact that working with simple straight line extrapolations can lead to such diverging conclusions suggests that we need to take a closer look at where the Chinese currency should stand, both over time and across countries.

2.2. *The real exchange rate–income relationship*

It is well-known that standard exchange rate models — including the fundamental/behavioral equilibrium exchange rate models commonplace in the practitioner literature — are not well-suited to explain exchange rate behavior of developing and transition economies. Thus, we opt to discuss some results from a more straightforward and robust relative price and relative output framework to highlight the issues in assessing the degree of RMB misalignment. Some brief remarks on results derived from standard exchange rate models will be discussed later.

The empirical real exchange rate–income relationship is documented in Summers and Heston (1991) using data from the Penn World Table. Apparently, Frankel (2006) is the first study exploiting this empirical regularity to assess the degree of RMB undervaluation. To be sure, this framework does not give a small estimate of RMB undervaluation — that is, choosing this model does not bias against the claim of undervaluation.

Specifically, Cheung *et al.* (2007a) consider a pooled time series cross-section regression, where all variables are expressed in terms relative to the US;

$$q_{it} = \beta_0 + \beta_1 y_{it} + u_{it}, \tag{1}$$

where q is expressed in real terms relative to the US price level, and y is real *per capita* income also relative to the US. The data are drawn from the Penn World Table. Not surprisingly and consistent with Frankel's results, estimates of Equation (1) show that the RMB is substantially undervalued by 54% in 2004.[2]

The results that are relevant to our discussion is highlighted in Figure 2, which plots the actual and resulting predicted rates and standard error bands derived from the regression results. There are a few observations. First, the observations are quite dispersedly scattered. The wide dispersion in the scatter plots should give pause to those who would make strong statements regarding the exact degree of misalignment. Second, the RMB misalignment has switched from overvaluation to undervaluation in the mid-1980s. Third, and perhaps most importantly, in 2004, the RMB was more than one standard error — but less than two standard errors — away from the predicted value, which in the present context is interpreted

---

[2]Cheung *et al.* (2007a) give a detailed discussion of empirical results obtained from Equation (1).

Relative price level

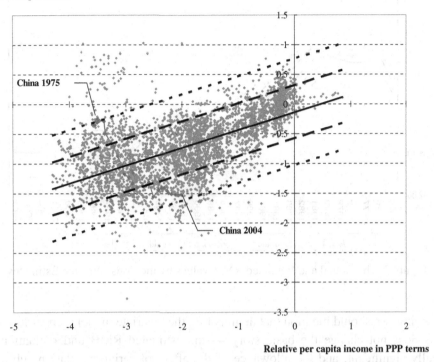

Figure 2. The Rate of RMB Misalignment Based on the Pooled OLS Estimates with the PPP-Based Per Capita Income

as the "equilibrium" value. In other words, by the standard statistical criterion that applied economists commonly appeal to, the RMB is not undervalued (as of 2004) in a statistically significant sense.

Before discussing whether the use of two standard errors is too stringent a criterion for assessing the degree of RMB misalignment, we note that the deviations from the estimated equilibrium exchange rates are persistent; that is, deviations from the real exchange rate–income relationship exhibit serial correlation. In order to obtain estimates that are statistically correct in the presence of serial correlation, we implemented a panel version of the Prais–Winsten procedure. Figure 3 offers a temporal dimension of the estimated misalignment that is not plagued by serial correlation problems — it traces the evolution of the RMB level over time, its predicted value, and the associated confidence bands.

The figure shows a striking feature — after controlling for serial correlation, the actual value of the RMB is mostly staying within one standard error prediction interval surrounding the (predicted) equilibrium value in the last 20 plus years — the two values virtually have converged by 2004 and there is little indication of undervaluation. In fact, the 2004 actual value slightly exceeds the predicted one, suggesting an *over*valuation of 0.2%, albeit statistically insignificant. Recalling the huge data dispersion observed in Figure 2, we believe the data are not informative for a sharp misalignment inference — not just for the recent period, but for most of the sample period.

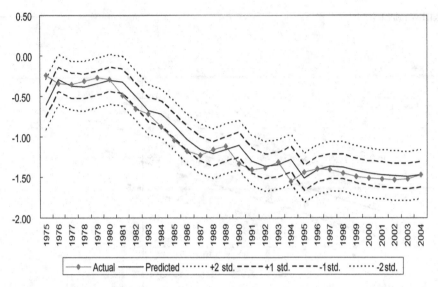

Figure 3. The Actual and Predicted RMB Values by the Prais–Winsten Estimates

In passing, we should mention that augmenting the bivariate model with various control variables does not change the basic story — the estimated RMB undervaluation is not statistically significant, and the allowance of the effect of serial correlation substantially reduces the estimated rate of undervaluation.

2.3. *Other approaches*

Most studies that made it into the headlines indicated a large degree of RMB undervaluation. Indeed, the pending Schumer–Graham bill cites the reported undervaluation estimates are between 15% to 40%, thus justifying the imposition of an across-the-board 27.5% tariff on imports from China.

Two recent IMF studies — Dunaway and Li (2005) and Dunaway *et al.* (2006) — assess the reliability of the reported RMB undervaluation estimates obtained from some typical modeling approaches, which are briefly reviewed in the Appendix.

These authors noted the difficulties, both methodological and empirical, in measuring an equilibrium exchange rate, and raised certain concerns about the robustness of the reported estimates of the degree of RMB undervaluation. For instance, it is puzzling to see that a given approach can give rise to a wide range of undervaluation estimates. They also reported that substantial changes in equilibrium exchange rate estimates resulted from minor changes in model specifications, variable definitions, and sample periods. In a sense, the two IMF studies reinforce the message from the seminal Meese and Rogoff (1983) article.

It is worth pointing out that most of these reported undervaluation estimates do not come with a measure of sampling uncertainty — a point stressed in the previous subsection. We anticipate that accounting for sampling uncertainty will reinforce the conclusion that a precise and accurate measure of the degree of RMB misalignment is a very elusive goal.

2.4. *Trade surplus*

The case for RMB undervaluation is built upon several arguments, in addition to direct estimation of the equilibrium exchange rate. One phenomenon is the large and growing trade surplus China has with the US. It is argued that the trade surplus persists because China enjoys an unfair trade advantage from its significantly undervalued currency. Economic theory, for instance, suggests that the RMB value should be linked to the magnitude of the overall trade balance instead of to the size of a specific bilateral trade balance.

Figure 4 shows the Chinese current account balance expressed in dollar terms and as a share of GDP. Note that the Chinese current account is mainly driven by its trade account performance. Clearly, the Chinese current account balance has ballooned in recent years. It should be noted that, however, China's external balances have not — until quite recently — constituted a *prima facie* case for RMB undervaluation. Yet in 2004, China's trade surplus relative to GDP was not particularly large compared with, say, those recorded by Japan and Germany. Indeed, Chinn and Ito (2007) argue that China's current account surplus over the 2000–2004 period — while exceeding the predicted value — was within the statistical margin of error, according to a model of the current account based upon the determinants of saving and investment.

China's trade surplus with the US should be viewed in light of China's role in the international production process. With its current framework of incentives and its abundant labor, China has grown into a global production/manufacturing hub. As it is developing its manufacturing capacity, China participates in the international production process and plays the role as the last leg of the production chain.

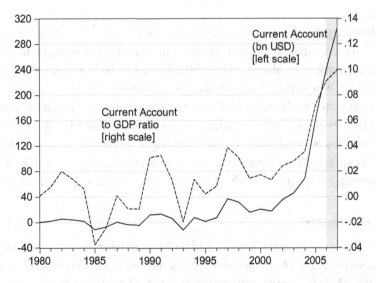

Figure 4. Current Account Balance (in billions of US dollars) and Current Account to GDP Ratio
Note: Statistics for 2006–2007 are IMF projections.
Source: IMF, *World Economic Outlook* (April 2007) and authors' calculations.

For example, in the case of the electronics industry, China imports primary materials and capital goods, implements labor-intensive processing and assembly of imported (high-end) components, and exports the final products to, say, end consumers. Thus, instead of exporting directly to, say, the United States, economies in Asia export raw materials and components to China, take advantage of the low labor cost and manufacture facilities, and export their products via China. As expected, China incurs large trade deficits with these countries and enjoys substantial trade surplus with, in this case, the United States. Thus, the observed China trade surplus with the United States may exaggerate the trade imbalance between these two countries.

The link between the trade surplus and an undervalued exchange rate is obscured by the difficulty in establishing a strong exchange rate effect on China's trade. Cheung *et al.* (2007b), for instance, represents a recent effort to determine the exchange rate effect on China's trade balance. Such an effort is hampered by data problems, including the lack of the relevant trade price indexes. Further, estimated conventional trade equations may be deprived of relevancy because of the drastic economic and structural changes experienced by China in recent years. Against this backdrop, Cheung *et al.* (2007b) obtains very different exchange rate effect estimates across some plausible trade equations — a result that echoes some other studies on exchange rate effects on China's trade balances.

With these caveats, there is some evidence that China's trade balance is affected by its exchange rate. Even with some possible estimates of trade elasticities, the exchange rate effect on overall trade flows is relatively small, and sometimes goes in the direction opposite of anticipated. When one ignores the "perverse" estimates and uses only plausible estimates from their study, one obtains for a 10% RMB real appreciation a US$46 billion (in year 2000 unit) reduction in the Chinese trade balance, which while not inconsequential, is still not tremendously large when measured against a 2006 balance of US$401 billion (again, in year 2000 unit).

These findings suggest that exchange rate policy alone will not be sufficient to reduce the Chinese trade balance, especially when taken in the context of a trend increase in China's manufacturing capacity. It is also worth mentioning an issue not commonly discussed in the debate. With its non-trivial shares of the global manufacturing capacity, China is not necessarily a price-taker in the world product market and its action can have implications for the world price level. For instance, while China has experienced real appreciation since 2005, its trade surplus is not dwindling, but swelling at a time the prices of its exports are not declining. It is likely that China's trade surplus is affected by, other than the exchange rate, factors including consumption behaviors and macro-policies of China and, say, the US.

2.5. *International reserves*

Another eye-catching situation is China's rapid build-up of international reserves. Some people consider China's recent phenomenal international reserve accumulation as *prima facie* evidence that the RMB is significantly undervalued. Nonetheless, official reserve holdings might be deemed insufficient as concerns over China's contingent liabilities come to the fore. For instance, one recent report (Ernst & Young, 2006) estimates that, in 2005, China's total non-performing loan liability, a key component of China's contingent liability, stood at $900 billion, a figure higher than its reserve holdings. The subsequent retraction of this report by the company does not negate the fact that there are substantial amounts of non-performing loans, the estimation of which is surrounded by considerable uncertainty.

Indeed, the claim that China's rapid international reserve accumulation is a proof of RMB undervaluation may require additional scrutiny. For instance, Prasad and Wei (2005), examining the composition of capital flows into and out of China, argue that much of the international reserve accumulation that has occurred in recent years is due to changes in the capital account rather than in the current account. These inflows are sensitive to expectations of the future RMB exchange rate and, thus, this component of build-up may be self-fulfilling.

The empirical evidence that China is holding an excessive amount of international reserves, indeed, is quite tenuous. Cheung and Ito (2007) trace the evolution of the theory of demand for international reserves and estimate several vintages of international reserve demand equations. These demand equations are used to illustrate the evolving roles of the traditional macro-variables, the financial variables and the institutional variables. Using data from more than 100 countries over the last 30 years, these authors report international reserve equations estimated from different sample periods, for developed and developing countries, and with different combinations of explanatory variables.

Interestingly, all these different specifications do not suggest that China was holding an excessive amount of international reserves during the 1999–2004 period. During this period, China is deemed to hold a level of international reserves (per GDP) that is 15.4% less than the level predicted by the model estimated using developing countries' data. If the model fitted to developed countries is used, the underhoarding is in the order of 30%. Further, using model specifications obtained from other historical periods tend to yield an even higher level of underhoarding. There is a possibility that China's recent large accumulation of international reserves is part of a catch-up process that the country is going through in the recent decades.

In the last two or three years, however, China experienced quite a drastic increase in its level of international reserve holding. It is not clear whether the results for 1999–2004 carry over to the post-2004 period. Apparently, the case for RMB undervaluation is, on this count, now stronger. Nonetheless, the experience suggests that it would be prudent to evaluate the conditions systematically before drawing conclusions.

2.6. *Interest rate dependence*

Instead of arguing that the RMB should be appreciated, some commentators call for a more flexible Chinese currency. In fact, there is no shortage of proposals in both the media and academia for China to reform its foreign exchange market and policy stance. Some recent examples are Eichengreen (2006), Goldstein (2004), Goodfriend and Prasad (2006), Roberts and Tyers (2003) and Williamson (2005). McKinnon (2005, 2006) and Mundell (2004) are among the few that favor RMB stability. McCallum (2004) and Schwartz (2005) represent yet another view on the issue: China, and not outside sovereignties, should determine the complex issue of reforming its foreign exchange policy.

One argument offered by advocates of a flexible RMB is that it is to China's benefit to float its currency. With a *de facto* fixed exchange rate, China has to give up monetary policy independence and follow the policy set by the US, which is the anchor currency country, in order to maintain the pegged exchange rate. Despite its increasing integration into the world economy, there is no apparent evidence that China and the US share common business cycles. In the absence of similar cyclical behavior, it is very costly for China to follow US monetary policy.

Will exchange rate flexibility allow China to pursue an independent monetary policy? Apparently, existing theoretical and empirical results are ambiguous regarding the link between exchange rate flexibility and policy independence, which is usually measured by interest rate independence. Without the benefit of foresight, one may like to ask whether China has lost its policy independence and, for example, followed the US interest rate policy under the current *de facto* pegged exchange rate arrangement.

In the case of China, even a casual observer will not rule out the possibility of imperfect interest rate pass through. For instance, despite China's capital account is perceived to be porous, its restrictions on capital flows are effective enough to yield a wedge between the Chinese and US interest rates. Figure 5 plots the Chinese one-month interbank and the US one-month Fed fund interest rates. There is no visual evidence that the Chinese interest rate follows the US rate.

Cheung *et al.* (forthcoming) offer a formal analysis of the interaction between the Chinese and US interest rates. To ensure the robustness, these authors consider results from the cointegration procedure, vector autogression models, and the bounds test approach. Together, these three types of econometric techniques cover various conceivable dynamic model specifications of interest rates.

In sum, there is no convincing evidence that the Chinese interest rate is affected by the US rate during the 1996 to 2005 period. All the three different econometric frameworks give

Figure 5. One-Month Chinese and US Interest Rates

the similar lack of dependence result.[3] If the current Chinese interest rate is not driven by the US rate and if the Chinese economy is performing reasonably well, then abandoning the peg for policy independence may not be a relevant argument.

While there is no substantial evidence of policy dependency, it is not our intention to argue in favor of an inflexible RMB exchange rate. What we meant is to discuss the RMB issue in a more informed manner. With both ambiguous theoretical and empirical results, a reasonable policy recommendation is, instead of a drastic change policy, a policy that allows for gradual changes with continual monitoring and assessment of the effects of the policy change.

3. Policy Concerns

Undeniably, the valuation of the Chinese currency is one of the most intensely debated issues in the international community. However, some of the arguments do not appear to hold water and some are likely to be *non sequiturs*. In the previous section, we discussed issues inherent to some arguments for the undervaluation of the Chinese currency.

One rationale for undertaking this exercise was our firmly held conviction that many strong policy recommendations were being made on the basis of weak empirical evidence. We believe the limitations of our knowledge regarding the appropriate model and the true nature of the relevant data needs to be acknowledged. At the same time, it is worth mentioning that our results, while highlighting the difficulty of drawing a clear verdict, do not necessarily mean that there is no undervaluation.

One message is that the evaluation of the equilibrium RMB exchange rate is far more complicated than it appears. Simply put, with current theoretical and empirical technologies, it is not feasible to deliver an RMB undervaluation verdict that meets the standards of empirical work expected of academic work.

Our preceding discussion has been somewhat academic, in that we focus on the strength of empirical evidence. But policymakers operate in the here and now of the real world. They need to take as given certain conditions, and may perceive the burgeoning trade/current account surpluses and foreign exchange reserves as indicators of RMB undervaluation. It is reasonable, then, for policymakers to ask for some currency adjustment, perhaps even more than what has taken place.

Relatedly, to the extent that one believes the value of the RMB is related to the Chinese current account surplus, one might believe RMB appreciation is desirable as it would reduce reserve accumulation, and the consequent ongoing credit boom that threatens to overheat the economy. This is not a policy implication leading from a finding, merely a description of how the exchange rate affects the economy, given the other policies in place.

At the same time, some concerns regarding RMB appreciation should be heeded. The first is that RMB appreciation in and of itself is unlikely to alter the basic problem of a massive and expanding US trade deficit. That problem is first and foremost a "made-in-America" issue, driven by collapsed household and public sector savings, and our heavy dependence

---

[3]These results are reported in Cheung, Tam and Yiu (forthcoming).

upon imported oil. The RMB is probably misaligned by at least one or two criteria. But it would be an enormous mistake to think a stronger RMB is a panacea for what ails America (or China, for that matter).

Another concern is the implications for regional economies. The extant discussion routinely stresses the impact of RMB valuation on global trade relationships and global trade imbalances. Given the role of modern China in East Asia, we cannot ignore the implications of China's foreign exchange policy for the region. In this regard, two observations are worth mentioning.

First, the Asian economies have tended to link their currencies to the US dollar via either a *de facto* or *de jure* peg, even after the 1997 financial crisis. To the extent that these currencies were stabilized at low values, the East Asian exchange rate regimes are often viewed as part of a mercantilist approach to economic development (Dooley *et al.*, 2005).

Second, the integration of China into the world economy has brought about substantial adjustment in production and trade in developing economies, especially those in East Asia. These economies, while sharing extensive production and trade linkages with China, possess both real and financial sectors that are less sophisticated than those in developed countries. Therefore, they are very susceptible to the (adverse) effects of RMB exchange rate volatility. It is highly possible that China's Asian trading partners would suffer more from a volatile RMB exchange rate than they would benefit from, say, a stronger RMB. A volatile RMB is likely to impose extra costs on the integration between China and its neighboring economies and hinder the cooperation between these economies.

The biggest uncertainty pertains to shocks that are difficult to model but could nonetheless induce large changes to the equilibrium value of the exchange rate — namely, the shocks that could spring from contingent liabilities and loopholes in capital controls. The mere act of quickly revaluing — or of moving to a relatively free float — might in itself change the equilibrium exchange rate if it triggers corporate defaults or causes changes in the balance sheets of unhedged firms. The end of capital controls, either by fiat or by slow erosion, might also alter the equilibrium exchange rate.

Thus, one natural concern is whether the Chinese economy, given its fragile financial systems and hidden domestic economic problems, is capable of handling a floating RMB exchange rate without incurring a substantial domestic economic backlash which would cause repercussions for the regional and even the global economies.

Even though some people perceive China to be a market economy, the reality is that China is still intrinsically a transition economy with a relatively primitive and inefficient banking and financial sector. It is also still in the early stages of devising and developing prudential legal and regulatory framework that promotes governance and financial stability. It is highly questionable whether the current Chinese economy could withstand the potential financial instability induced by full foreign exchange flexibility. A volatile RMB exchange rate would most likely hinder China's financial development. Systemic financial difficulties in China could in turn create ripple effects across the global economy.

That being said, we do believe that China should pursue a policy of gradually loosing its grip on the RMB. In a well-functioning foreign exchange market, a market-determined exchange rate enhances resource allocation and improves efficiency by providing correct price signals.

The pace of liberalizing its foreign exchange policy has to be linked to developments in its financial markets. With a growing role in an uncertain world, China's foreign exchange policy can have unexpected (instead of expected) effects on the world in general and to other regional economies in particular. Given the high degree of uncertainty surrounding the determination of the equilibrium exchange rate, and the potentially adverse implications of sharp exchange rate movements, it seems appropriate for a large transition economy like China to take a cautious approach to enhance exchange rate flexibility and, at the same time, augment the policy change with a parallel development of the sophistication of domestic financial markets. Continuous monitoring and assessment of the situation will be an essential adjunct in this process.

Acknowledgments

The views expressed are solely the responsibility of the authors, and do not necessarily reflect those of any other individuals or institutions the authors are associated with.

Appendix. A Brief Literature Review

A couple of surveys of the RMB misalignment literature have compared the estimates of the degree to which the RMB is misaligned. Government Accountability Office (2005) provides a comparison of the academic and policy literature, while Cairns (2005) briefly surveys recent point estimates obtained by different analysts. Here, we review the literature to focus on primarily theoretical papers and their economic and econometric distinctions.

Most of these papers fall into familiar categories, either relying upon some form of relative purchasing power parity (PPP) or cost competitiveness calculation, the modeling of deviations from absolute PPP, a composite model incorporating several channels of effects (sometimes called behavioral equilibrium exchange rate models), or flow equilibrium models.

The relative PPP comparisons are the easiest to make, in terms of calculations. Bilateral real exchange rates are easy to calculate, and there are now a number of trade-weighted series that incorporate China. On the other hand, relative PPP in levels requires the cointegration of the price indices with the nominal exchange rate (or, equivalently, the stationarity of the real exchange rate),[4] but these conditions do not necessarily hold, regardless of the deflator adopted in empirical analyses. Wang (2004) reports interesting IMF estimates of unit labor cost deflated RMB. This series has appreciated in real terms since 1997; of course, this comparison, like all other comparisons based upon indices, depends upon selecting a year that is deemed to represent equilibrium. Selecting a year before 1992 would imply that the RMB has depreciated over time.

Bosworth (2004), Frankel (2006), Coudert and Couharde (2005) and Cairns (2005) estimate the relationship between the deviation from absolute PPP and relative per capita

---

[4]For a technical discussion, see Chinn (2000).

income. All obtain similar results regarding the relationship between the two variables, although Coudert and Couharde fail to detect this link for the RMB.

Zhang (2001), Wang (2004) and Funke and Rahn (2005) implement what could broadly be described as behavioral equilibrium exchange rate (BEER) specifications.[5] These models incorporate a variety of channels through which the real exchange rate is affected. Since each author selects different variables to include, the implied misalignments will necessarily vary.

Other approaches center on flow equilibriums, considering savings and investment behavior and the resulting implied current account. The equilibrium exchange rate is derived from the implied medium-term current account using import and export elasticities. In the IMF's "macroeconomic approach", the "norms" are estimated, in the spirit of Chinn and Prasad (2003). Wang (2004) discusses the difficulties in using this approach for China, but does not present estimates of misalignment based upon this framework. Coudert and Couharde (2005) implement a similar approach. Finally, the external balances approach relies upon assessments of the persistent components of the balance of payments condition (Goldstein, 2004; Bosworth, 2004). This last set of approaches is perhaps most useful for conducting short-term analyses. But the wide dispersion in implied misalignments reflects the difficulties in making judgments about what constitutes persistent capital flows. For instance, Prasad and Wei (2005), examining the composition of capital inflows into and out of China, argue that much of the reserve accumulation that has occurred in recent years is due to speculative inflow; hence, the degree of misalignment is small.

Two observations are of interest. First, as noted by Cairns (2005), there is an interesting relationship between the particular approach adopted by a study and the degree of misalignment found.[6] Analyses implementing relative PPP and related approaches indicate the least misalignment. Those adopting approaches focusing on the external accounts (either the current account or the current account plus some persistent component of capital flows) yield estimates that are in the intermediate range. Finally, studies implementing an absolute PPP methodology result in the greatest degree of estimated undervaluation. Dunaway and Li (2005) make a similar observation.

Second, while all these papers make reference to the difficulty of applying such approaches in the context of an economy ridden with capital controls, state-owned banks and large contingent liabilities, few have attempted a closer examination of these issues. Cheung *et al.* (2007a) directly incorporate some institutional factors including corruption and capital controls in their analysis.

References

Bosworth, B (2004). Valuing the renminbi. Paper presented at the Tokyo Club Research Meeting, 9–10 February.
Cairns, J (2005). Fair value on global currencies: An assessment of valuation based on GDP and absolute price levels. *IDEAglobal Economic Research*, 10 May.

---

[5]Also known as BEERs, a composite of exchange rate models.
[6]All the studies reviewed by Cairns imply undervaluation or no misalignment.

Cheung, Y-W, M Chinn and E Fujii (2007a). The overvaluation of renminbi undervaluation. *Journal of International Money & Finance*, 26, 762–785.

Cheung, Y-W, M Chinn and E Fujii (2007b). China's current account and exchange rate. Paper presented in the NBER Conference on China's Growing Role in World Trade, Cape Cod, MA.

Cheung, Y-W, M Chinn and A Garcia Pascual (2005). Empirical exchange rate models of the nineties: Are any fit to survive? *Journal of International Money & Finance*, 24, 1150–1175.

Cheung, Y-W and H Ito (2007). A cross-country empirical analysis of international reserves. Manuscript, UCSC.

Cheung, Y-W, D Tam and MS Yiu (forthcoming). Does the Chinese interest rate follow the US interest rate? To appear in *International Journal of Finance and Economics*.

Chinn, M (2000). Before the fall: Were East Asian currencies overvalued? *Emerging Markets Review*, 1, 101–126.

Chinn, M and H Ito (2007). Current account balances, financial development and institutions: Assaying the world "saving glut". *Journal of International Money and Finance*, 26, 546–569.

Chinn, M and E Prasad (2003). Medium-term determinants of current accounts in industrial and developing countries: An empirical exploration. *Journal of International Economics*, 59, 47–76.

Coudert, V and C Couharde (2005). Real equilibrium exchange rate in China. CEPII Working Paper 2005-01, Paris, January.

Dooley, M, D Folkerts-Landau and P Garber (2005). *International Financial Stability: Asia, Interest Rates, and the Dollar*. Deutsche Bank Global Research.

Dunaway, S, L Leigh and X Li (2006). How robust are estimates of equilibrium real exchange rates: The case of China. IMF Working Paper.

Dunaway, S and X Li (2005). Estimating China's equilibrium real exchange rate. IMF Working Paper.

Eichengreen, B (2006). China's exchange rate regime: The long and short of it. Manuscript, University of California, Berkeley.

Ernst & Young (2006). *Global Nonperforming Loan Report 2006*. EYGM Limited.

Frankel, J (2006). On the yuan: The choice between adjustment under a fixed exchange rate and adjustment under a flexible rate. *CESifo Economic Studies*, 52(2), 246–275.

Frankel, JA and S-J Wei (2007). Assessing China's exchange rate regime. NBER Working Paper No. 13100, May.

Funke, M and J Rahn (2005). Just how undervalued is the Chinese renminbi? *World Economy*, 28, 465–489.

Goldstein, M (2004). China and the renminbi exchange rate. In *Dollar Adjustment: How Far? Against What?* Special Report No. 17, CF Bergsten and J Williamson (eds.). Washington, DC: Institute for International Economics.

Goodfriend, M and E Prasad (2006). A framework for independent monetary policy in China. IMF Working Paper WP/06/11.

Government Accountability Office (2005). International trade: Treasury assessments have not found currency manipulation, but concerns about exchange rates continue. *Report to Congressional Committees* GAO-05-351. Washington, DC: Government Accountability Office.

McCallum, BT (2004). China's exchange rate and monetary policy. Shadow Open Market Committee.

McKinnon, RI (2005). Exchange rates, wages, and international adjustment: Japan and China versus the United States. *China & World Economy*, 13, 11–27.

McKinnon, RI (2006). China's new exchange rate policy: Will China follow Japan into a liquidity trap? *The Economists' Voice*, 3, Article 2.

Meese, R and K Rogoff (1983). Empirical exchange rate models of the seventies: Do they fit out of sample? *Journal of International Economics*, 14, 3–24.

Mundell, R (2004). China's exchange rate: The case for the status quo. Paper presented at IMF seminar on The Foreign Exchange System, Dalian, China, 26–27 May.

Prasad, E and S-J Wei (2005). The Chinese approach to capital inflows: Patterns and possible explanations. NBER Working Paper No. 11306, April.

Roberts, I and R Tyers (2003). China's exchange rate policy: The case for greater flexibility. *Asian Economic Journal*, 17, 155–184.

Schwartz, AJ (2005). Dealing with exchange rate protectionism. *Cato Journal*, 25, 97–106.

Summers, R and A Heston (1991). The Penn World Table (mark 5): An expanded set of international comparisons. *Quarterly Journal of Economics*, 106, 327–368.

The Treasury Department (2006). *Report to Congress on International Economic and Exchange Rate Policies, December 2006*. The US Treasury Department, Office of International Affairs. http://www.treas.gov/offices/international-affairs/economic-exchange-rates/pdf/2006_FXReport.pdf.

Wang, T (2004). Exchange rate dynamics. In *China's Growth and Integration into the World Economy*, Occasional Paper No. 232, E Prasad (ed.), pp. 21–28. Washington, DC: IMF.

Williamson, J (2005). The choice of exchange rate regime: The relevance of international experience to China's decision. *China & World Economy*, 13, 17–33.

Zhang, Z (2001). Real exchange rate misalignment in China: An empirical investigation. *Journal of Comparative Economics*, 29, 80–94.

INSULATION OF INDIA FROM THE EAST ASIAN CRISIS: AN ANALYSIS

PAMI DUA

Department of Economics, Delhi School of Economics
University of Delhi, Delhi 110007, India
dua@econdse.org

ARUNIMA SINHA

Department of Economics
Columbia University, New York, NY, USA

This paper investigates the effects of the East Asian crisis on the Indian economy and exchange rate movements. Despite the contagion effects that profoundly affected the other crisis-hit countries, the Indian economy and the rupee were found less affected. Reforms after the 1990–1991 crisis, control of capital flows, weak economic linkages with crisis-affected countries and stabilization policies that include intervention in the foreign exchange market and tightening of monetary policy are reasons for the insulation of the Indian economy from the crisis.

Keywords: Contagion; currency pressure; liberalization and reforms; policy intervention.

1. Introduction

This paper examines the effects of the 1997 East Asian financial crisis on the Indian economy and exchange rate movements. It seeks to identify the reasons for the insulation of the Indian economy from the crisis. The main findings suggest that reforms undertaken in response to the domestic crisis in 1991 and the Mexican crisis in 1994–1995 as well as stabilization policies adopted during the crisis period helped to shield the Indian economy from most of the effects of the financial crisis in 1997.

The paper is organized as follows. Section 2 gives a brief background of the East Asian crisis and introduces the concept of contagion and its role in the crisis. The impact of the contagion effect on India is also discussed. Section 3 gives an overview of the Indian exchange rate system since the early 1990s. Reasons for the insulation of the Indian economy from the East Asian crisis are discussed in Section 4. Section 5 concludes.

2. The East Asian Crisis

The East Asian financial crisis of 1997–1998 came close on the heels of the Latin American crisis of 1994–1995. Both crises were triggered by the sudden collapse of major regional currencies: the Mexican peso and the Thai baht. Prior to the crisis, several similarities between the two catalyst countries were identified. Both Mexico and Thailand had received large capital inflows and foreign investment in the 1990s and had been highly regarded by international investors. However, both had experienced deterioration in their export growth rates and rise in current account deficits in the years before the crises. The real exchange rate in Mexico and Thailand had also appreciated significantly. Overvalued exchange rates, speculative attacks and investor panic all led to currency depreciation.

There were, at the same time, significant differences between the two crises. Before the financial crisis of 1997, the model of development adopted by the East Asian economies was widely accepted as being extremely conducive for sustained economic growth over a long period. Unlike the Latin American countries, these economies were distinguished by their high rates of capital accumulation and savings, and strong cooperation between the state and the private sector. They experienced high growth rates, low rates of inflation and balanced government budgets. For example, the Thai economy had a budget surplus of 2.6% of GDP in the 1991 to 1996 period. Malaysia recorded an inflation rate of 4.2%, while Korea had a savings rate of 34.8% in the same period (Desai, 2003). In fact, as Radelet and Sachs (1998) argue, many of the usual macroeconomic indicators of any financial crisis did not register any significant changes for the East Asian economies. Thus, the crisis caught most of the global financial system.

It was, however, the factors that had made the East Asian economies such stellar successes, widely promoted by the IMF and the World Bank, which became the reasons for the financial crisis that was to follow. There was rapid capital accumulation, but it was mostly by highly leveraged industries in exports and real estate.

The most important warning sign of the impending crisis was the fragility of the financial system. Credit extended by the banks to the private sector expanded very rapidly, financed mostly by the banks' huge offshore borrowings. Financial sector claims on the private sector increased from 100% in 1990 to approximately 140% in Malaysia, Thailand and Korea. Programs of partial financial liberalization in the late 1980s and early 1990s had allowed the banks to channel foreign money into the domestic sector. For example, in Thailand, foreign liabilities of commercial banks increased from 5.9% to 28.4% of GDP between 1992 and 1995 (Radelet and Sachs, 1998). As the numbers in Table 1 show, the total international claims held by foreign banks increased from about US$185 billion for Thailand, Korea and Indonesia in the end of 1995 to US$231 billion in mid-1997. A large part of this bank credit was used by the private sector for real estate investment. Real estate loans ranged from 30% to 40% in Thailand and 15% to 25% in South Korea by late 1997 (Desai, 2003). Significant amounts of foreign capital were flowing into the real estate sector of the East Asian economies due to the abnormally high rates of return that were offered. For instance, in the mid-1990s, the annual return on building a skyscraper in Bangkok was close to 20%.

The problem of moral hazard afflicted much of the credit extended to the private sector. As the finance companies and banks borrowed heavily from abroad, they accumulated short-term unhedged liabilities and lent long-term to finance projects with questionable viability, and soon the borrowers missed repayments. These structural imperfections led to

Table 1. International Claims Held by
Foreign Banks: Total Outstanding

Country	End 1995	End 1996	Mid-1997
Thailand	62.8	70.2	69.4
Indonesia	44.5	55.5	58.7
Malaysia	16.8	22.2	28.8
Philippines	8.3	13.3	14.1
Korea	77.5	100.0	103.4

Note: Figures are in US$ billion.
Source: Bank for International Settlements.

distortions where the ratios of corporate debt-to-equity averaged 395% in South Korea and 450% in Thailand as the borrowing boom accelerated, compared to 106% in USA.

The large capital inflows created an investment boom in East Asia. Although the investment boom represented a significant positive shock to these economies, it contributed to asset price and widened their current account deficits at the same time.

The borrowing boom, therefore, was in several ways, the catalyst of the East Asian financial crisis. Although the economies had strong fundamentals, their financial excesses made them vulnerable to external shocks. Borrowing short-term, lending long-term, borrowing in dollars and yen and investing in assets which yielded returns in domestic currencies made them even more so. In 1995, the strengthening dollar (against the yen) led to an appreciation of the East Asian currencies that were quasi-fixed against the dollar. The appreciation and the weaker external demand since 1996 weakened their exports and threatened the stability of the domestic currencies. There were additional risks — banks in the debtor Asian five countries (Thailand, Indonesia, South Korea, Philippines and Malaysia) could not hedge their net holdings of short-term dollar liabilities in the pre-crisis period. Risk premiums in the domestic interest rates of debtor economies with original sin[1] were also higher than on dollar assets of comparable maturity. Therefore, the banks tended to overborrow in dollars without covering for exchange rate risk. When a speculative currency attack occurred in this situation, it forced an immediate repayment of short-term dollar debts. The banks could have tried to defend the respective currencies by running down the reserves, but eventually the currency would have to be devalued. The combination of these factors initiated the East Asian crisis in Thailand.

Table 2 shows the change in some of the crisis indicators in the five East Asian countries and India. In Malaysia, the ratio of financial institutions' claims-to-domestic GDP had increased to 144.6% by 1996. The Thai current account deficit reached 8% of the GDP in late 1996, prompting foreign creditors to withdraw their Thai stockholdings. Thailand's central

---

[1]The concept of "original sin" is discussed by Eichengreen *et al.* (2003). It is a situation in which the domestic currency cannot be used to borrow abroad or long-term domestically. In the presence of this incompleteness, financial fragility is unavoidable because all domestic investments will have either a currency mismatch or a maturity mismatch.

Table 2. Selected Crisis Indicators

Country	Indicators			
	Current Account/GDP (%) 1996	Capital Account/GDP (%) 1996	Financial Inst. Claims on Private Sector/GDP (%)	
			1990	1996
Thailand	−8.0	10.6	83.1	141.9
Indonesia	−3.5	4.9	50.6	55.4
Malaysia	−5.3	9.4	71.4	144.6
Philippines	−4.3	11.0	19.3	48.4
Korea	−4.8	4.8	56.8	65.7
India	−1.6	3.1	26.8	24.7

Source: Radelet and Sachs (1998).

bank tried to initially support the baht in the face of declining inflows of foreign exchange, but then gave up.

The collapse of the Thai baht formally initiated the East Asian financial crisis. Other regional currencies followed suit, and the financial crisis rapidly turned into a full-blown downturn, with significant effects on the real sector.

Contagion, which may be defined as the transmission of a crisis to a particular country due to its real and financial interdependence with countries that are already experiencing a crisis (Fratzcher, 1998), was clearly evident in the case of the East Asian economies. Although the crisis was triggered off in Thailand's financial markets, it spread fairly quickly to Malaysia, Korea, Philippines and Indonesia. Real linkages between the economies meant that the effects were not delimited to the financial sector only. The affected economies witnessed a sharp decline in output, employment and standards of living.

The failure of the Thai central bank to support the baht and its subsequent float, or more correctly, depreciation on 2 July 1997, had an impact on the currencies of the neighboring countries such as Malaysia, Indonesia and Philippines.[2] By the early last quarter of 1997, the ringgit had lost 30% of its value (Table 3). In South Korea, the widespread bankruptcies of corporations sent stock prices spiraling downwards, which prompted foreign investors to dump their holdings. After initial attempts by the central bank to support the won by running down reserves and raising the interest rates, South Korea also abandoned the defense of its currency in November 1997. Hence, the financial interlinkages between the East Asian economies led to the transmission of the crisis that began in Thailand to the entire region, with the exceptions of Japan and Singapore.

From Table 3, it is shown that the highest percentage change in the baht occurred in January 1998, and this followed a persistent decline in foreign reserves from a high of more than $31 billion in October 1997. Both these facts illustrate the advent of the currency

---

[2]Contagion is first manifested through the depreciation (sudden and large) in currencies across countries that have financial interlinkages.

Table 3. Foreign Exchange Reserves and Percentage Change in Exchange Rates

	India		South Korea		Malaysia		Thailand	
	% Change in Exchange Rate (from June 1997)	Foreign Exchange Reserves ($bn)	% Change in Exchange Rate (from June 1997)	Foreign Exchange Reserves ($bn)	% Change in Exchange Rate (from June 1997)	Foreign Exchange Reserves ($bn)	% Change in Exchange Rate (from June 1997)	Foreign Exchange Reserves ($bn)
Jul-97	−0.22	29.64	0.23	33.45	2.45	21.82	23.60	30.35
Aug-97	0.29	**29.85**	0.90	31.14	9.66	22.11	32.58	25.86
Sep-97	1.59	29.15	2.41	30.43	19.91	22.27	44.30	29.54
Oct-97	1.18	29.65	4.13	30.51	30.61	22.34	53.05	**31.21**
Nov-97	3.94	27.61	15.97	24.40	34.13	21.88	59.96	26.18
Dec-97	9.36	27.57	65.68	20.40	49.49	20.90	80.25	26.89
Jan-98	9.31	27.60	**90.56**	23.51	**73.63**	19.82	**116.03**	26.57
Feb-98	8.51	27.18	82.62	26.71	51.23	19.92	87.61	26.08
Mar-98	10.32	28.76	67.11	29.75	48.14	19.91	68.34	27.61
Apr-98	10.67	29.04	56.33	35.54	48.07	19.86	62.36	29.46
May-98	12.76	28.35	56.78	38.76	50.91	19.83	60.45	27.38
Jun-98	17.79	26.77	57.12	40.90	58.49	19.81	73.39	26.50
Jul-98	18.69	26.82	45.04	43.02	64.95	19.65	69.16	26.70
Aug-98	**19.29**	27.59	47.84	45.09	66.71	19.69	71.24	27.79
Sep-98	18.68	28.90	54.70	46.98	51.38	20.82	65.64	27.29
Oct-98	18.13	29.44	51.10	48.83	51.04	22.86	56.43	28.48
Nov-98	18.36	29.40	45.00	50.02	50.94	23.09	49.91	28.89
Dec-98	18.97	29.83	36.58	**52.04**	51.03	**25.68**	48.94	29.54

Note: Bold numbers denote maximum levels.
Source: Various Central Banks and IFS.

crisis in Thailand. Malaysia and South Korea also saw the maximum depreciation in their respective currencies in January 1998. The foreign reserves in South Korea began to fall in October 1997. Unlike Malaysia, however, where the decline in reserves was not reversed almost until the last quarter of 1998, Korean reserves recovered almost immediately in April 1998. The Indian rupee did not experience such extreme depreciation. The maximum percentage change was only about 20%, and this occurred well after baht, won and ringgit had experienced their deepest depreciation. Foreign reserves did not fluctuate widely. These factors together suggest that India remained relatively immune from the contagion effect.

Table 3 shows some interesting results: Thailand, Malaysia and South Korea all experienced large deviations in the exchange rates[3] from the trend level in June 1997. In contrast, India witnessed a comparatively mild change in the rupee–dollar rate during the same period.

---

[3]Exchange rates in Table 3 measure price of the US dollar in terms of the domestic currency. For example, the rupee–dollar exchange rate is the amount of US dollar per rupee. A fall in *e* therefore implies a depreciation of the domestic currency.

This reinforces the conclusions of Table 2: India was relatively isolated from the East Asian crisis.

To capture the effect of the depreciation of the baht on the other East Asian currencies during the crisis period, an index of currency pressure is developed in Dua and Sinha (2007). They first introduce a measure of currency pressure, a weighted average of the percentage devaluation of the domestic currency above its trend and the percentage loss in reserves. The weights used are measured as the inverse of the variance for each variable. e is the exchange rate in US dollars per unit of the domestic currency. $\overset{o}{e}$ measures the effect of an overvalued currency and is calculated using the difference of the average real exchange rate over the period prior to the crisis (September 1994 to May 1997) and the actual real exchange rate during each month of the crisis. The trend of the exchange rate $((\Sigma \overset{o}{e})/n)$ is measured as the average rate of nominal depreciation or appreciation prior to the crisis. Thus, the numerator of the first term $((\overset{o}{e} - (\Sigma \overset{o}{e})/n))$ in Equation (1) measures the percentage devaluation of the domestic currency above its trend. *Res* is the amount of foreign exchange reserves in billions of dollars. $\overset{o}{Res}$ is calculated using the difference of the average foreign reserves over the period prior to the crisis (September 1994 to May 1997) and the actual reserves during each month of the crisis:

$$CC_t = \frac{(\overset{o}{e} - (\Sigma \overset{o}{e})/n)}{\sigma_e} + \frac{(\overset{o}{Res})}{\sigma_{res}}, \tag{1}$$

where n is the number of time periods and σ_e and σ_{res} are the standard deviations of the percentage changes in the exchange rate and reserves over the period January 1993 to May 1997. The measure may be interpreted as follows: a depreciation of the domestic currency, i.e., a fall in e and a fall in reserves *res*, reduces the value of CC and hence represents higher currency crisis. A higher value of the currency pressure measure indicates a lower contagion level.

The index of currency pressure is constructed for India, South Korea, Malaysia and Thailand. As monthly data is irregular for the Philippines and Indonesia for the period of analysis, these two countries are excluded from our analysis.

We provide a graphical analysis of the crisis using Figures 1–8. These illustrate the impact of the crisis in two sub-periods — July 1997 to February 1998, and March to December 1998. For country-specific discussion, we refer to figures for Thailand (Figures 1 and 2), Malaysia (Figures 3 and 4), South Korea (Figures 5 and 6) and India (Figures 7 and 8). The first set of the figures in each pair refers to the corresponding graphs of exchange rate and foreign reserves movement; the second set is the path of the index of currency pressure. Pair-wise figures capture the fluctuations in the exchange rates, foreign reserves and the index of currency pressure in each country.

Although the baht experienced its biggest depreciation in January 1998, the currency pressure index fluctuated wildly between July 1997 and March 1998. It is noted from Figure 1 that the baht depreciated by almost 50% in July 1997 at the onset of the crisis. Corresponding to this time, Figure 2 shows that the index attained its lowest value, i.e., currency pressure was very high.

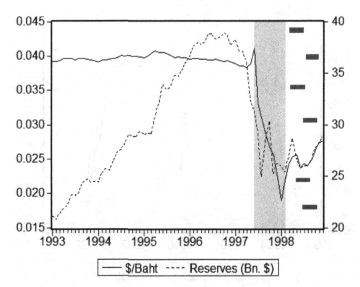

Figure 1. Exchange Rate and Foreign Exchange Reserves in Thailand
Note: The light grey shaded region denotes the first sub-period of the crisis (July 1997 to February 1998). The dotted region is the second sub-period (March 1998 to December 1998).

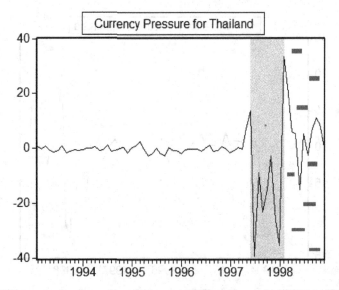

Figure 2. Index of Currency Pressure from February 1993 to December 1998 in Thailand
Note: The light grey shaded region denotes the first sub-period of the crisis (July 1997 to February 1998). The dotted region is the second sub-period (March 1998 to December 1998).

For the case of Korea, as mentioned earlier, the central bank tried to defend the currency against early speculative attacks. It can be seen from Figure 5 that when the bank abandoned the defense of the won in November 1997, it plummeted. At this time, Figure 6 shows that the currency pressure index attained its lowest values in December 1997 and January 1998.

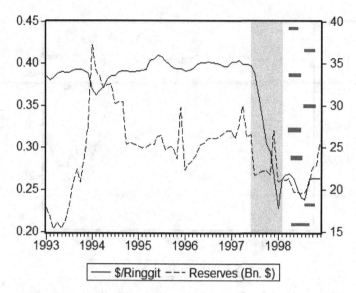

Figure 3. Exchange Rate and Foreign Exchange Reserves in Malaysia
Note: The light grey shaded region denotes the first sub-period of the crisis (July 1997 to February 1998). The dotted region is the second sub-period (March 1998 to December 1998).

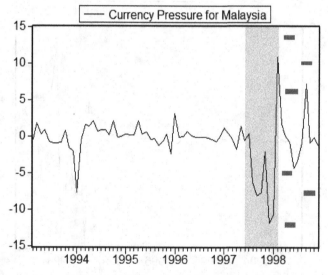

Figure 4. Index of Currency Pressure from February 1993 to December 1998 in Malaysia
Note: The light grey shaded region denotes the first sub-period of the crisis (July 1997 to February 1998). The dotted region is the second sub-period (March 1998 to December 1998).

Although the case of Malaysia was different from the other affected countries by the management of the crisis later, it also abandoned its quasi-currency peg. Within days of the Thai baht devaluation, the Malaysian ringgit was hit by a speculative attack. For the period of analysis, Figure 4 shows that the index for Malaysia fell to its lowest values, coinciding

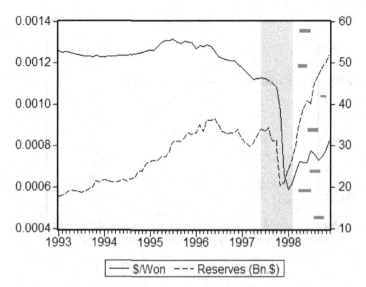

Figure 5. Exchange Rate and Foreign Exchange Reserves in Korea
Note: The light grey shaded region denotes the first sub-period of the crisis (July 1997 to February 1998). The dotted region is the second sub-period (March 1998 to December 1998).

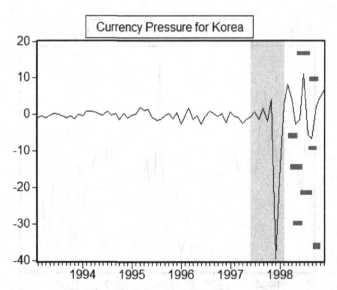

Figure 6. Index of Currency Pressure from February 1993 to December 1998 in Korea
Note: The light grey shaded region denotes the first sub-period of the crisis (July 1997 to February 1998). The dotted region is the second sub-period (March 1998 to December 1998).

with the largest depreciation of the ringgit. It can also be seen from Figure 3 that foreign reserves had fallen at the time the country was trying to maintain the currency peg.

India experienced some of the fluctuations in the currency pressure index that affected the East Asian economies, but these were not as sharp as in the crisis-hit economies. The index did see some falls in November and December 1997 and later in June 1998 as evident

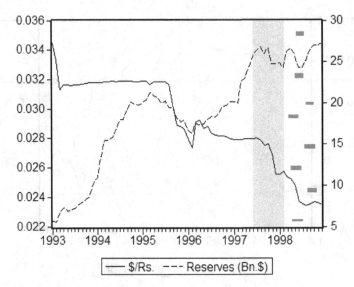

Figure 7. Exchange Rate and Foreign Exchange Reserves in India
Note: The light grey shaded region denotes the first sub-period of the crisis (July 1997 to February 1998). The dotted region is the second sub-period (March 1998 to December 1998).

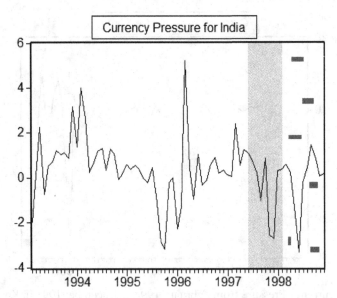

Figure 8. Index of Currency Pressure from February 1993 to December 1998 in India
Note: The light grey shaded region denotes the first sub-period of the crisis (July 1997 to February 1998). The dotted region is the second sub-period (March 1998 to December 1998).

from Figure 8. The largest depreciation of the rupee came in August 1998. It is interesting to note that the rupee appreciated marginally in July 1997, at a time when Thailand, South Korea and Malaysia experienced depreciation. From Figure 7, it can be seen that after the depreciation of the rupee, foreign reserves began to increase again.

Korea led a temporary turnaround in the Asian financial markets. As can be seen from Figures 5 and 6, the exchange rate and currency crisis measure recovered slightly after December 1997. By March 1998, however, the Asian financial markets suffered another setback, and the values of relevant variables (exchange rates, foreign reserves and currency crisis measure) worsened rapidly again. The renewed financial pressure began to abate about May/June 1998. The won began to stabilize, gaining against the US dollar, and was followed by other Asian currencies recovering.

By November 1998 and January 1999, Thailand and Korea were well on their way to recovery. In case of Malaysia, the ringgit had bottomed out by June 1998.

2.1. *Contagion effects*

The measure of currency pressure developed above is now used to analyze the contagion effects. From mid-August 1997, the contagion spread rapidly to other ASEAN economies and by October, its effects were felt outside this bloc of countries. The East Asian economies continued to feel the effects of contagion until December 1997 and January 1998.

In the first period, as seen in Figure 2, Thailand experienced significant currency pressure through all the three channels — money supply, foreign reserves and the exchange rate. The path of the currency pressure index is extremely volatile. Similarly, the index was volatile for Malaysia and Korea (Figures 4 and 6). However, it can be seen that India did not experience wild fluctuations in the currency pressure index (Figure 8).

Currency pressure in Thailand and Korea tapered off in the second sub-period. Malaysia, however, continued to experience a volatile index, even though the fluctuations were less extreme compared to the first part of the crisis period. This period did see more fluctuations in the index for India — both with respect to the other economies, as well as compared to the previous sub-period.

Dua and Sinha (2007) study the contagion effects of the East Asian crisis for Thailand, Korea, Malaysia and India using panel data analysis. As Thailand was where the crisis originated, it is treated as a case of currency pressure rather than contagion. Malaysia and Korea showed significant contagion effects between June 1997 and December 1998. However, India did not exhibit any such effects for the period.[4] GDP growth rates of the affected countries in the neighborhood of the crisis period shown in Table 4 illustrate India's relative insulation. The five crisis-hit East Asian countries (Thailand, Korea, Malaysia, Indonesia and Philippines) as well as India clocked GDP growth rates of over 6% in 1996. By 1998,

---

[4] A detailed analysis of the contagion effect is present in Dua and Sinha (2007). The contagion model is estimated using panel data for the four countries — India, Thailand, Korea and Malaysia — over the period June 1997 and December 1998 as follows:

$$CC_{it} = \alpha_{it} + \beta_{1i}m_{it} + \beta_{2i}res_{it} + \beta_{3i}e_{it} + u_{it},$$

where i is the index of countries and t is the time index in months. Three economic fundamentals are used to examine the contagion effect: m is the ratio of money supply, M3, to the index of industrial production (y); res is the ratio of foreign reserves to y; and e is the real exchange rate. The literature on contagion models expects CC to be negatively related to m and e, and positively related to res. The estimation results indicate that there was only weak contagion effect in India. This is in sharp contrast to the results of other countries.

Table 4. GDP Growth During the East
Asian Crisis Period

Country	GDP Growth Rate (%)		
	1996	1997	1998
Thailand	6	−1	−11
Malaysia	10	7	−7
Korea	7	5	−7
Indonesia	8	5	−13
Philippines	6	5	−1
India	7	4	6

Source: World Development Indicators.

the East Asian countries recorded negative growth rates, while India's growth rate remained robust.

3. India's Prelude to the East Asian Crisis

It is clear from Section 2 that there was very little contagion in India. As figures in Table 2 reiterate, India did not exhibit similar crisis indicators.

India had learnt from the lessons drawn from its own external crisis in 1991, several of which were reinforced by the Mexican peso crisis. In this section, we first present a brief overview of the Indian exchange rate experience. This is followed by a discussion of the exchange rate policies adopted by the central bank in the 1990s, many of which helped India to insulate itself from the East Asian crisis.

We begin with some background on India's economy leading to the liberalization measures. Preceding the first economic crisis in 1965–1967, which was a result of two successive droughts, independent India suffered a "quiet" balance of payments (BOP) crisis. Slow growths of agriculture and exports combined with the large investment demands of the third Five-Year Plan led to a balance of payments deficit that was contained using import controls. These were extremely severe and hampered both production and exports. Even before the crisis of 1965 was fully realized, there were already concerns about the low level of foreign reserves.

In June 1966, India experienced its first major devaluation, following the recommendations of the World Bank. Reserves had, by this time, hit rock bottom. In nominal terms, the devaluation was massive: from 4.76 to 7.5 rupees (36.5%) per US dollar. This was accompanied by other liberalization measures. Between 1965 and 1970, the balance of payments situation improved, despite large falls in the net foreign aid disbursed. Foreign reserves increased, reaching some of the highest levels seen in the past decade. However, reserves fell again in 1971.

The second macroeconomic crisis hit the country between 1973–1975. The balance of payments started to deteriorate in October 1973 as a result of oil price increases. Terms of trade worsened by 40% between 1972 and 1975, and the current account deficit increased from $455 million to $951 million during the same period. The fall in the current account occurred despite the increase in exports. However, a combination of policies ensured that the deficit fell to $91 million in 1975–1976.

The role of the exchange rate policy was also very important. Between December 1971 and September 1975, the rupee was pegged to the pound sterling. As the sterling was weak during this period, the rupee could depreciate with it, without setting off alarm bells. Thus, the fall in the nominal exchange rate from 1972 to mid-1975 was more than necessary to compensate for the high domestic inflation, and real exchange rate depreciated by about 10% (Joshi and Little, 1994). In September 1975, India switched to a multi-currency peg with undisclosed weights.

The crisis of 1979–1981 was similar to the previous one. The current account went from a surplus to a deficit of 26% in one year (between 1978–1979 and 1979–1980). The role of the government was significantly less interventionist during this third crisis compared to the previous ones. Inflation rose for close to three years, starting in 1979. The oil price shock pushed up import prices by approximately 50%. However, as there had been a large accumulation of foreign reserves at the beginning of the crisis, import controls did not need to be tightened. By 1981–1982, however, reserves had fallen by more than $2 billion. Even though the worsening terms of trade required its devaluation, the real effective exchange rate appreciated by approximately 15% between 1979 and 1981. As India's domestic inflation was higher than its trading partners, to stop the real exchange rate from appreciating would have required a devaluation of the nominal effective exchange rate in 1980. This was problematic since the rupee was pegged to an undisclosed basket of currencies and a devaluation would have required a change of peg or a devaluation by stealth (Joshi and Little, 1994). Moreover, at that time, a devaluation was a sensitive issue politically. Finally, a policy of devaluation by stealth was undertaken after 1982.

In 1983, the management of the exchange rate became more sophisticated. One of the positive developments was that the real exchange rate became the variable in focus, and the determination of the nominal exchange rate became less politicized. However, despite the current account adjustment in 1982–1984, current account deficit as a proportion of GDP increased sharply between 1985 and 1990. Additionally, exports stagnated towards the end of the 1980s decade due to the real exchange rate appreciation. Thus, the seeds of the 1991 crisis were sown in the previous decade.

3.1. *Crisis of 1990–1991*

The Indian economy experienced its most far-reaching balance of payments crisis in 1990–1991. The crisis was mainly due to a combination of internal weaknesses along with problems of the external sector. Within the economy, the main causes were excessive regulation of private industry and trade by the government, a weak financial system and high fiscal deficits. In the external sector, the primary contributing factor was an overvalued exchange rate. At the same time, two external shocks acted as a catalyst to push the economy into a crisis. First, the Gulf War caused oil prices to rise and increased the value of India's oil imports. The Gulf War also caused a sharp fall in the remittances from Indians in the

Gulf region, thus increasing the pressure on India's balance of payments. The global slow-down during this period exacerbated the crisis by causing a slowdown in the growth rate of India's export volumes. The result was a loss of investor confidence that resulted in a credit downgrade.

The government undertook a comprehensive plan to deal with the crisis, among which, one was to devalue the exchange rate and transform the system from a discretionary, basket-pegged system, to a market-determined, unified exchange rate, following a short intermediate period of dual rates.

3.2. *How the crisis built up*

At the end of the 1980s, domestic demand increased due to the drop in the volatility of the agricultural sector in 1989–1990 as well as the expansion in domestic credit creation. Government spending was very significant during this time, and the fiscal deficit rose to 10% of the GDP. Domestic inflation rate was over 12% and the current account deficit was increasing to about 3% of the GDP. In addition, by September 1990, the net capital inflows of Non-Resident Indians, which had been significant, turned negative. Access to short-term credit and commercial borrowings were extremely restricted and difficult. Thus, this time round, macroeconomic policy mismanagement played a much more central role. As India's creditworthiness was downgraded by international agencies, foreign investment dried up. India's foreign reserves reached one of the lowest levels in recent history — approximately US$1 billion, which was just enough for a two-week imports. The Reserve Bank of India (RBI) was forced to send gold to the Bank of England and the country was almost defaulting on its foreign liabilities. At this time, the government turned to the IMF for help.

Fiscal policy was extremely lax: the fiscal deficit increased from 8%–10% of the GDP between 1980 and 1989. In the 1970s, the fiscal deficit had averaged about 4.5%. Balance of payments worsened despite rapid growth in exports and a fall in oil prices. According to Joshi and Little (1994), the crisis of 1990 originated in the mismanaged policy decisions taken after the second oil shock. Real exchange rate appreciation resulted in stagnation in exports. Fiscal deterioration was unchecked and led to a worsening current account deficit, even as domestic and foreign debts increased rapidly.

Domestic demand pushed up the overall growth in the economy, but it had other adverse effects. The liberal trade regime made it difficult for the government to use traditional policies to control the burgeoning current account deficit. Therefore, the policy response hinged on using quantitative restrictions on imports. Other IMF-recommended policies included restricting domestic demand via reducing credit expansion and intense fiscal tightening. These resulted in dismal rates of growth: real GDP growth slowed down to less than 1%. The same period also saw a 19% devaluation of the rupee, backed with IMF credit.

Even though overall growth slowed down, the balance of payments situation improved dramatically. The deficit of 3.5% of the GDP in 1990–1991 fell to about 0.7% in 1991–1992. Foreign reserves increased to about $6 billion. In July 1991, the rupee was devalued by 18% and this became one of the first actions of the liberalization program.

3.3. *Liberalization of the Indian economy*

By 1991, an ambitious plan for the liberalization of the Indian economy was introduced by the new government. The aim was to liberalize markets and introduce greater market orientation into the system. The main policy measures aimed at reducing high fiscal deficit, controlling high inflation levels and regulating monetary policy further. Some of the reforms are discussed below.

3.3.1. *Financial sector reforms with market-determined interest rates*

The banking sector was one of the biggest beneficiaries of the reform program. The banking sector forms the largest part of the financial sector in India. More than 80% of the funds flowing through the financial sector are accounted for by the banks. In 1969, most major banks had been nationalized, and the share of private sector banks fell to about 11%. Bank activities such as setting interest rates and commercial borrowings were heavily regulated.

In the 1991 reform program, the policymakers gave considerable importance to the banking sector. At the time, investor and deposit protection was mostly non-existent, and the sector was plagued with low profitability. Some of the measures put in place were: financial and accounting statements of banks were made more transparent and aligned to international standards; the administrated interest rate structure was dismantled and most important interest rates such as the deposit rate were market-determined; criterion for determining Non-Performing Loans (NPL) was tightened and the 364-day Treasury bills and 5- and 10-year bonds were introduced by the government. Public sector banks were allowed to access the capital markets and the reduction of mandatory allocation of their credit to priority sectors improved profitability. There were also stringent, prudential limits on the exposure of financial intermediaries to stocks and real estate.

These reforms undertaken from 1991 through 1997 improved the financial soundness and credibility of banks, increased competitiveness within the system and made the institutional framework more resilient to crises.

3.3.2. *Monetary policy reforms and diversification of monetary instruments*

Prior to 1991, the main goal of monetary policy was to neutralize the impact of the fiscal deficits. Money supply was driven largely by the government resorting to central bank borrowing through automatic monetization and *ad hoc* bill issuance. Thus, there was a close link between fiscal and monetary policies. This was gradually phased out of the system with restraints on automatic monetization of budget deficits. There was also emphasis on the development of money and financial markets including those for government securities and bills. Open market operations were activated to impact liquidity and the central bank increasingly used the repo (repurchase agreements) rate as well as overnight call money intervention. The Bank Rate was also restored as a signaling instrument for monetary policy and there was a phased reduction in the reserve requirement ratios of the cash reserve ratio and the statutory liquidity requirement. As we shall see later, monetary policy was used actively during the crisis period to stabilize the volatility in the foreign exchange market.

3.3.3. *Capital account reforms with reasonable degree of capital control*

Although wide-ranging measures were taken in the financial sector, the role of the central bank, and monetary and fiscal policies, the government remained cautious about full capital account convertibility. Foreign direct investment (FDI) was allowed into the country only after 1991. The current account was made fully convertible in August 1994, following the IMF program. Further deregulation measures were adopted by the RBI following the slowdown of foreign capital after the Mexican crisis. Despite significant liberalization measures, restrictions remained. We briefly discuss the specific capital controls imposed in India as well as their selective relaxation.

Before 1991–1992, FDI was controlled on a case-by-case basis and was therefore reduced to a trickle. In the liberalization program, automatic approval of foreign investment for up to 51% of shareholding was allowed for a wide range of industries. By 1996, the number of industries where FDI was allowed was expanded considerably, and in some cases, foreign equity of up to 74% was allowed.

Prior to the reform measures of 1991–1992, foreign portfolio investment was mostly not allowed. In 1992, some foreign institutional investors (FIIs) such as pension funds and mutual funds were permitted to invest in listed securities in the primary and secondary markets in equities and bonds. By 1997, the FIIs could invest in government securities and Treasury bills as well. Capital income and capital gains could also be repatriated at the market exchange rate.

Several other kinds of capital controls did not see much relaxation. Offshore borrowing by Indian companies continued to be controlled on a case-by-case basis by the government. An overall annual ceiling for external commercial borrowing was also maintained. Commercial banks were not allowed to maintain deposits or make loans in foreign currencies. Their foreign assets and liabilities were also strictly controlled. Thus, overall, the internationalization of the rupee was strictly controlled. Offshore trading of the rupee was prohibited. Policy was generally directed towards limiting forward trading in the foreign exchange to hedging current account transactions. Thus, the forward market lacked depth and was liquidity-deficient. In fact, all of these controls on capital market liberalization helped to insulate India from the East Asian crisis.

3.3.4. *Reform towards greater exchange rate flexibility*

The RBI undertook policies to move towards a market-determined exchange rate system along with the liberalization measures discussed above. This was a marked contrast from the pegged regime before. As shown in Table 5, India had put in place a rupee exchange rate system whereby the currency was pegged against a basket of international currencies. In the early 1990s, amongst the several measures taken to tide over the crisis was a devaluation of the rupee in July 1991 to maintain the competitiveness of Indian exports. This initiated the move towards greater exchange rate flexibility. A liberalized exchange rate management system (LERMS) was put in place in March 1992 along with other measures to liberalize trade, industry and foreign investment. This made the rupee partially convertible on the current account through a dual exchange rate.

Table 5. Chronology of the Indian Exchange Rate

Year	The Foreign Exchange Rate Market and Exchange Rate
1947–1971	Par Value system of exchange rate. Rupee's external par value was fixed in terms of gold with the pound sterling as the intervention currency.
1971	Breakdown of the Bretton Woods system and floatation of major currencies. Rupee was linked to the pound sterling in December 1971.
1975	To ensure stability of the rupee, and avoid the weaknesses associated with a single currency peg, the rupee was pegged to a basket of currencies. Currency selection and weight assignment was left to the discretion of the RBI and not publicly announced.
1978	RBI allowed the domestic banks to undertake intra-day trading in foreign exchange.
1978–1992	Banks began to start quoting two-way prices against the rupee as well as in other currencies. As trading volumes increased, the "Guidelines for Internal Control over Foreign Exchange Business" were framed in 1981. The foreign exchange market was still highly regulated with several restrictions on external transactions, entry barriers and transactions costs. Foreign exchange transactions were controlled through the Foreign Exchange Regulations Act (FERA). These restrictions resulted in an extremely efficient unofficial parallel (*hawala*) market for foreign exchange.
1990–1991	Balance of Payments crisis (see above).
July 1991	To stabilize the exchange rate market, a two-step downward exchange rate adjustment was done (9% and 11%). This was a decisive end to the pegged exchange rate regime.
March 1992	To ease the transition to a market-determined exchange rate system, the Liberalized Exchange Rate Management System (LERMS) was put in place, which used a dual exchange rate system. This was mostly a transitional system.
March 1993	The dual rates converged, and the market-determined exchange rate regime was introduced. All foreign exchange receipts could now be converted at market-determined exchange rates.

Source: Reserve Bank of India.

In March 1993, India switched over to a unified market-determined exchange rate system from the existing dual rate regime. Since 1993, the exchange rate has exhibited fluctuations that have been more severe during the crisis period. For instance, it depreciated by 6.31% between July 1997 and March 1998 and by approximately 11% from July 1997 to December 1998 (Table 3). Foreign currency reserves fell from $29 billion to $26.77 billion between July 1997 and June 1998. But by December 1998, reserves increased to $29.83 billion.

As the capital account was liberalized and capital inflows increased, there was increasing pressure on the rupee to appreciate. To prevent a decline in competitiveness due to this, the RBI purchased some of these inflows and added them to the foreign reserves. The subsequent increase in reserves led to an extended period of stability of the currency.

Until July 1995, the exchange rate markets were fairly stable. As the capital account was liberalized, capital inflows increased enormously during this period. Foreign currency assets of the RBI increased from US$6.4 billion to US$20.8 billion between March 1993 and March 1995. This helped in maintaining the stability of the rupee.

Between August 1995 and March 1996, a change in international capital flows following the Mexican crisis, a rise in the current account deficit, and an appreciation of the US dollar put pressure on the rupee, ending the previous phase of stability. The size and frequency of direct interventions by the RBI increased during this time (see below).

In the period immediately preceding the East Asian crisis (April 1996 to mid-August 1997), the foreign exchange market regained most of its previous stability. Capital flows and reserves also reached their previous levels.

The East Asian crisis and the subsequent contagion effects had significant effects on the Indian foreign exchange rate market. For instance, the rupee depreciated by over 9% between June 1997 and December 1997 and by approximately 19% from June 1997 to December 1998 (Table 3). Foreign currency reserves fell between July 1997 and June 1998, but reversed by December 1998. These effects were, however, small compared to the corresponding changes in Thailand, South Korea and Malaysia as indicated in Table 3.

4. How Did India Insulate Herself from the East Asian Crisis?

Some of the factors that helped to insulate India relatively from the crisis include the following: (1) India's progression towards a flexible exchange rate with timely exchange market intervention and implementation of monetary policy measures by the central bank; (2) limited capital liberalization with restrictions on capital flows; (3) financial reforms towards strengthening the institutional framework, improving transparency and imposing prudential limits on exposure to real estate and stocks; and (4) India's weak trade linkages with the crisis-hit East Asian economies. The liberalization program undertaken after the BOP crisis in 1990–1991 also contributed towards ensuring strong macroeconomic fundamentals in the Indian economy.

While the crisis-hit East Asian countries also exhibited strong macroeconomic fundamentals before the crisis, a stark difference between India and the five Asian economies is that capital flows (including portfolio equity investment) into these economies were large and variable. The juxtaposition of high private credit and volatile capital flows in response to opportunities for profits leading to asset price inflation fueled the crisis.

Nevertheless, although India was relatively closed in terms of capital liberalization, it was not totally immune from the crisis. Some of the policy measures that provided support to India during the crisis period are explained below. The intervention policy adopted by the central bank is described in detail followed by a brief discussion on monetary policy measures and capital controls.

4.1. *Intervention by the RBI*

Since August 1994, the rupee has been convertible on the current account and the process of integration of the Indian financial market with the rest of the world has been underway. Capital account convertibility is allowed for foreigners, foreign-based corporate and non-resident Indians. Several types of exchange controls have been dismantled and the Indian rupee is no longer pegged. The RBI, however, continues to follow a policy of managed float. The managed float of the rupee has two objectives — to foster international competitiveness and to limit daily market volatility.

The exchange rate regime can be interpreted as "more flexible" during normal market conditions, and "managed" when chaos prevails. In the former case, exchange rate changes may be viewed as "passive", while in the latter case, central bank's intervention is "active". The objective behind the passive exchange rate changes is to avoid persistent misalignment, whereas in the case of active intervention, the objective is to avoid disruptive market corrections. During the phases of active intervention, measures of "leaning against the wind" may be applied, while "leaning with the wind" would be the theme of the passive episode. Intervention is used for several reasons: evening out the volatility of the exchange rate and correcting the misalignment in relation to fundamentals, as well as to prevent depreciation of the rupee and keep it along the desired macroeconomic path.

We use the empirical observations on intervention and exchange rate volatility to show that the Bank was generally averse to excessive fluctuations of the exchange rate during the crisis, and took measures to moderate the movements in the case of volatility in the foreign exchange market. The high correlation between volatility and monthly changes can be easily seen from Figure 9, which shows the level of RBI intervention during the East Asian crisis period as measured by sales and purchases of the US dollar. Gross intervention is the sum of purchases and sales of the US dollar, irrespective of the sign. Net intervention is the same, except that the sum takes account of the signs. The monthly percentage changes and volatility[5] of the exchange rate is plotted in Figure 10. Using Figures 9 and 10, we note the close association between the Bank's intervention and the volatility of the exchange rate — higher level of intervention in January 1998 was used in view of the significantly higher volatility of the rupee–dollar exchange rate between November–December 1997. High volatility between May–July 1998 resulted in the second major spike in intervention activity between July and September 1998. Thus, the RBI used its intervention strategy

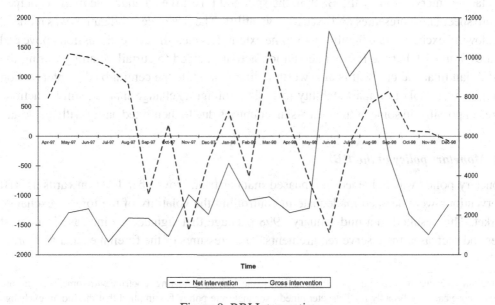

Figure 9. RBI Intervention

---

[5]Volatility is measured by the moving three-month standard deviation of the exchange rate.

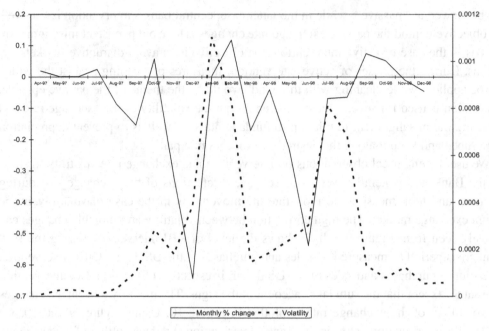

Figure 10. Exchange Rate Monthly Changes and Volatility

to temper the volatility of the exchange rate following periods of large fluctuations in the exchange rate during the crisis period.[6]

This intervention strategy thus played an important stabilizing role during the crisis. Substantial intervention by the Bank in the spot and forward exchange rate markets helped to curb speculative pressures and excessive volatility. The risk of destabilization was reduced by allowing exchange rate flexibility to some extent. It is clear from the discussion above and Figures 9 and 10 that the RBI's intervention activity helped to curtail volatility during the East Asian financial crisis. It is also worth noting that while the central bank's intervention activities were able to impart stability to India's foreign exchange market, similar actions were not possible in some of the East Asian countries due to their fixed parity with the dollar.

4.2. *Monetary policy of the RBI*

Monetary policy was tightened in a phased manner from November 1997 onwards as RBI interventions were deemed inadequate in controlling the volatility of the foreign exchange market. This resulted in a mid-January 1998 package that signaled an increase in interest rates and increased the reserve requirements. The pressures of the foreign exchange market

---

[6]In the current exchange rate regime, the bank adheres to the "managed floating" doctrine with some intervention. Over recent years, the broadly market-determined exchange rate policy has implied that the Indian exchange rate has demonstrated adequate flexibility against major world currencies. The central bank has been selling and buying US dollars in the foreign exchange market to reduce volatility caused by the demand-supply mismatch. It is important to note, however, that such interventions are not to maintain the exchange rate in any predetermined band. In recent years, as capital movements have increased, the exchange rate has become more volatile.

Table 6. Share of East Asian Countries in India's
Exports and Imports

Country	Exports (%)	Imports (%)
Thailand	1.03	0.90
Malaysia	1.12	1.79
Korea	1.77	3.25
Indonesia	1.33	2.20
Philippines	0.48	0.15

Source: Centre for Monitoring Indian Economy, *Monthly Review*.

Note: Figures are for 2005–2006 fiscal year.

forced the RBI to resort to the "announcement effects" of the Cash Reserve Ratio (CRR), despite its previous commitment to use Open Market Operations (OMO) as the preferred indirect instrument of monetary policy. Other than the CRR and repurchase operations, the RBI also used export credit and surcharges on import finance. The program of reducing the CRR was deferred to the future in November 1997. Additionally, a fixed repo rate of 4.5% was introduced to absorb surplus liquidity. In December 1997 and January 1998, the CRR was increased by 1%. Similarly, the interest rates on repos were further increased: first to 5% and then further to 9%. The reverse repo facility was made available to Primary Dealers in Government Securities market at the Bank Rate on a discretionary basis. The Bank rate rose from 9% to 11% in January 1998. In April 1998, the monetary measures were eased and the CRR was reduced to its pre-crisis levels. Interest rate on fixed repos was reduced to 7% and later to 6%. Monetary policy was tightened again in August 1998 (Acharya, 2006). As a result of these measures, the rupee began to stabilize and market expectations of further depreciation were reversed.

4.3. *Trade linkages with East Asian countries*

India's relative isolation from the contagion effects of the East Asian crisis can also be explained by her weak trade linkages with the other affected countries. Exports of 10 major East Asian countries (Thailand, Malaysia, Korea, Indonesia, Philippines, China, Hong Kong, Singapore, Japan and Taiwan) amongst themselves account for about 50% of their total exports. Trade ties are thus strong. However, as can be seen from Table 6,[7] the East Asian economies affected by the crisis account for only a small portion of India's foreign trade.

4.4. *Restrictions on capital flows*

Traditionally, there have been two kinds of capital controls: (1) targeted measures to regulate short-term inflows and outflows, and (2) pervasive restrictions on all sorts of capital transactions.

---

[7]Ratios are indicative of trade for the past few years.

Targeted measures include unremunerated reserve requirements, limits on open currency positions, taxes on cross-border flows and quantitative restrictions on portfolio transactions.[8] These kinds of measures are usually used in episodes of "overheated" portfolio inflows, or large capital outflows in a crisis period, when there are concerns about the effect of such flows on domestic interest rates and money growth.

Pervasive restrictions have usually been used to allow full use of domestic resources, without worrying about external volatility and influence. These include prohibitions on capital inflows and outflows, requiring approval for capital transactions, multiple exchange rate regimes, and often, current account restrictions. These kinds of measures were present in India before and during the East Asian crisis and helped to limit the contagion effect of the East Asian financial crisis in India.

5. Conclusions

This paper analyzes the effect of the East Asian financial crisis on the Indian exchange rate movements *vis-à-vis* those of the three other affected countries. Active intervention by the Reserve Bank of India, controls on capital flows, weak trade linkages, financial sector reforms and strong macroeconomic fundamentals helped India to be relatively immune from the East Asian crisis. Before the onset of the crisis, unlike the other afflicted East Asian countries, India was also able to keep short-term debt under control in relation to foreign reserves and total debt. This in turn enabled India to avoid an unstable debt structure. This was a direct result of controls on debt-creating short-term inflows.

Financial markets in India also saw a paradigm shift. In the pre-liberalization era, they were characterized by administered interest rates, quantitative ceilings, captive markets for government securities, pegged exchange rate, current and capital account restrictions. Various reforms have ensured that the markets have made the transition to a regime of market-determined interest and exchange rates, price-based instruments of monetary policy, current account convertibility and phased liberalization of the capital account.

While India was able to insulate herself from the East Asian crisis to a large extent, the imperative question a decade after the East Asian crisis is whether India is equipped to avert any future crises. As India moves towards greater integration with the global economy, several lessons from her own 1990–1991 crisis, the Latin American crisis as well as the East Asian crisis have been learnt. These include the importance of ensuring prudential norms in the financial and banking sectors, reducing the exposure of the financial sector to speculative markets including real estate and stocks; maintaining fiscal stringency; keeping external debt and the current account deficit at a low level; reducing volatility in the foreign exchange markets; as well as ensuring stability in capital flows.

To better understand the current state of the Indian economy, we examine first, the macroeconomic fundamentals of the economy, and second, the exposure of the economy to foreign capital inflows.

---

[8] Among the East Asian countries, Thailand and Malaysia are good examples of countries that used targeted measures during the 1997 crisis. Both economies have been fairly open to portfolio capital flows.

Table 7. Indian Economy — Key Variables

	External Indicators									
	1990–1991	1995–1996	1996–1997	1997–1998	1998–1999	1999–2000	2000–2001	2003–2004	2004–2005	2005–2006
Trade Balance*	14.6	21.5	18.8	18.7	18.3	19.4	22.4	24.3	29.3	32.9
Exports*	5.8	9.1	8.7	8.5	8.0	8.2	9.9	11	12.2	13.2
Imports *	8.8	12.4	10.2	10.1	10.2	11.1	12.5	13.3	17.1	19.7
Current Account Deficit*	−3.1	−2.7	−1.2	−1.4	−1.0	−1.0	−0.8	2.6	−0.4	−1.3
REER	99.98	100.97	98.95	103.07	94.34	95.28	99.3	99.04	99.68	102.27
NEER	88.04	89.09	89.03	91.97	90.34	90.42	88.48	88	90.5	88.96
Exchange Rate: Re/$	17.94	35.69	35.49	37.16	42.07	43.33	47.07	45.6	44.63	45.29
Foreign Exchange Reserves (billion $)	5.8	21.7	26.4	29.3	32.5	38	42.3	113	141.5	151.6
External Debt*	28.7	26.2	23.4	22.1	21.2	21.2	20.5	19.6	18.1	15.8

	Key Economic Indicators									
	1990–1991	1995–1996	1996–1997	1997–1998	1998–1999	1999–2000	2000–2001	2003–2004	2004–2005	2005–2006
Real GDP Growth	5.6	7.3	7.8	4.8	6.5	6.1	4.4	7.5	8.5	9
Saving*	23.1	25.1	23.2	23.1	21.5	24.2	23.4	29.7	31.1	32.4
Investment*	26.3	26.9	24.5	24.6	22.6	25.3	24	28	31.5	33.8
Fiscal Deficit (of Center and State)*	9.4	6.5	6.4	7.3	9.0	9.5	9.4	8.5	7.5	7.4
Inflation (WPI)**	—	8.0	4.6	4.4	5.9	3.3	7.2	5.5	6.4	4.4

Source: Reserve Bank of India, *Handbook of Statistics; Economic Survey, 2007*.
*Expressed as % of GDP; **WPI for All Commodities with 1993–1994 as base year.

India's current macroeconomic fundamentals are shown in Table 7. These show that India's macroeconomic fundamentals should be able to hold it in good stead in the years to come. The growth indicators show that the GDP growth approximately doubled between 1990–1991 and 2005–2006. The rate of GDP growth rose from about 3% in the 1950–1980 period to 6% in the 1980s and 1990s. In the last four years, between 2003 and 2007, the economy grew at 8.5% on average. Thus, there is tangible evidence of self-accelerating growth. The ratios of savings and investment to GDP have grown and inflation has been kept in check. Prices have been mostly stable. In line with the growing economy, the share of agriculture in GDP has also reduced to 20% from 40% in the 1970s, while the services sector is burgeoning to 60%.

The fiscal position of the government has also improved considerably. The deficit of the central and state governments reached unprecedented levels after the 1990–1991 crisis. Since then, efforts have been made to control this. Under the Fiscal Responsibility and Budget Management Act of 2003, the government intends to reduce the ratio of the gross fiscal deficit to GDP to 3%.

Trade in goods (exports plus imports) as a percentage of GDP has increased from 14.6% in 1990–1991 to 32.9% in 2005–2006. Exports have grown from 5.8% of GDP in 1990–1991 to 13.2% in 2005–2006, while imports have risen from 8.8% to 19.7% over the same period. Current account deficit has decreased over the years, showing the buoyant trade in services as well as remittances. On the other hand, foreign exchange reserves have seen a quantum jump from US$5.8 billion in 1990–1991 to US$151.6 billion in 2005–2006, reflecting the comfortable external position of the Indian economy.

The Indian economy also experienced a large increase in net capital flows following the introduction of reforms in the 1990s. Net capital inflows more than doubled from an average of US$4 billion in the 1980s to an average of approximately US$9 billion during 1993–2000. The proportion of non-debt flows in total capital flows increased from 5% in the second part of 1980s to 43% during 1990s and further to about 70% in 2000–2006. Table 8 shows the details of the division between non-debt and debt-creating flows.

As shown in Table 8, within non-debt-creating flows, the proportion of portfolio investment in total capital flows was more than 50% in 2003–2004 to 2005–2006, up from 28% in

Table 8. Composition of Capital Inflows to India

	1990–1991	1995–1996	1996–1997	1997–1998	1998–1999	1999–2000	2000–2001	2003–2004	2004–2005	2005–2006
Total Capital Inflows (Net) (US$ billion)	7.1	4.1	12	9.8	8.4	10.4	10	17.3	28.6	24.2
Composition of Capital Flows (% to Total)										
1. Non-debt-creating inflows	1.5	117.5	51.3	54.8	28.6	49.7	67.8	93.7	54.6	86.1
a. Foreign direct investment	1.4	52.4	23.7	36.2	29.4	20.7	40.2	25.8	21.4	32.7
b. Portfolio investment	0.1	65.1	27.6	18.6	−0.8	29	27.6	67.9	33.2	53.7
2. Debt-creating inflows*	83.3	57.7	61.7	52.4	54.4	23.1	59.4	−6.0	35.2	37.0
3. Other capital	15.2	−75.2	−13	−7.2	17	27.2	−27.2	12.3	10.2	−23.1
4. Total (1 to 3)	100	100	100	100	100	100	100	100	100	100

*Debt-creating inflows include the following: external assistance; external commercial borrowings; short-term credit; non-resident Indian deposits; and rupee debt service.

1990–1991 to 1996–1997 and 18% in 1997–1998 to 2002–2003. This temporary drop in the 1997–1998 through 2002–2003 period was possibly due to the East Asian crisis as reflected in the data given in Table 8. The rise in the proportion of portfolio investment has also imparted increased volatility to the total capital flows, which in turn increases the volatility of the exchange rate. While the RBI has been playing an important role in the stabilization of capital flows via sterilization activities, with increased capital liberalization and global integration, India is now exposed to the volatility of foreign capital flows and, in general, that of the international financial environment.

Thus, despite the strong economic fundamentals, a sound financial architecture and active intervention by the central bank, a decade after the East Asian crisis, it is difficult to predict if India will be able to avert financial crises in the future. Due to the increase in the openness of the economy, India is now more vulnerable to external shocks than it was a decade ago. The key issue is that financial contagion is difficult to anticipate, especially since, to some extent, it depends on investor confidence, market sentiment and trust in financial markets, institutions as well as policy measures. With a change in confidence, Keynes' "animal spirits" may come into play that can make investors susceptible to herd behavior and speculative bubbles that can turn out to be self-fulfilling.

References

Acharya, S (2006). Managing India's external economic challenges in the 1990s. In *Essays on Macroeconomic Policy and Growth in India*, pp. 124–154. New Delhi: Oxford University Press.

Desai, P (2003). *Financial Crisis, Contagion and Containment: From Asia to Argentina*. New Jersey: Princeton University Press.

Dua, P and A Sinha (2007). East Asian crisis and currency pressure: The case of India. Centre for Development Economics, Delhi School of Economics, Working Paper No. 158.

Eichengreen, B, R Hausman and U Panizza (2003). Currency mismatches, debt intolerance and original sin: Why they are not the same and why it matters. NBER Working Paper No. 10036.

Fratzcher, M (1998). Why are currency crisis contagious? *Weltwirtschaftliches Archiv*, 134(4), 664–691.

Joshi, V and IMD Little (eds.) (1994). *India: Macroeconomics and Political Economy, 1964–1991*. New York: Oxford University Press.

Radelet, S and J Sachs (1998). The onset of the East Asian financial crisis. NBER Working Paper No. 6680.

Reserve Bank of India (2005–2006). *Report on Currency and Finance, 2005–2006*.

SINGAPORE'S EXCHANGE RATE POLICY: SOME IMPLEMENTATION ISSUES

HWEE-KWAN CHOW

School of Economics, Singapore Management University
90 Stamford Road, Singapore 178903
hkchow@smu.edu.sg

Reflecting the small open nature of its economy, Singapore has adopted an exchange rate-centered monetary policy framework since 1981. The exchange rate regime in Singapore is an intermediate regime that follows the basket-band-crawl system. With this managed float system, the MAS has successfully deterred speculators from attacking the domestic currency for most of the past three decades. At the same time, the flexibility accorded by the managed float system aided Singapore in escaping from the 1997–1998 Asian crisis relatively unscathed. In order to advance our understanding of the hitherto successful operation of Singapore's exchange rate policy, we examine the following three aspects of its implementation: (i) the use of the exchange rate instead of the interest rate as the key monetary policy instrument; (ii) the management of the currency basket in terms of foreign exchange intervention operations; and (iii) regulating the level of domestic liquidity alongside exchange rate policy. This paper also provides some insights on the challenges ahead that potentially face policymakers when implementing Singapore's exchange rate policy.

Keywords: Exchange rate targeting; intervention operations; domestic liquidity.

1. Background

When the Monetary Authority of Singapore (MAS) was first established in 1971, Singapore operated a currency board system. With the collapse of the Bretton Woods system in the early 1970s, instabilities in the world currencies led Singapore to develop its own exchange rate policy framework. The Singapore dollar has officially been on a managed float by the MAS since June 1973. By 1981, an exchange rate-centered monetary policy framework had been adopted.

In view of its small and open nature, it is not surprising that the exchange rate plays a key role in the Singaporean economy. Singapore's high degree of openness to trade is captured by its trade to GDP ratio. The size of total imports and exports has been approximately three times that of GDP over the past three decades. In relation to capital flows, almost all forms of capital restrictions and foreign exchange controls have been eradicated since 1978. Even the restrictions on the non-internationalization of the Singapore dollar, imposed to deter currency speculation, have been progressively removed over the years to facilitate the development of Singapore's capital markets. As a major financial center, Singapore has free capital mobility.

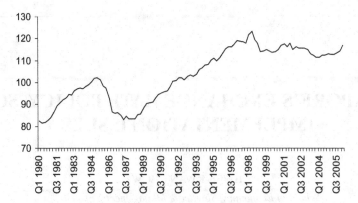

Figure 1. Singapore's Nominal Effective Exchange Rate
Source: International Financial Statistics.

Countries with an export-led growth strategy would typically maintain a low international value of their domestic currency to prevent a loss of competitiveness (Calvo *et al.*, 1995). However, despite its openness and reliance on export growth, Singapore maintains a strong Singapore dollar policy. Figure 1 depicts a time series of Singapore's nominal effective exchange rate (NEER).[1] The exchange rate variable has been defined such that a rise in its value signals an appreciation of the Singapore dollar. It is clear from the secular upward trend in Figure 1 that the Singapore dollar has been appreciating against its major trading partners over the past three decades. Key considerations behind the strong Singapore dollar policy are the desire to maintain confidence in the domestic currency and to ensure price stability. After all, liberalized capital flows and a stable currency are important requirements for Singapore's role as an international financial center and the development of a large offshore banking sector.

Although the exchange rate has not been used to safeguard competitiveness, Singapore's exports continue to exhibit robust growth. In other words, Singapore's competitiveness does not seem to have been compromised by the strong Singapore dollar policy (Abeysinghe and Wilson, 2002). Yip and Wang (2001) and Yip (2002) also found no empirical evidence of a long-run tradeoff, but only a short-run tradeoff, between Singapore dollar appreciation and export competitiveness. A plausible explanation for this is that the appreciation of the Singapore dollar was accompanied by lower inflation, leaving Singapore's relative price competitiveness unaffected by the appreciation. Meanwhile, the secular appreciation of the domestic currency has the advantageous effect of pushing Singaporean companies to move up the value chain to focus on higher value-added industries. Hence, compared with some other East Asian countries, Singapore's exports tend to be more technology-, skill- and capital-intensive. This, as well as Singapore's more moderate inflation, enables Singapore to maintain its international competitiveness despite the secular rise of its nominal exchange rate and the quasi-fixed exchange rate systems of some other regional countries.

---

[1]The NEER series has been computed by the IMF based on recently updated trade weights (Bayoumi *et al.*, 2006).

The MAS adopts an intermediate exchange rate regime by managing the Singapore dollar under a basket-band-crawl (BBC) system (Khor *et al.*, 2004; Williamson, 1999). Under this managed float system, the Singapore dollar is related to a trade-weighted basket of currencies of its major trading partners and competitors. Additionally, the domestic currency is (more than) fully backed by Singapore's foreign reserves. With the exception of the Asian crisis period, the MAS has successfully deterred speculators from attacking the domestic currency over the past three decades. Even during the crisis period, the flexibility accorded by the managed float system aided Singapore in escaping from the crisis relatively unscathed.

Unlike the crisis economies which initially defended their currencies, Singapore's acceptance of market-driven depreciations at the wake of and amid the deepening crisis could have deterred currency speculators from engineering overdepreciation in the domestic currency (Yip, 2005). The immediate depreciations brought about a sufficiently depreciated Singapore dollar that would have lowered the benefit of further speculation. This also alleviated the need for a steep interest rate hike that was crucial during speculative attacks in Hong Kong.[2] Of course, Singapore's substantial amount of foreign reserves played a critical role in deterring speculative attacks. Further, strong economic fundamentals such as consistent fiscal surpluses, large current account surpluses, maintenance of stable and consistent macroeconomic policies, and a robust financial system are important reasons why Singapore was relatively less affected by the Asian crisis.

After the weakening of the currency during the crisis, the value of the Singapore dollar leveled off in the post-crisis period (see Figure 1). As the managed float system had served Singapore well, the central bank continues to manage the Singapore dollar under the BBC system. Meanwhile, the region's exchange rate regimes have become more diverse after the crisis. The crisis countries of Indonesia, (South) Korea, Philippines and Thailand have adopted greater flexibility in their exchange rate management. By contrast, Malaysia and China maintained a rigid US dollar peg until July 2005, after which both announced a shift in their exchange rate regimes to a basket peg and a managed float respectively.

In order to advance our understanding of the hitherto successful operation of Singapore's exchange rate system, we examine three distinct aspects of its implementation. Specifically, this paper addresses the following issues: first, the use of the exchange rate instead of the interest rate as the key monetary policy instrument; second, the management of a currency basket in terms of foreign exchange intervention operations; and third, regulating the level of domestic liquidity alongside exchange rate policy. The balance of this paper is organized as follows. In the next section, we discuss the choice between the exchange rate *vis-à-vis* the interest rate as an intermediate target for monetary policy. Section 3 describes the intervention operations that arise when managing the currency basket. Domestic liquidity considerations in relation to foreign exchange interventions are examined in Section 4. We conclude with some comments on the challenges ahead for operating Singapore's exchange rate system.

---

[2]Nevertheless, monetary conditions in Singapore did tighten, with the domestic 3-month interbank rate rising from an average of 3.3% before the crisis to a high of 9.3% in January 1998.

2. The Exchange Rate as Monetary Policy Instrument

With the Singapore economy being buffeted by recurrent shocks from the external environment, the primary role of monetary policy is to react to cyclical fluctuations in inflation and output in order to compensate, at least partially, for the impact of exogenous shocks.[3] However, for a small open economy like Singapore, it is not feasible to operate an independent monetary policy under a fixed exchange rate. With reference to the open economy trilemma, monetary policy can only fully achieve two of the following three dimensions: monetary policy independence, fixed exchange rates, and open capital accounts. (See Obstfeld *et al.*, 2004 for a treatise on the open economy trilemma.) Given that Singapore has chosen free capital mobility, it can only choose to target either the exchange rate or one monetary variable, but not both.

The policymakers' inability to control interest rates, exchange rates, and maintain an open capital account simultaneously means that the central bank has to choose between interest rate targeting *vis-à-vis* exchange rate targeting. The MAS has chosen to use the exchange rate as opposed to the more conventional benchmark policy interest rate as its policy-operating tool since the early 1980s (MAS, 2000). It is the use of the exchange rate as an intermediate target that contributes to the unique nature of monetary policy in Singapore. The rationale of this decision is revealed when we consider the structure of the Singaporean economy as well as its monetary transmission mechanism. Firstly, Singapore is highly dependent on external demand, which constitutes two-thirds of aggregate demand. Secondly, domestic consumption has a high import content — out of every Singapore dollar spent in Singapore, about 50 cents go to imports. Being a price-taker in the international markets, it follows that Singapore is highly susceptible to imported inflation. Hence, the highly open and trade-dependent nature of the economy implies that the exchange rate is the most effective tool for controlling inflation.

By comparison, the Singapore economy is less interest rate sensitive, notwithstanding its status as a financial hub. Figure 2 provides a schematic illustration of the interactions amongst the key macroeconomic variables as a monetary policy shock is propagated through the Singapore economy. Chow (2005) provides a detailed description of Singapore's monetary transmission mechanism. In that study, the findings from a vector autoregressive analysis suggest that the exchange rate is more influential than the interest rate as a source of macroeconomic fluctuations. In fact, the interest rate does not even appear to be an important channel for transmitting the effects of exchange rate changes to the real economy.

Such a result is not in the least unexpected, given that domestic investment is not particularly sensitive to the interest rate because Singapore's heavy reliance on foreign direct investment limits the impact of the cost of domestic borrowing. As for domestic consumption, houses are a major component of personal wealth in Singapore, but a decline in housing wealth — plausibly caused by a rise in mortgage rates — does not seem to have significant dampening effects on aggregate consumption (Abeysinghe and Choy, 2004). This rather

---

[3]Parrado (2004) uses a monetary reaction function to show the counter-cyclicality of Singapore's monetary policy.

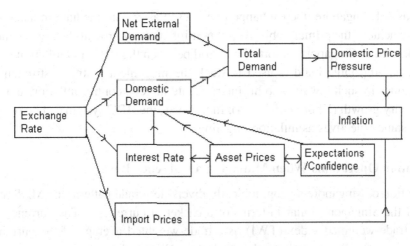

Figure 2. Monetary Transmission Mechanism
Note: This diagram is modified from MAS (1999)
and for simplicity, does not show all interactions
between variables.

unusual finding has been attributed to the illiquid nature of Singapore's housing assets as well as the strong bequest motives of Singaporean households (Phang, 2004).

The choice between exchange rate targeting and interest rate targeting is also an important issue for the regional countries. The Asian crisis has prompted the central banks in East Asia to shift their focus from exchange rate stability to price stability. In particular, the crisis-hit countries like Indonesia, Korea, Philippines and Thailand announced the explicit adoption of inflation targeting and the move towards using interest rates as the key monetary policy instrument. After all, the nearly pegged exchange rates and their attendant insurance effect exacerbated the boom-bust cycles associated with capital flows, thereby contributing to the crisis (Corsetti *et al.*, 1999). However, unless capital controls are imposed, the open economy trilemma dictates that those countries that adopt inflation targeting would tend to have a freely floating exchange rate regime as well.

In view of the openness of these regional economies, an increase in exchange rate volatility will have adverse effects on their financial stability as well as their current account position. More importantly, the central banks of these countries will find it a challenge to meet the inflation target when there are large exchange rate movements. Ho and McCauley (2003) found that an appreciation (depreciation) of at least 10% tends to be associated with an inflation target undershoot (overshoot). Hence, notwithstanding the adoption of inflation targeting, there is a need to pay attention to exchange rate stability. In fact, international reserves in East Asia are rising significantly, suggesting active interventions in the foreign exchange markets to moderate the appreciation of domestic currencies. In practice, a number of East Asian economies have not completely lifted capital controls but have maintained a managed float after the crisis (Reinhart and Rogoff, 2001). In other words, regional central banks continued to place emphasis on the management of exchange rates within their monetary policy frameworks.

In the case of Singapore, the exchange rate is used as an intermediate monetary policy instrument to achieve the primary objective of non-inflationary growth. In a sense, monetary policy is operated in Singapore as sort of a hybrid between the BBC and inflation targeting. In practice, an adjustable band is used to track the movement of this instrument, while setting its values in such a way as to hit intermediate targets, control inflation and achieve non-inflationary growth (Khor *et al.*, 2004). In this way, the BBC system can be operated to achieve the same objectives as inflation targeting.

3. Intervention Operations When Managing a Currency Basket

In consideration of Singapore's geographically diversified trade pattern, the MAS monitors the value of the Singapore dollar in terms of a basket of currencies. The currency basket, termed the trade-weighted index (TWI), is a trade-weighted average of the currencies of Singapore's major trading partners and competitors. Neither the component currencies nor their assigned weights in the basket are disclosed by the MAS. The band is centered at a parity which is the target exchange rate for the TWI. This target rate is reflective of the long-run equilibrium exchange rate[4] and is allowed to crawl over time. Such periodic adjustments in small steps keep the band in line with Singapore's long-term economic fundamentals. This circumvents the emergence of a situation where the Singapore dollar becomes significantly overvalued or undervalued, which would leave the currency vulnerable to speculative attacks.

The MAS uses a prescribed policy band in its monetary policy operations (see MAS, 2003). The Singapore dollar is allowed to float within the band, but like the central rate, the band limits are not publicly announced. The MAS avoids intervening within the band except to prevent unwarranted volatility in the TWI. However, when the TWI approaches or exceeds the boundaries of the policy band, the MAS may carry out intervention operations in order to "lean against the wind" and defend the band. Williamson (1998) makes a distinction between a crawling band whereby the central bank is obliged to carry out foreign exchange intervention whenever the bounds are breached, versus a monitoring band whereby the central bank is obliged to avoid intervening within the band except to smooth out exchange rate volatility. Singapore's exchange rate framework is more akin to that of a monitoring band than a crawling band (Yip, 2005).

Over the years, Singapore has maintained a conservative fiscal policy as well as a commitment to low inflation and a strong Singapore dollar which helped to build the central bank's credibility. Since market participants are mostly convinced of MAS' commitment to enforce the policy band, they tend to keep within it. Such market discipline in turn alleviates the need for frequent central bank intervention operations in the foreign exchange markets (Krugman, 1991). In addition, Singapore's large foreign reserves, as depicted in Figure 3, serve to deter currency speculators.

Despite adopting a basket numeraire, it is not necessary to carry out intervention operations using all the component currencies of the basket. Rather, the central bank can conduct foreign exchange intervention in a single currency that it finds most convenient to transact

---

[4]See MacDonald (2004) for a MAS study on Singapore's equilibrium real effective exchange rate.

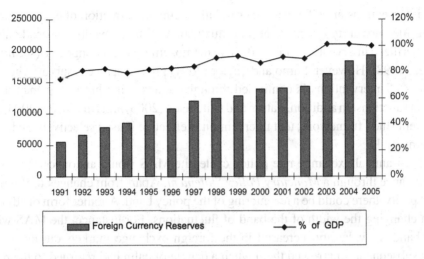

Figure 3. Foreign Reserves (S$ million)
Source: Monetary Authority of Singapore and International Financial Statistics.

with. This implies that the central bank could, if it wishes, hold foreign reserves entirely in that particular currency for the purpose of intervention operations (Williamson, 2005). Not surprisingly, the MAS intervenes in the US dollar (USD) exchange market as it is the most liquid (MAS, 2003). Following Desai and Veblen (2004), we use a stylized example to illustrate how the authorities can manage the entire currency basket with the use of a single exchange rate. In particular, all of MAS' intervention activities can be accomplished by directing intervention at the Singapore dollar (SGD) bilateral rate with the USD, scaled by observable market levels of the other bilateral rates against the USD.

Suppose the currency basket comprises only two currencies, the US dollar (USD) and the Japanese yen (JPY) with weights w_{USD} and w_{JPY} respectively. The magnitude of these weights reflects the relative importance of the USD and the JPY to Singapore's trading relationships, and they add up to one. The TWI is computed as the geometric mean of the SGD bilateral rates with the USD and the JPY as follows:

$$TWI = \left(\frac{USD}{SGD}\right)^{w_{USD}} \times \left(\frac{JPY}{SGD}\right)^{w_{JPY}}.$$

By expressing the non-USD bilateral rate in terms of cross-rates through the USD, i.e.,

$$TWI = \left(\frac{USD}{SGD}\right)^{w_{USD}} \times \left(\frac{JPY}{USD} \times \frac{USD}{SGD}\right)^{w_{JPY}},$$

all of the USD exposure can be factored out as follows:

$$TWI = \left(\frac{USD}{SGD}\right) \times \left(\frac{JPY}{USD}\right)^{w_{JPY}}.$$

In this way, the central bank can use the USD/SGD exchange rate alone to influence the outcome of the domestic currency on a trade-weighted basis.

Central banks, in general, have often cited exchange rate misalignments and disorderly markets as common justifications for intervention. There is thus, an implicit belief that foreign exchange interventions are effective either in influencing the direction of exchange rates or dampening the variability of exchange rate fluctuations. The conventional academic view holds that sterilized interventions are ineffective in impacting the exchange rate (see *inter alia* Dominguez, 1998). However, Sarno and Taylor (2001) provide a recent survey whereby the effectiveness of interventions is confirmed through studies using high frequency data and intervention functions. In addition, Fatum and Hutchison (2003) and Hutchison (2003) found, using an event study framework, that intervention is effective if used selectively and directed to short-term goals.

In its semi-annual exchange rate policy cycle, the MAS would announce the exchange rate policy stance through a *Monetary Policy Statement*. Apart from changes to the crawl in the central parity, there could be a recentering of the policy band. Another form of adjustment is through changing the width of the band of fluctuations. For instance, the MAS widened its policy bands as volatility increased in the foreign exchange markets during the Asian crisis, and subsequently narrowed them when a degree of calm had returned to the regional markets. Some market participants have advocated a wider band to guard against the risk of policymakers misjudging the level of Singapore's equilibrium exchange rate. However, others have pointed out that broadening the policy band would increase the risk of the Singapore dollar overshooting and is thus, destabilizing. After all, the Singapore dollar is frequently used as a proxy for broader Asian currency risk, which means that changes in the fundamentals of other regional currencies could lead to overshooting of the Singapore dollar.

4. Domestic Liquidity Considerations

Reflecting the strong and improving fundamentals of the Singaporean economy over the past decades, the TWI has historically exhibited an upward trend. Correspondingly, the foreign exchange intervention operations carried out by the MAS have mostly been to mitigate the appreciation of the domestic currency. This, in turn, leads to a rise in foreign reserves (see Figure 3) and an increase in the monetary base. One macroeconomic implication of defending appreciations is thus an increase in inflationary pressures, unless the MAS carries out sterilization of its foreign exchange interventions. The MAS can in fact counteract the impact on domestic liquidity through the conduct of money market operations. Instruments used for money market operations include foreign exchange (reverse) swaps, direct lending to or borrowing from banks, direct purchases or sales of Singapore Government Securities (SGS) and repurchase agreements on SGS (MAS, 2003). With the use of market operations, the MAS has been able to mop up liquidity from the domestic banking system on a large scale in reaction to economic and financial developments.

Two aspects of the macroeconomic environment are important in impacting liquidity conditions in the Singapore economy. First, the government maintains a strong fiscal position and with few exceptions, has run persistent budget surpluses of over 5% of GDP since the early 1990s (see Figure 4). This, along with the Central Provident Fund (CPF) system described below, contributed to a high national savings rate of above 40% for most of that time period (see Figure 5). The fiscal surplus means that the MAS, as the government's financial agent, is in receipt of deposits from the government. This in effect represents

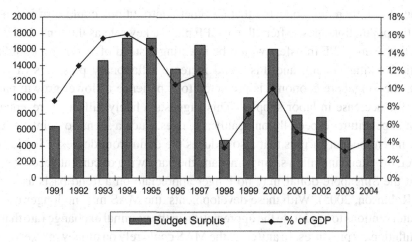

Figure 4. Government Budget Surpluses (S$ million)
Source: International Financial Statistics.

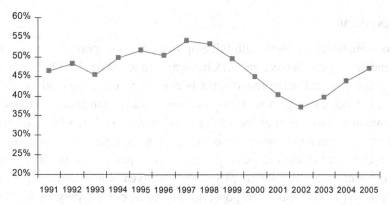

Figure 5. Gross National Savings Rate (as % of GDP)
Source: Asian Development Bank.

a withdrawal of funds from the domestic financial system. Second, contributions to the CPF — a government-administered fully-funded mandatory retirement program — tend to be in excess of withdrawals due to the relatively youthful profiles of its members. These net contributions also effectively remove liquidity from the domestic banking system.

Since both CPF contributions and public funds transfers represent a substantial liquidity drain out of the economic system, the money supply tends to shrink through these two channels. In order to overcome this liquidity drain, the MAS can actively counteract it through foreign exchange operations (i.e., use the Singapore dollar to purchase the US dollar) to ensure there is sufficient liquidity circulating in the domestic economy. As pointed out earlier, MAS' foreign exchange intervention operations to moderate the appreciation of the Singapore dollar increases the monetary base. This helps to channel funds back into the domestic banking system and offset the liquidity drain from government budget surpluses and CPF net contributions.

Looking ahead, there are concerns that CPF net contributions could turn into net withdrawals as the population ages. After all, the CPF plays a key role as the fund for retirement income. In this event, CPF transfers would be injecting instead of removing liquidity from the domestic banking system, and this could increase inflationary pressures (Yip, 2005). Meanwhile, the Singapore economy is projected to experience a slower growth path associated with the decrease in labor supply.[5] This suggests a likely fall in tax revenues while government expenditure, especially on healthcare, rises. Such a scenario points to a decline in the government budget surplus that also reduces the drain from domestic liquidity.

However, the attendant fall in savings rate and the narrowing of current account surpluses implies that the Singapore dollar may no longer appreciate on a trend basis as in the past (Khor and Robinson, 2005). With these developments, the MAS may no longer use foreign exchange interventions to moderate the appreciation in the nominal exchange rate that adds to excessive inflationary pressures. In any case, the MAS could rely on money market operations to regulate the level of liquidity in the domestic economy alongside exchange rate policy to foster stable money market conditions and to keep the financial system functioning smoothly.

5. Challenges Ahead

To achieve non-inflationary growth with full employment, Singapore's monetary policy has been complemented by a proactive and flexible wage policy (Wu, 1999). The coordination between exchange rate and wage movements is evident in the appreciation of the Singapore dollar while labor earnings rose during business cycle expansions. Conversely, during severe economic downturns such as the 1985 recession and the Asian financial crisis, nominal exchange rate depreciation was accompanied by wage cuts in the form of downward adjustments to CPF contribution rates. In particular, a 15 percentage point reduction in the employer's contribution to the CPF coupled with a two-year wage restraint policy was initiated to bring down labor costs in response to the Asian crisis (Abeysinghe and Wilson, 2002). Other administrative policy measures such as cost-cutting and budgetary measures were also employed. Contemporaneously, the MAS allowed the nominal exchange rate to depreciate by widening the band of fluctuation for the trade-weighted index.

The simultaneous cuts in wages and NEER depreciation during the mid-1980s recession and the Asian crisis helped to alleviate the need for huge adjustments in the nominal exchange rate, typically taken to preserve international competitiveness as an economy faces negative shocks. On both occasions, Singapore's real exchange rate depreciations were effected primarily through deflationary price and wage adjustments (see Figure 6).

Looking ahead, there are limitations to the use of domestic cost-cutting measures to substitute for external exchange rate policy. In particular, an ageing population dictates an increasing need for the CPF to focus on its role as a fund for retirement income, rendering CPF cuts less feasible. Nonetheless, a significant fall in the value of the domestic currency is detrimental to the purchasing power of Singapore's overseas investments. The extent to which a real depreciation can be purchased without a nominal depreciation would then depend on

---

[5]This is due to the ageing population, but can be counteracted by immigration policies.

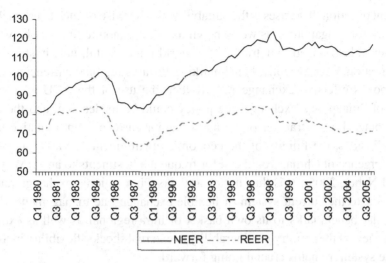

Figure 6. Singapore's Nominal and Real Effective Exchange Rate
Source: International Financial Statistics.

the flexibility of Singapore's wage structure that links income to the domestic growth cycle, as well as the future degree of flexibility of domestic factor and product markets.

Another challenge faced by policymakers when implementing Singapore's exchange rate policy is related to the recent renewed focus on developing regional exchange rate cooperation (Ogawa, Ito and Sasaki, 2004). There are concerns related to export competitiveness in light of some regional currencies being more flexible and, as a result, appreciating more than others. For instance, both the Singapore dollar and Korean won have risen against the US dollar more than the Chinese yuan and the Malaysian ringgit in the post-crisis period. One way of preventing this from harming Singapore's export competitiveness, as well as the competitiveness of other countries with rising currencies, would be to foster closer exchange rate cooperation among East Asian countries.

However, studies on the feasibility of a monetary union in East Asia have invariably deemed it to be a very distant prospect.[6] This is not surprising given the region's economic and institutional diversity, particularly the substantial variation in trade patterns within East Asia. In the case of Singapore, Chow and Kim (2001) found a lack of empirical support for it to enter a common currency peg with the other East Asian countries. Since a full monetary union for East Asia is not a viable option, a common loose arrangement such as an EMS-type system has been considered for maintaining intra-regional exchange rate stability (see *inter alia* Wyplosz, 2004). To this end, some have proposed the creation of an Asian currency unit (ACU) — a weighted index of East Asian currencies — to be used as a benchmark for monitoring the movements of regional currencies (Ogawa and Shimizu, 2005).

---

[6]For instance, Chow and Kim (2003) applied the Optimum Currency Area (OCA) criteria and found the region to be dominated by domestic rather than common regional shocks, thereby concluding that a common currency would be costly for the region. Additionally, Eichengreen and Bayoumi (1996) argued that the region was not ready for monetary union in view of political considerations.

A pertinent question that arises is the suitability or otherwise of such a regional exchange rate framework for Singapore. It is well-known that the economic linkages between Singapore and other industrialized countries of the world remain vital, notwithstanding greater regional integration. Consequently, benchmarking towards regional currencies will not stabilize Singapore's effective exchange rate. Rather, the use of the ACU as a tool for the surveillance of Singapore's exchange rate policy could be misleading, and the authorities will be confronted by the transfer of swings in major currencies into relative trade competitiveness. Besides, the fluidity of the economic environment in East Asia, such as the economic emergence of China, would call for frequent adjustments to an ERM-type system (Hefeker and Nabor, 2005). It is thus not clear that such a regional exchange rate arrangement is superior to the current system of flexible exchange rate management whereby the Singapore dollar benchmarks to its own basket of intra-regional as well as extra-regional currencies. In view of the country's vulnerability to external shocks, flexibility in Singapore's exchange rate system remains crucial going forward.[7]

Acknowledgments

The author would like to thank the editor and two anonymous referees for helpful comments and suggestions.

References

Abeysinghe, T and KM Choy (2004). The aggregate consumption puzzle in Singapore. *Journal of Asian Economics*, 15(3), 563–578.

Abeysinghe, T and P Wilson (2002). International competitiveness. In *Singapore Economy in the 21st Century: Issues and Strategies*, AT Koh, KL Lim, WT Hui, B Rao and MK Chng (eds.). Singapore: McGraw-Hill.

Bayoumi, T, J Lee and S Jayanthi (2006). New rates from new weights. *IMF Staff Papers*, 53(2).

Calvo, G, C Reinhart and C Vegh (1995). Targeting the real exchange rate: Theory and evidence. *Journal of Development Economics*, 47, 97–133.

Chow, HK (2005). A VAR analysis of Singapore's monetary transmission mechanism. In *The Economic Prospects of Singapore*, WTH Koh and RS Mariano (eds.), pp. 274–298. Singapore: Addison Wesley.

Chow, HK and Y Kim (2001). Exchange rate policy in Singapore: Prospects for a common currency peg in East Asia. *Singapore Economic Review*, 45(2), 1–26.

Chow, HK and Y Kim (2003). A common currency peg in East Asia? Perspectives from Western Europe. *Journal of Macroeconomics*, 5(3), 331–350.

Corsetti, G, P Pesenti and N Roubini (1999). What caused the Asian currency and financial crisis? *Japan and the World Economy*, 11, 305–373.

Desai, MA and MF Veblen (2004). Exchange rate policy at the Monetary Authority of Singapore. Harvard Business School Case 204-037.

Dominguez, K (1998). Central bank intervention and exchange rate volatility. *Journal of International Money and Finance*, 17, 161–190.

---

[7]This is not in any way at odds with Singapore's official support for regional integration efforts such as the Chiang Mai Initiative. In fact, Singapore has been and remains a champion of greater trade liberalization, especially among the ASEAN countries.

Eichengreen, B and T Bayoumi (1996). Is Asia an optimum currency area? Can it become one? Regional, global and historical perspectives on Asian monetary relations. In *Exchange Rate Policies in Emerging Asian Countries*, S Collignon *et al.* (eds.). London: Routledge.

Fatum, R and MM Hutchison (2003). Is sterilized foreign exchange intervention effective after all? An event study approach. *The Economic Journal*, 113(487), 390–411.

Hefeker, C and A Nabor (2005). China's role in East Asian monetary integration. *International Journal of Finance and Economics*, 10, 157–166.

Ho, C and R McCauley (2003). Living with flexible exchange rates: Issues and recent experience in inflation targeting emerging market economies. BIS Working Paper, Bank of International Settlements.

Hutchison, MM (2003). Intervention and exchange rate stabilization policy in developing countries. *International Finance*, 6, 41–59.

Khor, HE and E Robinson (2005). Exchange rates and price stability. *Business Times*, August.

Khor, HE, E Robinson and J Lee (2004). Managed floating and intermediate exchange rate systems: The Singapore experience. MAS Staff Paper No. 37.

Krugman, P (1991). Target zones and exchange rate dynamics. *The Quarterly Journal of Economics*, 106(3), 669–682.

MacDonald, R (2004). The long run real effective exchange rate of Singapore — A behavioural approach. MAS Staff Paper No. 36.

MAS (Monetary Authority of Singapore) (1999). Monetary policy and the economy. MAS Economics Explorer Series No. 2.

MAS (Monetary Authority of Singapore) (2000). A survey of Singapore's monetary history. MAS Occasional Paper No. 18.

MAS (Monetary Authority of Singapore) (2003). *Monetary Policy Operations in Singapore*. MAS monograph.

Obstfeld, M, JC Shambaugh and AM Taylor (2004). The trilemma in history: Tradeoffs among exchange rates, monetary policies, and capital mobility. Mimeo, University of California, Berkeley, Dartmouth College, March.

Ogawa, E, T Ito and YN Sasaki (2004). Cost, benefits, and constraints of the currency basket regime for East Asia. In *Monetary and Financial Integration in East Asia: The Way Ahead*, Vol. 2, Asian Development Bank (ed.), pp. 209–239. Palgrave.

Ogawa, E and J Shimizu (2005). A deviation measurement for coordinated exchange rate policies in East Asia. REITI Discussion Paper Series 05-E-017.

Parrado, E (2004). Singapore's unique monetary policy: How does it work? IMF Working Paper No. 04/10.

Phang, S (2004). House prices and aggregate consumption: Do they move together? Evidence from Singapore. *Journal of Housing Economics*, 13(2), 101–119.

Reinhart, CM and K Rogoff (2001). The modern history of exchange rate arrangements: A reinterpretation. NBER Working Paper No. 8963.

Sarno, L and M Taylor (2001). Official intervention in the foreign exchange market: Is it effective, and if so, how does it work? *Journal of Economic Literature*, 39, 208–244.

Williamson, J (1998). Crawling bands and monitoring bands: How to manage exchange rates in a world of capital mobility. *International Finance*, 1(1), 59–79.

Williamson, J (1999). Future exchange rate regimes for developing East Asia: Exploring the policy options. Paper presented to a Conference on Asia in Economic Recovery: Policy Options for Growth and Stability, Institute of Policy Studies, Singapore, 21–22 June.

Williamson, J (2005). A currency basket for East Asia, not just China. Policy Briefs in International Economics, PB05-1, Institute of International Economics.

Wu, Y (1999). Macroeconomic coordination of exchange rate and wage movements under quasi-sterilization: Singapore experience. *Pacific Economic Review*, 4(2), 185–201.

Wyplosz, C (2004). Regional exchange rate arrangements: Lessons from Europe for East Asia. In *Monetary and Financial Integration in East Asia: The Way Ahead*, Vol. 2, Asian Development Bank (ed.), pp. 241–284. Palgrave.

Yip, PSL (2002). A note on Singapore's exchange rate policy: Empirical foundation, past performance and outlook. *Singapore Economic Review*, 47(1), 173–182.

Yip, PSL (2005). *The Exchange Rate Systems in Hong Kong and Singapore: Currency Board vs Monitoring Band*. Singapore: Prentice Hall.

Yip, PSL and RF Wang (2001). On the neutrality of Singapore's exchange rate policy. *ASEAN Economic Bulletin*, 18(3), 251–262.